Multilingual High

Education

BILINGUAL EDUCATION AND BILINGUALISM
Series Editors: Nancy H. Hornberger, *University of Pennsylvania, USA*
and Colin Baker, *Bangor University, Wales, UK*

Bilingual Education and Bilingualism is an international, multidisciplinary series publishing research on the philosophy, politics, policy, provision and practice of language planning, global English, indigenous and minority language education, multilingualism, multiculturalism, biliteracy, bilingualism and bilingual education. The series aims to mirror current debates and discussions.

Full details of all the books in this series and of all our other publications can be found on http://www.multilingual-matters.com, or by writing to Multilingual Matters, St Nicholas House, 31–34 High Street, Bristol BS1 2AW, UK.

Multilingual Higher Education

Beyond English Medium Orientations

Christa van der Walt

MULTILINGUAL MATTERS
Bristol • Buffalo • Toronto

Library of Congress Cataloging in Publication Data
A catalog record for this book is available from the Library of Congress.
Van der Walt, C. (Christa)
Multilingual Higher Education: Beyond English Medium Orientations/Christa van der Walt.
Bilingual Education and Bilingualism: 91
Includes bibliographical references and index.
1. Multilingualism—South Africa. 2. Language and languages—Study and teaching (Higher)—South Africa. 3. Language and education—South Africa. 4. Multicultural education—South Africa. 5. Language planning—South Africa. I. Title.
P115.5.S6V36 2013
378.017–dc23 201204414

British Library Cataloguing in Publication Data
A catalogue entry for this book is available from the British Library.

ISBN-13: 978-1-84769-919-0 (hbk)
ISBN-13: 978-1-84769-918-3 (pbk)

Multilingual Matters
UK: St Nicholas House, 31–34 High Street, Bristol BS1 2AW, UK.
USA: UTP, 2250 Military Road, Tonawanda, NY 14150, USA.
Canada: UTP, 5201 Dufferin Street, North York, Ontario M3H 5T8, Canada.

Typeset by Exeter Premedia Services Private Ltd.

Contents

    Approaches and Techniques   125
        Institutional Policies and Classroom Practices   125
        Conceptualising Multilingual Pedagogy in Higher
            Education Classroom Settings   130
        Proposed Strategies and Practices in Multilingual
            Classrooms   141
        Conclusion   161

5   From *Mono* to *Multi*: New Thinking about Higher Education   163
        Introduction: Higher Education, Prestige and Power   163
        From *Mono* to *Multi:* Arguments against
            False Dichotomies   163
        Moving Forward: Future Directions for Research
            in Multilingual Higher Education   175
        Conclusion   180

    References   181
    Subject Index   201
    Country Index   203

Preface

This book was written at a time when I attended a variety of conferences, some on bilingualism, others on bi-/multilingual higher education (HE), still others on English-medium universities and a substantial number on the problems of writing centres and their view of academic literacy development at the HE level in English. Each of these conferences seemed to attract a different group of participants despite the fact that the same themes emerged, albeit framed from the perspective of the organisers. My attempt here is to merge some of these themes, notably from HE studies, bilingual education, bilingualism and sociocultural theories of learning. I realise that I run the risk of not letting any one of these emerge clearly, but even the labour of writing this book has not dampened my conviction that these aspects need to be merged to guide multilingual HE teaching and learning practices.

The challenges of multilingual HE contexts grow particularly in times and places where money is tight, more so when the discourse of education is increasingly couched in market terms and linguistic diversity is seen as a liability rather than an asset. For the past 30 years, these are the issues that HE institutions have faced to varying degrees: from the Sorbonne in Paris to the School of Planning and Architecture in New Delhi, from the City University of New York to the City University of Hong Kong, from the Islamic College of Southern Africa in Cape Town to the International Christian University in Tokyo.

The spotlight here is on bi-/multilingual students and lecturers and the practices they develop when they take the liberty of using the languages they have at their disposal to make sense of academic discourse. My own experiences and current institution obviously colour my perceptions and I set out to include specifically African and European authors, also those who write in languages (other than English) that I can read. My only regret is that I did not do justice to the literature in other languages. My ideal of a multilingual text could not be realised this time, but that will come.

My purpose is to inform classroom practice rather than provide guidelines for institutional policies. Institutional, top-down policies seem time-consuming and rigid to me and they cannot allow for ever-changing classrooms and contexts. Furthermore, I see lecturers making decisions – some good, some (for me) not so good – and I am not convinced that policies will affect this state of affairs either way. For HE practitioners, I hope that the language arrangements and multilingual teaching scenarios will be of use. The ideas expressed here continue to be shaped by three people in particular: Ofelia García, who constantly urged me to write the book; Colin Baker, who encouraged me in this area of study; and Neville Alexander, whose work in South Africa was a constant inspiration. With his passing away in August 2012, the South African educational and political scene lost a brilliant mind and an inspiring academic.

This book would not have been possible without the constant support of my husband André (*dankie – hoe sou ek dit sonder jou doen*¿!), my closest colleagues Renée Nathanson, Marguerite MacRobert, Phumla Kese and John Ruiters (thanks for the million cups of coffee and for knowing when to leave me alone), Liesel Hibbert (for her critical reading and valuable discussions), Nanda Klapwijk (for helping with teaching and serving as inspiration for the final chapter and, above all, for helping with the reference list). For my students, particularly the ones in the Multilingual Education modules since 2009: you challenged me by living out your multilingual identities.

I received financial support from the Von Humboldt Foundation, the National Research Foundation and my own institution, Stellenbosch University, for which I'm extremely grateful.

Christa van der Walt
June 2012

1 The Special Place of Higher Education

Context

In my own multilingual country, South Africa, language has a tangible presence that announces itself in virtually every encounter. When I buy something I try to guess the shop assistant's preferred language from the customary, bland 'Hi'; when students come to my office they seem to visibly calculate the possible advantages of a particular language choice; when I meet my departmental chair in his office I will speak English, but when he is in a predominantly Afrikaans group, we will probably address him in Afrikaans. My colleague, who is a home language speaker of Xhosa, will address her daughter alternately in English and Xhosa, and I will speak to my husband in English in her presence although our normal conversations are in Afrikaans. At my officially multilingual university, language is often the scapegoat for other, ideological disagreements; we often use English to hide and protect other identities. Language is also the ultimate olive branch, when, after a heated debate, a colleague uses a variety of Afrikaans to defuse the situation.

This pervasive and ubiquitous multiplicity of languages is typical of African societies and although my multilingualism does not even approach that of my African-language-speaking colleagues, I share the lived experience characterised by 'language mediation and translation [which] are common communicative bridges of everyday life' (Ouane, 2009: 59). In contrast to the often-pathologised vision of Africa as chaotic or underdeveloped because of its multilingual nature, I see language diversity as normative for 21st century societies. Ouane (2009: 57, emphasis added) provides the contrast between viewing societies through a monolingual lens as opposed to a multilingual view:

> Therefore the multilingual ethos refuses to see and interpret linguistic issues through the lens of one language, singling it out of the language *constellations*. It claims that multilingualism is not the juxtaposition or additive of many individual languages, but a *composite state* resulting from the interaction with a given number of languages within a *common* space.

The words that I italicised in this quotation reflect a multilingual *ethos* (Ouane, 2009: 59) by foregrounding the way in which languages interact in multiple ways (*constellation*) to form a picture of multiplicity (*a composite state*) that is shared by a (relatively) stable community of users (a *common space*).

Such a multilingual ethos sees nominally monolingual higher education (HE) as restrictive of learning and teaching. In the course of this book I will argue that a value-driven stance towards multilingualism, which pays attention to social justice and equity (García, 2009: 336, Skutnab-Kangas *et al.*, 2009), prevents a perception of multilingual students and academic staff as problems that need to be 'fixed' by providing academic or language support of some kind. A multilingual ethos, as it emerges in many African societies, can provide the impetus for re-conceptualising multilingual education worldwide in a way that balances local and global interests.

One of the aims of this book is to demonstrate how two processes, one global and the other local, demand such re-conceptualisation if HE is to improve learning environments and, consequently, its throughput. The drive towards internationalisation is the first process. This is seen mainly as a response to global or globalising demands to be competitive (see Chapters 2 and 3). The second process, which is a local and regional process to widen participation of minoritised communities, is often a response to local and national government initiatives to increase participation rates in HE. The argument is that internationalisation of HE does not inevitably mean a bigger place for English but, in fact, increases the multilingual nature of HE (as shown by scholars such as Haberland & Risager, 2008: 43). At the same time, attempts at widening participation locally require an increased awareness and acknowledgement of bi-/multilingual teaching and learning practices to enable *epistemological access* (see Morrow, 1993; Boughey, 2002; Makoni & Pennycook, 2007) and thus improve students' chances of success. The theoretical justification for this claim draws on two perspectives: a multilingual perspective on education and the sociocultural perspective on learning. This book focuses on the overlap between these two perspectives that HE learning and teaching demands in an age of increasing international mobility and widened access:

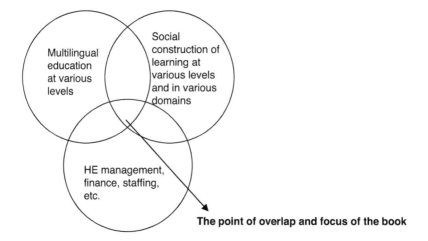

The point of overlap and focus of the book

Terminological Issues

Although terms will be clarified throughout the book, the use of certain terms needs to be clarified since they are used in a particular way for a particular reason.

- The term *language of learning and teaching* (LoLT) is used rather than the term *medium of instruction* to focus on the way in which language is used by both students and the lecturer. A language is not a neutral conduit for ideas, as implied by the term *medium of instruction.*
- The term *higher education* is used to refer to post-secondary education. By this is meant education that is mostly entered into voluntarily (in contrast to primary and, to an extent, secondary education that may be compulsory to differing degrees). Preparation for a particular profession or vocation is seen as the main task of such institutions, whether they be universities or colleges. In the literature, the term *post-secondary* is sometimes used to refer to any training after secondary school, but I prefer HE because it is more familiar. I am mindful of the perception that HE is mainly university-based education and, indeed, many of the examples in the book refer to universities. However, I attempted to include colleges and vocational training institutions in Chapter 2 and, as far as observations about the social nature of learning and the extent of multilingualism in post-school education are concerned, all HE institutions (HEIs) are assumed to be concerned with the promotion of student success.
- *Globalisation*: This term is used in the market economy sense and particularly in the context of neoliberal discourses about HE. References to HE as a commodity and academics (including students) as tradable products form part of this discourse.
- *Internationalisation* refers to the international exchange of students and academics as the continuation of a centuries-old tradition, which now includes possibilities of virtual collaborative research and teaching and dual-degree programmes, among others.

Although the last two terms cannot always be disentangled, I agree with Altman and Knight (2007: 291) that '[g]lobalization may be unalterable, but internationalization involves many choices'. I strongly endorse their conclusion that 'today's emerging programs and practices must ensure that international higher education benefits the public and not simply be a profit center' (Altman & Knight 2007: 304). This view of internationalisation is to be inferred when the term is used in this book, without losing sight of its liberal, market-related link to globalisation and the criticism by Scott (2000: 4) that the use of *internationalisation*, in the 21st century, 'conjures up a world of diplomatic exchanges and international agencies in which the interests of ex-colonial and great powers still linger'.

- The term *student* is used to refer to HE students and the term *learners* to refer to students at school level. This distinction is necessary because bi-/multilingual education is still seen as a 'schooling' practice and research on bi-/multilingual teaching and learning is done mostly at school level. The distinction also becomes important when discussing the application of school practices to HE.
- The term *multilingual* education will include officially *bi*lingual institutions, unless a specific point is made about bilingual education. Even officially bilingual institutions may have some faculties that are introducing a third language, for example, the University of Fribourg, which is introducing English in addition to German and French. Moreover, the existence of an officially bilingual language policy does not mean that no other languages are used for learning and teaching purposes.
- *Minoritised* is the term used to refer to languages and communities that are generally perceived to be disadvantaged in terms of social recognition. There are many reasons for such perceptions; a language could be minoritised because of the recent immigrant status of its speakers (e.g. Xhosa in Germany), but the same language is minoritised in South African education despite its official status and its number of speakers because the language may not be regarded as suitable for secondary or HE teaching (see later on in this chapter). The term indicates that minority status is not a property of a community or a language, but is assigned to it.

A Multilingual Perspective on Learning: Language as a Resource

It is generally accepted that there are more multilingual than monolingual individuals worldwide (Romaine, 2008). Aronin and Singleton (2008) argue that the scale and significance of multilingualism can be linked to 'dramatic social changes' (2008: 1) that characterise globalisation. Although their claim for the uniqueness of the current sociolinguistic landscape (in terms of its multilingual nature) may be overstated – multilingualism has been a feature of African and Indian societies for centuries – the degree to which multilinguals are able to interact physically and virtually can be seen as unprecedented. However, not all forms of multilingualism are necessarily valued equally highly. In Chapter 2, the point is made that English-plus multilingualism is becoming the norm for multilingual individuals and, generally speaking, the inclusion of high-status languages will be seen as constituting a more valuable multilingual repertoire, one that is mostly available for elites and their children (Nelde, 1991: 69). Research done in such educational environments has been presented as models for teaching colonial languages to African communities where multilinguals use minoritised languages, with disastrous consequences (Brock-Utne, 2009).

New conceptions of multilingualism

When do we call ourselves bi- or multilingual? I regularly ask students this question when they plot their language biographies. Although some of them grew up using Cape Flats Afrikaans, this variety of Afrikaans has never appeared on their biographies. Similarly, students would not consider their basic knowledge of Xhosa or German, which many would have encountered at school or undergraduate level, as evidence of their being multilingual. The idea of 'balanced bilingualism', that is, the ability to use languages equally well in all domains and modes, is pervasive and seen as the ultimate target for bi-/multilinguals.

Emerging research done in Europe on third-language acquisition and its implications for multilingual education (Jessner, 2008: 45) indicates that comfortable assumptions about learners or students developing mirror competencies in two languages that are kept strictly separate do not correspond to the language use and practices of bi- or multilinguals. From such a monolingual perspective, bi- and trilingual people are perceived as two or three monolinguals in one, who add languages one by one to a fully formed 'mother tongue'. The reality is far more complex, with multilinguals developing a repertoire of language practices, and becoming 'competent but specific speaker-hearers' (Jessner, 2008: 20). This is clearly illustrated in Ouane's (2009: 53) description of what he calls an African multilingualism:

> [I]n some places in Africa or India, a child can grow up with up to six languages at the same time. Each of these languages represents a different part of the culture in these areas. Cultural identity has several markers at various levels from local to community, national and even international. Each layer could be reflected or carried by a language in a multilingual set-up.

From the perspective of a *constellation* of languages (see the section 'Context' above), Ouane (2009: 59) criticises the 'monolingual, compartmentalising habitus' of Western theories of bilingualism and bilingual education, which do not take everyday practices of language mediation and translation into account. By keeping languages apart, Ouane argues, the monolingual view of teaching and curricula '[leads] to a dead end and inhibits its [multilingualism's] further expansion' (Ouane, 2009: 59).

Instead, Herdina and Jessner (2002: 151) argue, we need a dynamic systems model of multilingualism to explain the psycholinguistic processes and to underpin empirical investigations into particular instances of multilingualism. Although they admit that research into the psycholinguistics of multilingualism is still in its infancy, a dynamic systems model is hoped to 'provide an innovative theoretical framework in which it is possible to ask meaningful questions concerning multilingual development to obtain more satisfactory answers to the plethora of questions surrounding multilingualism as a psycholinguistic phenomenon with sociolinguistic consequences' (Herdina & Jessner, 2002: 152).

Multilingualism in education

Dominant paradigms of foreign language teaching are largely to blame for the tradition of keeping learners' existing languages apart from the target language. The fear of 'negative interference' from the home and other languages leads to punitive practices, for example, making learners pay fines when they use their home language in a foreign language class. Perceptions of code switching as a sign of limited language proficiency or as undesirable in educational contexts (see Chapter 4), particularly in language teaching classes, have spilled over into content subject teaching. The existence of other languages is constructed as undesirable and problematic.

In an analysis of language in education policies in the USA, Ruiz (1994) compares a language-as-resource paradigm to (among others) that of language-as-a-problem. In the case of a language-as-resource paradigm, the existence of many languages in a particular community is seen as supportive of learning and teaching. In the case of a language-as-problem paradigm, multilingual students are constructed as lacking certain skills and competencies and therefore needing special programmes or interventions. This orientation has led to the development of English for academic purposes programmes and, more recently, programmes in academic literacy, as discussed in Chapter 3. Ouane's view adds a dimension to the language as a resource paradigm by arguing that not only language but multilingual competence itself are resources.

García (2009: 7) emphasises that 'bilingual education is not simply about *one language plus a second language equals two languages*' (her emphasis), but that students use a multiplicity of language practices, in different modes, calling on their available languages as well as varieties of languages to manage their learning and achieve their goals. For example, receptive proficiency in one language does not preclude its use in education, because a more nuanced view of multilingualism (as argued later on) means that listening in one language and writing in another exploit the individual's repertoire of language use (as argued in Chapters 3 and 4). This view extends the language-as-resource paradigm to bilingual education, and links up with a view of multilingual communication as a dynamic and recursive process. García's image (2009: 8) of bilingual education as an all-terrain vehicle rather than a bicycle is striking in this regard and links up with Canagarajah's (2011: 403) view of multilingual language practices as codemeshing. He contrasts this idea with more traditional views: 'Whereas code switching treats language alternation as involving bilingual competence and switches between two different systems, codemeshing treats the languages as part of a single integrated system'.

As educators and language teachers, we need to emphasise, and do so repeatedly, that a focus in education on the use of one particular language (and only very specific forms and registers of that language at that) is a violation of social justice, effective learning and access to knowledge (Skutnab-Kangas *et al.*, 2009). When students are discouraged from using the languages at their disposal for learning, either actively or merely by pretending that other languages do not exist, they are deprived of practices and tools that they can access and mobilise with relative ease. Furthermore, students who use the LoLT as an additional language are often put through entry or placement tests such as the International English Language Testing System or the standardized tests used in the TESOL (Teaching English to Speakers of Other Languages) framework. The languages that they bring with them and which may have helped them gain access to HE disappear in the process of these students being classified as 'second language students' or 'international students' or 'academic support students'. Chapter 3 will show that students' struggle to be successful in HE is often constructed as an inability to use the LoLT well. Although proficiency in the LoLT is a legitimate concern in HE, minority, transnationally mobile (the term proposed by Haberland & Risager (2008: 42) for 'international' or 'foreign' students) or first-generation students' feelings of alienation cannot be ascribed merely to lack of proficiency in the LoLT. As Boughey (2002: 305) notes, 'the 'naming' of students' language-related experiences, and the initiatives intended to remediate the problems which result from that 'naming', require further interrogation if epistemological access is to be granted'. HE practitioners often reduce learning to the mastery of certain forms of language use by merely offering 'academic support' or 'academic writing courses'. When such 'interventions' are imposed on students who have successfully gained access to HE based on prior performance in another language, a monolingual focus becomes particularly problematic.

For me, as a researcher in a multilingual community and a citizen of a country that acknowledges 11 official languages, an orientation that sees language-as-a-resource is natural, even normative, although such a view may not be widespread. However, the orientation towards language-as-a-resource is not as unproblematic as it may sound. It is more than the trite statement, 'It's not a problem, it's a challenge!' and far more than the warm glow of political correctness when people proclaim the advantages of multilingualism while expressing mock modesty at their own lack of knowing more than English. When language is seen as a resource for bi-/multilinguals only, the language-as-a-resource paradigm runs the risk of being contaminated by what Torres-Guzmán (2007: 54) calls a view of bi-/multilingualism as a compensatory strategy rather than 'a socially desirable commodity'. This point is important for my argument: a (low-status) language is not merely a bridge or a support for another (high-status, academic) language; community languages contextualise and feed HE in very real ways – they form part of the 'common space' identified by Ouane (2009: 57). When students from a community surrounding the HEI enrol for courses and programmes, they provide the lifeblood of that institution. When students graduate, they go back into a variety of communities where they have to interact in a variety of languages, serving a community that supported their training in different ways.

My own perspective on the language-as-a-resource orientation is shaped by Torres-Guzmán's view, particularly when she links the societal value of bilingualism to Bourdieu's view of languages as symbolic capital. However, I treat this perspective with the caution that emerges from my own position in a country where high-status languages are spoken by a minority. Bourdieu argues (1991: 55, original italics),

> the competence that we have to produce sentences that are likely to be understood might be quite inadequate to produce sentences that are likely to be *listened* to…speakers lacking the legitimate competence are *de facto* excluded from the social domains in which this competence is required.

Despite the careful formulation here, it has become commonplace to reduce Bourdieu's argument to a blanket assignation of status to particular languages. I would caution against a reductionist view of, for example, English being more valuable than Sesotho sa Lebowa in Pretoria/Tswane.[1] English may be highly desirable, but will have little power (and airtime!) when tempers rise in faculty board meetings and other languages are used to claim a particular advantage. A reductionist view does not take the covert prestige and speakers' power into account when a junior employee can use Xhosa to narrow the status gap between her and her Xhosa-speaking supervisor. These kinds of interaction are well known the world over. I am reminded of a Latino immigrant in New York offering to clear my Spanish-speaking host's snowed-in driveway and neighbours begging her to ask him (in Spanish) to clear their driveways too. (English was powerless in this case!) I agree with Pennycook (1998: 165) that we need a more nuanced view of language and culture (in the context of colonialism and culture) 'whereby culture is not seen merely as a reflex of material conditions, and power operates in more complex ways than simply as something possessed by the "powerful"'.

In an educational context where language use is regulated more strictly than on the streets of New York, the language-as-a-resource orientation is less obvious, and restrictions on language use (as well as the use of particular registers of language) increase from primary to secondary to tertiary education levels. An illustration of one such restriction is nowhere more clearly evident than in the availability of literature on bi-/multilingual education. There is no shortage of books and academic articles about bi-/multilingual models and practices at primary school level. At secondary school level the volume decreases sharply and at HE level there are significantly fewer books. Existing edited volumes are mostly descriptions of *particular* bi-/multilingual HE settings. The aim in this book is to put multilingual HE on the agenda as a serious enterprise by arguing that all HE is inherently multilingual. Only by accepting this we can move beyond current debates on the 'problem' of limited English proficiency as well as the perception that bi-/multilingual HE is the province of the current network of explicitly bi-/multilingual universities such as Helsinki, Fribourg, Luxemburg and others.

The seemingly simplistic statement that HE is multilingual implies that we deal with a range of issues that centre around language-related constructions of opportunity, privilege and, subsequently, inequality, because such constructions are often based on institutional rather than personal aspirations to 'internationalise' or 'widen access'. When such aspirations result in additional demands on staff and students because a language such as English is added to (an) existing institutional language(s) or because students are encouraged or forced to improve their academic language proficiency, the multilingual nature of HE becomes a crucial and core factor in throughput rates, institutional rankings on league tables and, consequently, funding at national and international levels.

Globalisation and English-plus multilingualism

When national governments require 'accountability' and 'a good return on investment' from HEIs (demands that are, of course, related to the degree to which a particular HE is dependent on public funding), challenges of access and throughput converge to put pressure on each member of the academic staff. Implementation of government-led initiatives, in synergy with market discourses, is almost inevitably encouraged by offering funding incentives.

A case in point

The Dearing Report (1998) on the state of HE in England is a good example of the process whereby government initiatives compel changes with subsequent funding implications. The Summary Report (Dearing Report, 1998) notes, '[i]n the future, competitive advantage for advanced economies will lie in the quality, effectiveness and relevance of their provision for education and training'. In the section on 'Future demand for higher education', the report links a growth in participation rates in HE to national competitiveness, particularly in comparison to 'advanced nations' (referring mainly to Europe and Japan), leading to Recommendation 2 and a call for 'widening participation', particularly for ethnic minorities, disabled and mature students. Fifteen years down the line, Bourn (2010: 19) describes the policy support for a 'global citizenship' and internationalisation that comes, significantly, from the Higher Education Funding Council for England.

Examples like these are commonplace. Attempts to increase access and widen participation (also referred to as 'massification') in Europe are linked not only to competitiveness in the HE 'market', but also to equity and social cohesion, particularly 'by including those groups who have traditionally been excluded' (ethnic minorities and mature students) and with a view to democratic citizenship (Osborne, 2003: 6). HE, as a space where a particular kind of citizenry is created, is demanded by governments with increasingly tight budgets. Amaral and Maassen (2004: xi) conclude that '[m]assification of higher education has led to increasing costs of the system which, according to governments, can no longer be carried only by the public purse'.

By demanding massification or widening participation and, in so doing, changing the profile of HE students, governments are looking for diplomats and graduates who will serve the country on a globalising stage or, in market speech, the global markets. Entrance and interaction at that level are, of course, intimately linked to knowledge of global languages, and many HEIs argue, together with their students and, in turn, their parents or care-givers, that global competitiveness is best served by an education that is con-ducted in the language(s) of the global market. The institutional LoLTs, seen as the primary carriers or mediators of knowledge, skills and values, are the centripetal forces where student throughput rates coincide with educational accountability towards the government (as seen from the institution's per-spective) and with job market opportunities that can be accessed in global languages (as seen from the students' perspective). HE, as a costly exercise (for either a government or parents), promises a bright future and its unique nature will be discussed later in this chapter to show how perceptions of job preparation and the fiscal responsibility of students and parents create very definite expectations of the structure and delivery of academic programmes.

Speaking from a European perspective, Van Leeuwen (2004: 577) argues that '[n]ot only the changed political reality and the globalized economy, but also changes in the academic world itself, have gradually impelled European universities to abandon the monolingual approach and try to accord some place to other languages in their institutional design'. Except for a two-page discussion on explicitly bi-/multilingual universities in countries (e.g. Switzerland) and regions (e.g. north-east Italy) that are multilingual, his treatment of multilingual universities focuses mainly on the way in which monolingual institutions try to include English in their programme offerings.

A case in point

In a report on the progress that HEIs are making in terms of imple-menting the Bologna process (Crosier et al., 2007), progress is explicitly linked to the introduction of programme offerings in English. The authors (2007: 45) note, regarding student mobility in Europe, that '[l]anguage barriers therefore continue to pose major obstacles to mobility, *even where programmes are now offered through English*' (emphasis added). The impor-tance of English is emphasised when they report on, for example, the University of Ljubljana by noting that, '[n]ext to international pro-grammes like ERASMUS, the university, with support of external stake-holders, initiated special funds to attract students from former Yugoslav republics and invested its own resources to offer courses and programmes in foreign languages. However the number of English taught programmes is still very limited' (Crosier et al., 2007: 556).

The focus on English may obscure the fact that academic language pro-ficiency in the widest sense of the word is the central access mechanism to HE worldwide. Even exceptional secondary school exit results may become secondary if a student's language proficiency in the institutional LoLT is not regarded as sufficient. Cummins's (1979 and 1981) distinction between basic interpersonal communication skills (BICS) and cognitive academic language proficiency (CALP) is often invoked to explain the difference between using a language for communication and using it as a LoLT. For students to participate successfully in HE, sufficiently high levels of CALP are needed to be regarded as 'academically literate'.

We would do well to heed Brock-Utne's warning (2009: 29) against an uncritical application of these terms that were developed in Canada in the context of immigrant and minoritised students. First, McSwan and Rollstadt (2005) make the valid point that the BICS/CALP distinction requires of immigrant or other minoritised learners to demonstrate a developmental pattern that is similar to that of home language speakers, that is, to develop BICS from which CALP can develop. With reference to school education in Africa, Brock-Utne notes that, 'learners are supposed to acquire CALP in a language in which they do not have BICS'. African children, particularly in rural areas, are multilingual before they start their schooling, but, unlike immigrant children, they will not necessarily have exposure outside the classroom to a dominant LoLT, usually a colonial language such as French, English or Portuguese. As they enter school, they need to learn a new language and develop CALP at the same time. The participation rate in African HE, which officially uses colonial languages for teaching and learning, shows the effect of these practices: between 0.33% in Mozambique and 9.11% in South Africa according to statistics reported by Pillay (2008). Of course, language proficiency is not the only reason for low participation in HE, but its effect on dismal school exit results, which may act as a barrier to access HE, cannot be denied.

The point (elaborated in Chapter 3) is that a lack of academic language proficiency must be seen as a problem not only for students who have used academic languages other than the HE LoLT but also for students who use varieties of the LoLT. With regard to English in the UK, Preece (2009: 29) notes, 'the language of the institution as "proper English" of "good quality" conforms to dominant institutional norms regulating English and highlights the marginalised status of vernacular varieties of English and its negative connotations within educational settings'. In such settings, being a home language speaker of the LoLT is not enough; speakers of varieties of English can be at a disadvantage and may be required to attend additional 'academic language' courses. When one observes the problems that speakers of non-standard varieties have with academic language use at HE level, it is clear that the concept of a 'home language speaker' requires careful and critical attention, as the discussion in Chapter 3 will show. It is this state of affairs that calls into question a view of multilingualism as *not* being the same as multi-dialecticism as Ouane (2009: 53) claims.

Students, their parents/caregivers and their lecturers know that one particular form of bi-/multilingualism is required to succeed at HE level: one of the languages needs to be *academic* English. Jenkins (2003: 141) refers to *English-knowing bilinguals* to indicate that bi-/multilingualism does not necessarily imply knowledge of *any* number of languages: in internationalised HE contexts, it means *academic* English *plus* other languages.

What this could mean for HEIs is that, if students used a LoLT other than English to complete their school studies, they are not simply bi-/multilingual but also biliterate to varying degrees. This powerful resource is often pushed aside as institutions develop English for Academic Purposes courses or academic literacy programmes in English, as Chapter 3 will show.

A Sociocultural Perspective on Learning

From the preceding sections, the complexity of multilingualism in HE emerges clearly: the introduction of English at many European institutions to support and encourage *transnational* student mobility is a completely different phenomenon to the drive in many African countries (and elsewhere) to push up *national* HE participation rates. In the case of universities in the USA and Britain, which attract the highest number of transnationally mobile students (Varghese, 2008: 16, 18), the lucrative international student market is offset by students' perceived language problems. In both cases, successful completion of courses and programmes is a priority. To complicate this picture even further, we need to acknowledge Hanks' (1991: 24) introductory words to Lave and Wenger's (1991) work, *Situated Learning*:

> Learners, like observers more generally, are engaged both in the contexts of their learning and in the broader social world within which these contexts are produced. Without this engagement, there is no learning, and where the proper engagement is sustained, learning will occur.

It is this perspective on learning, I will argue below, that allows us, at a meta-level, to conceptualise multilingual HE as a situation where students, using the languages they know and those they are getting to know, are enabled to succeed.

The social embeddedness of learning: Classrooms as communities of practice

Söderlundh (2008) describes students at a Swedish HEI using Swedish for classroom presentations despite the fact that the official LoLT is supposed to be English. Due South, at the other end of the globe, Hornberger (2007: 177) describes a grouping of pre-service teacher education students based on shared languages: 'four Nguni speakers (one Zulu, one Xhosa, two Swati), two Gujarati speaking women, three Afrikaans speakers, and one Portuguese speaker (who talks with me) form groups, while the rest of the class members chat to each other in small groups in English'. Officially, the HEI where this occurred uses Afrikaans and English as LoLTs.

Generally speaking, institutional language policies offer only the faintest of outlines of what is actually happening in classrooms. Language education policies are probably only invoked or developed when language 'problems' arise. When proficiency or use of a particular language is required as part of a language policy, this is evidence of the language-as-a-problem orientation because of the impulse to find a solution (in the form of a policy) for a particular language 'problem'. As Shohamy (2006: 77) notes of language in education policies, they 'can create and impose language behaviour' when they aim to 'manage' perceived problems. These problems can emerge at different levels and for a variety of reasons, from the problem of a language being under threat (e.g. using a policy to ensure that Afrikaans is used at South African HEIs) or a language not being used enough (e.g. using a policy to ensure that English is used in postgraduate programmes at some European universities). In between, lecturers and students manage translations, code switches and translanguaging in an effort to get to grips with their academic courses. There must surely be as many examples of multilingual classroom practices as there are classrooms, just as there are many examples of classrooms in which the use of only one language can be demonstrated.

Across these contexts we need to find a heuristic that makes it possible to analyse and evaluate the role of languages in learning in a way that is neither too general for meaningful analysis nor so specific as to yield results that are not relevant for most cases. Lave and Wenger's (1991) concept of *situated learning* offers a way to understand and think about multilingual HE without getting side-tracked by discussions about how a policy can possibly account for all the ways in which languages can be used in classrooms. The concept of *situated learning* focuses on the way in which learning develops and is tightly interwoven with specific communities of practice. This view takes on particular significance for managing languages in HE, since each HEI is embedded in an immediate community from which it draws at least some of its students, and on which it depends for goods and services. Each community differs just as each HEI and each classroom within that institution differs from the next. Transnationally mobile students add to the complexity as the number of students as well as their countries of origin changes from one semester to the next. From the perspective of policy makers, it is clearly impossible to formulate directives for the use of particular languages when the language profile of students is so contingent and fluid. Small wonder then that the use of one, international language seems like an attractive option.

By linking a situated learning perspective with academic literacy, Street (2011) and authors who follow in this tradition, such as Gee (1996 and 2004) and Barton *et al.* (2000), open up the possibility of seeing languages in HE not as an issue that can be dealt with by means of national or institutional language policies, but one that needs to be managed at the level of individual classrooms within the institution. Street (2011) aligns himself with Barton *et al.'s* (2000) recognition of the 'situatedness' of literacy as well as with Hornberger (2009) and her insistence on 'literacy as social practice'.

Developing multiple academic literacies in higher education

Chapter 3 will focus on the concept of academic literacy and its link to programmes that develop language proficiency for specific purposes. At this point, a brief introduction is important to underline the link between academic literacy and multilingual education. Transnationally mobile students are often confronted with programmes in English for academic purposes. Linking up with the phenomenon of massification and transnational student mobility, the language-as-a-resource orientation requires that HE acknowledges the literacies that students have already developed so that learning and achievement can be improved at that level. A monolingual orientation to education sees students and lecturers trying to shut out other literacies ostensibly to boost or foster learning of and through the dominant LoLT. An increasingly globalising and, therefore, multilingual HE situation needs to acknowledge what many Africans already know, which is that 'the monolingual habitus does not take into account the intermeshing of languages *within* multilinguals and in communities, across social domains and communicative practices' (Ouane, 2009: 59, emphasis added). Of course, this is a phenomenon that Africans themselves need to acknowledge and exploit! However, the movement among the African elite seems to be in the opposite direction, with more families moving towards using English as the only language of communication within the family (Bobda, 2006; Dzahene-Quarshie, 2010).

Hornberger (2009: 198) provides the heuristic by means of which different types and levels of literacy can be integrated in learning and teaching. Her continua of biliteracy model (see Figure 1.1) acts as a framework for multilingual environments (not necessarily educational environments) by means of which particular situations can be analysed and evaluated as a possible space that can be opened up for students who use minoritised, foreign and/or low-status languages. Hornberger conceptualises this process as a series of interconnected (or 'nested' as she calls it) relationships on a continuum of biliteracy by enumerating the factors that need to be taken into account when managing multilingual HE:

- the contexts of biliteracy (i.e. the communities within which students communicate on a daily basis, which can range from oral and multilingual at the one end of the continuum to literate and monolingual at the other);
- the media of biliteracy (with simultaneous exposure to more than one language at one end of the continuum and successive exposure at the other);
- the content of biliteracy (moving between minority and majority languages, the vernacular and the literary);
- the development of biliteracy (from reception to production, oral to written). (Hornberger, 2007: 184)

From the perspective of a sociocultural learning theory, the development of academic literacy or CALP (depending on one's ideological orientation) depends on ongoing engagement with particular academic specialisms; this

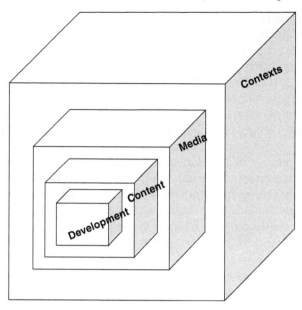

Figure 1.1 Nested relationships among the continua of biliteracy (Hornberger, 2002: 37)

is a prerequisite for students' (critical) socialisation into the discourse of their chosen academic direction. The complexity of multilingual academic environments requires the acknowledgement that academic language itself is a particular variety of a standard language and as such favours those students who use a variety perceived to be close to the high-status LoLT. Furthermore, transnational HE students will already have developed academic literacy in another language as well as a degree of fluency in the LoLT that they will be using at another HEI. They cannot, therefore, be seen as 'language deficient' but rather as emerging biliterates.

Becoming a member of an academic community requires the development of multi-literacies or literacy practices and knowledge that may not be familiar to students from minoritised communities, whether they be immigrant or first-generation students. Although they are not only concerned with literacy practices in HE, Barton and Hamilton's (2000: 8) six statements about literacy give an intimation of where students, who have no prior knowledge or second-hand experiences of HE studies, will struggle to feel part of an HEI:

- 'Literacy is best understood as a set of social practices: these can be inferred from events which are mediated by written texts' (Barton & Hamilton, 2000: 8). At a basic level, the practice of making notes in a classroom and filing them with course handouts in an orderly fashion may be foreign to students who come from a school background where there are no books or additional study material, and each subject simply has a workbook. The practice is often for the teacher to make sure that handouts are pasted into such a workbook.

- 'There are different literacies associated with different domains of life' (Barton & Hamilton, 2000: 8). The extent of domain specificity can be surprising for all first-year undergraduates, not only those from minoritised groups. Negotiating the intricacies of subject-specific discourse depends on students' willingness to ask questions and engage with their lecturers and fellow students. Students who have prior, even second-hand experience of the hierarchical nature of HE will probably be more willing to contact and interact with faculty members. If a prospective student has never heard family stories of asking permission to hand in an assignment late or if reading non-fiction is not an everyday experience (to mention only a fraction of the literacy practices that students engage in) he or she will struggle to manage an academic programme of study.

- 'Literacy practices are patterned by social institutions and power relationships, and some literacies are more dominant, visible and influential than others' (Barton & Hamilton, 2000: 8). At a basic level, majority or high-status languages will be more visible in a particular HE context. Within those dominant languages, certain registers dominate. The power of extended academic writing may be overwhelming for students who are used to writing no more than three or four paragraphs. Well-resourced schools with a tradition of preparing their students for HE access may have focused on academic skills like proper referencing and using an academic style (e.g. not using colloquial forms or personal pronouns, using passive voice and so on). The importance of *oral* presentation and assessment is well known to students at European universities, whereas most HEIs in the Anglo-Saxon world privilege the ability to *write* examinations and tests.

- 'Literacy practices are purposeful and embedded in broader social goals and cultural practices' (Barton & Hamilton, 2000: 8). Although national governments may have broad goals to improve participations rates and throughput, cultural practices at HEIs will determine their interpretation of such broad, social goals. For example, a distinct difference can usually be seen between rural and urban campuses. Where student residences are in close proximity to the campus, which is often the case in rural areas, students may have more contact after formal class hours and more opportunities to form study groups. Students who have family responsibilities or who cannot afford to stay in such residences may miss out on such additional study opportunities (McGhie, 2012).

- 'Literacy is historically situated' (Barton & Hamilton, 2000: 8). Except for the obvious fact that academic ways of writing and referencing developed over several hundred years, departments and units within an institution will have a history that determines, for example, how lectures are presented and which ways of writing and presenting are accepted as good practice. For example, students who enter Stellenbosch University with no knowledge of Afrikaans will be confused by lecturers' code switching between English and Afrikaans.

• 'Literacy practices change and new ones are frequently acquired through processes of informal learning and sense making' (Barton & Hamilton, 2000: 8). This is nowhere more obvious than in advances in technology. For example, students from backgrounds with no access to computers and other electronic devices, downloading electronic material to prepare for classes or uploading a completed assignment can become a serious barrier to successful study. Even experienced academics, who may have been schooled in the tradition of 'reading' a paper at a conference – where reading a paper meant actually reading a paper – now find themselves having to 'present' a paper using a computer programme. The opportunity to learn from others depends on spaces and opportunities to do so. If students feel alienated or not part of a group, their opportunity to learn in this way is compromised.

The link between situated academic learning and the language-as-a-resource paradigm is found in the social construction of literacy. Barton and Hamilton (2000: 13) capture this link succinctly when they say,

It is important to shift from a conception of literacy located in individuals to examine ways in which people in groups utilise literacy. In this way literacy becomes a community resource, realised in social relationships rather than a property of individuals.

In multilingual HE, the languages that students and lecturers share, among themselves and/or with a community outside the HEI, form a resource that Moll (2007: 274) calls a funds-of-knowledge perspective. Arguing from a sociocultural approach for bilingual education at school level in the USA, Moll (2007: 277) insists that from a funds-of-knowledge perspective 'the emphasis is not solely on remediating students' English language limitations, but on utilizing available resources, including the children's or the parents' language and knowledge, in creating new, advanced instructional circumstances for the students' academic development'. In interviews with multilingual HE students, we have shown how they too exploit each other's language proficiency to make sense of lectures, texts and assignments (Van der Walt & Dornbrack, 2011). Students' multilingual abilities and their latent or developed biliteracy is an untapped source that HEIs cannot afford to ignore.

And yet they do. Societal or individual multilingualism is ignored officially in the majority of HEIs and the push to use only English, particularly at postgraduate level, continues unabated in European HE. African HE, as Chapter 2 will show, is mainly English or French, with the latter also including English programmes. English is increasingly introduced in Latin American HE (Gacel-Ávila et al., 2005). Despite perceptions and the active promotion of English as an indication of sophistication and international relevance, Pennycook (1998: 156), in a critical analysis of the imagery by means of which English is presented in popular literature, warns:

> The main points I wish to draw attention to here are, first, the way in which a construction of English as a superior language, when coupled to a belief that to know English is to have available a better way of describing the world, makes of the native speaker of English not merely a supposedly better teacher of English but also somebody endowed with superior knowledge about the world… to try to change the beliefs and practices around these constructs will require a major battle against deeply embedded cultural patterns.

It would be foolish to deny the reality of the power and importance of English (and other dominant languages of learning and teaching in HE), but to pretend that it is the only language in an HE classroom would require quite astonishing powers of imagination. As will be shown in Chapter 4, many lecturers already acknowledge the presence of other languages in their classrooms, and the main challenge may rather be in developing appropriate, multilingual teaching and learning practices for widely divergent contexts.

As Chapter 2 (on multilingual institutions worldwide) will show, attempts to include low-status or indigenous languages in HE continue to fail in Africa as well as India. Although English as a LoLT cannot be singled out as the only reason for low participation and throughput rates in Africa, it is certainly a formidable barrier to overcome. Acknowledging the full repertoire or constellation of languages that are available in HE results in a validation of such languages alongside English and may be a first step towards a more formal acknowledgement of their status as languages of HE.

Moving from Primary and Secondary Bi-/Multilingual Education to Multilingual Higher Education

Publications on bilingual education and bi-/multilingualism have mushroomed in the past decade as a result of increasing interest in multilingualism, and Jessner (2008: 15) claims this is as a direct result of the European Union's commitment to multilingualism. Bi-/multilingualism and bi-/multilingual education seem to be a topic or theme at every language-related conference, to the extent that Ortega (2010) titled her plenary address to the conference of the American Association of Applied Linguists, *The bilingual turn*. It has long been a topic of discussion in Africa, particularly in education, as can be seen in the proceedings of the joint *Third International Conference of the Association for the Development of African Languages in Education, Science and Technology* and the *Fifth Malawian National Languages*

Symposium, where the theme of the joint conference was *Making Multilingual Education a Reality for All: Operationalizing Good Intentions* (Pfaffe, 2004).

The text that can be regarded as the standard in bi-/multilingual education is Colin Baker's *Foundations of Bilingual Education and Bilingualism*, which was first published in 1993 and is now in its fifth edition, with the last four editions being published since 2000. Building on an earlier publication, *Key Issues in Bilingualism and Bilingual Education* (1988), it was (in the 1990s) and still is the definitive British publication linking up with North American predecessors and counterparts such as Christina Bratt-Paulston (1980), Bernhard Spolsky and Robert L. Cooper (1978), and Jim Cummins (1986). In the USA and Canada, bilingual primary, and to some degree secondary, education programmes blossomed in the 1980s and the bulk of the literature on bilingual education was published in these contexts from a variety of perspectives, including educational, political, historical, psychological (including psychometric) and human rights.

The picture is very different in the case of HE. For various reasons, which will be discussed below, publications on the 'problem' of HE students not being primary users of the LoLT have only recently increased in number. In fact, in his definition of bilingual education in the 2008 *Encyclopedia of Language and Education*, Cummins (as co-editor with Nancy Hornberger of volume 5 on bilingual education) links bilingual education specifically to school education: 'The term *bilingual education* refers to the use of two (or more) languages of instruction at some point in a student's school career' (2008: xii).

Officially bi-/multilingual HEIs have existed for a long time, of course, but government initiatives to widen access to HE coupled with the fact and desirability of international student mobility have changed the nature of HEIs so that they are *all* becoming multilingual sites of education. This does not mean that such HEIs were previously mainly monolingual – just that national HEIs have been compelled to acknowledge multilingualism as a result of, first, government calls to widen access to so-called minority students within the country and, second, the presence of so-called international students from outside the country. As institutions turned their attention to language programmes for foreign students, entrance test results and throughput rates forced them to acknowledge domestic students who were not primary users of the institutional LoLT, as, for example, Dustmann *et al.* (2008) show. Preece's (2009) study, which shows that users of local varieties of English in the UK have emerged as students in need of 'language support', underlines the monolithic nature of academic language.

The history and current state of language in education debates cannot be divorced from the 19th century ideal of nation states with national languages, where schooling is an integral part of the development of a citizenry that uses a national language. Institutions of HE are similar to schools in that they are primarily seen as bound to national states and, therefore, not only to (a) national language(s) but, as academic institutions, to *the* particular standard of such (a) language(s). The link between nation states and a national language is the creation of modern times, and the imposition of such national languages on colonised nations is a legacy that education institutions in multilingual communities in, for example, Africa and India, struggle, wrestle and agonise with and ultimately manage as a matter of routine each and every day.

Discussions about language in education, therefore, are ultimately about a kind of projection: where do we (as a community, a region or a country) want to go and what should we look like when we get there? Describing attempts in the 18th century to standardise French, Bourdieu (1991: 49) describes the schools' pressure on parents 'to speak "French" to their children or requiring them to speak "French" at home, with the more or less explicit intention of increasing their value on the educational market'. The parallels with parental, school and government aspiration for learners in the 21st century are clear. A hundred years later and with reference to the USA, Ruiz (1994: 112) claims that '[a]t the root of any new language policy will be some fundamental assumptions about the future of the United States'. The forward-looking nature of policy injunctions is influenced by national and international trends that cascade down from supra-national governments to national governments and further on to universities and schools. What language in education policy statements offer is the implicit promise, first, of a better job and concomitant higher economic status and, second, in the case of less powerful, 'developing' states, citizenship of that nebulous community referred to as 'the global market'. Parents and students in both cases cannot remain unaffected and demand a dispensation that they perceive as economically and professionally advantageous.

HE, because it is seen as the final and best opportunity for formal professional and vocational training, concentrates these expectations to an extraordinary degree. We need only witness the industry that mushroomed around university entrance tests such as the Cambridge International Examinations (CIE) that reports in its quarterly publication *Achieve* (2010), 'Cambridge IGCSE [International General Certificate of Secondary Education] is increasingly adopted by schools in the UK and Europe, as well as countries including Egypt, India and Saudi Arabia – and CIE expects growth to increase in 2010'. Successful completion of the IGCSE allows students access to the university and builds on the good name and reputation of Cambridge University in the UK (http://www.cie.org.uk/).

In the following sections, the argument is made for seeing HE as a very particular kind of multilingual education. Taking a multilingual perspective on HE requires more than the extension and application of primary and secondary school models of bilingual education; it requires a careful investigation into the demands of HE in a globalising and increasingly mobile student body that requires language in highly specialised domains. Whereas internationalisation drives in HE constitute a crucial difference from school education, widening access to local, minoritised students is a shared concern.

Higher Education as a Specific Case in Education

The role of language in HE has been seen not only as empowering (from an Erasmian perspective) but also as a form of elite closure[2] and exclusion. In this regard, the debates are no different from those for primary- and secondary-level schooling. The degree of similarity that emerges in arguments for economic growth and citizenship demonstrates the importance of seeing HE in terms of its continuation of schooling, which emphasises the dependence of HE on lower levels of schooling. However, HE distinguishes itself from the school education in a number of ways that influence language in education choices profoundly. In the discussion that follows, the very obvious differences will be problematised particularly with regard to their far-reaching influence on HE.

Legislative frameworks

As has been alluded to above, an obvious difference between higher and lower levels of education can be found in the legislative imperatives that govern primary education in most nation states. Primary education and, depending on the economic health of a country, secondary education up to a certain level are legislated as compulsory, partly in accordance with the UN Universal Declaration of Human Rights (Article 26:1 and 2):

> Everyone has the right to education. [It] shall be free, at least in the elementary and fundamental stages. Elementary education shall be compulsory ... directed to the full development of the human personality and to the strengthening of respect for human rights and fundamental freedoms...

In line with this declaration, Walters (2001: 35) puts the responsibility to realise the declaration on the shoulders of the state: 'In modern societies public education is a social good, perhaps even a social right, the provision of which is a responsibility of the state'. Cochran-Smith's (2001: 91) fundamental question about school education in the USA is true for schooling all over the world, which is 'how to educate all children well'. The emphasis here is on *all*, with the duration of compulsory schooling mostly determined by the state's ability to support it.[3]

In developed and many developing countries, governments and education departments try to set a general agenda for education up to the age when learners will enter HE, with the motivation of working towards more unified educational goals from primary school through to HE. The results of the Programme for International Student Assessment tests of 15-year-olds' educational achievements in Europe have started discussions on more uniform curricula even before the traditional age of compulsory, formal schooling. Oberhuemer (2005: 29) points out that, '[t]he early years of childhood are receiving increased public policy attention and governments are becoming more aware that investment in early years provision contributes towards an important range of societal goals', particularly by introducing curriculum frameworks. She also notes efforts to integrate various levels of education, 'formulating goals for the education system from birth to 18, as in Sweden and in South Australia, [while] some have issued guidelines for the years from birth up to compulsory schooling, as in Norway'.

Although these steps do not constitute compulsory education, the establishment of core curricula for educational contexts outside of formal schooling can be seen as precursors to extending compulsory schooling. Thus, primary school teachers come to depend on, and expect of, learners to have followed a particular (voluntary) pre-primary, core curriculum, making it difficult for parents to opt out of pre-primary education. Similarly, the receivers of secondary education students (i.e. HEIs) demand and expect certain competencies that non-compulsory, formal secondary education may find difficult to ignore.

Compulsory education, when seen purely as a legislative, UN Declaration issue, masks the social, cultural and economic obstacles to full participation. One has to agree with Law (2007) that making schooling compulsory is more than a matter of legislative procedures. The argument that Law (2007) makes about China is made by Achoka et al. (2007) about Kenya, which is that social and cultural conditions play as large a role as do the legislative measures in getting children into schools. These factors are crucial in the process of learners continuing beyond compulsory schooling to upper secondary education and further on to HE.

What happens after compulsory schooling is largely up to individual communities' cultural practices (e.g. whether to send girls or boys for further education), available financing (by the state and families) and individual intellectual ability and motivation (e.g. by passing school exit examinations at a certain level). A high degree of personal choice to take up HE means that HEIs locate the responsibility to succeed in the individual student who needs to qualify to enrol and to progress at each level of a particular programme. The question 'Who belongs in higher education?' may mean at an institutional level that HEIs do not feel much pressure to create an inclusive environment that would allow bigger numbers of students to succeed. Judging by the literature on participation rates and concerns about drop out and failure rates worldwide, the point that Scott (2009: 25) makes about South African universities regarding the students who are admitted, can be applied to HEIs across the world:

> Perhaps the most fundamental factor, however, is psychological ownership of the student intake, that is, the extent to which the academic community intrinsically accepts responsibility for accommodating the student body that is admitted to the sector.

The fact that such responsibility is often delegated to 'academic support' or 'academic development' units outside academic departments indicates that 'intrinsically accepting responsibility', as Scott calls it, is not widespread.

For South Africa, as is the case for institutions that accept minoritised and transnational students worldwide, epistemological access means taking responsibility for success beyond entrance requirements.

Seen from the perspective of compulsory primary and secondary education, HE seems blissfully free of government or supra-national organisations' interference. Marginson and Van der Wende (2007: 3) claim, 'Higher education was always more internationally open than most sectors because of its immersion in knowledge, which never showed much respect for juridical boundaries'. Varghese (2008: 10) agrees, pointing out that, '[u]niversities, although they are national entities, have been recognized as some of the most international institutions, even in periods of aggressive nationalism'.

The reality is, of course, far from simple. Despite its 'autonomy' and 'academic freedom', HEIs, particularly universities, are not immune to government-imposed curricula and assessment strategies. Government investigations into the spending of public funds for teaching as well as research, government initiatives to assure the quality of education and national policy drives to widen access (nationally as well as internationally) mean that HE cannot ignore legislation and government initiatives.

A case in point

The subtle and often not-so-subtle ways in which government intervention directs HE policy and practice are exemplified by a Finnish representative of the Ministry of Education, Anita Lehikoinen, who describes her government's steering of a new strategy for internationalisation in Finnish HE (Lehikoinen, 2004: 45):

> However, all 20 universities and all 29 polytechnics now offer courses in English. This is due to the fact that the national government still sees the internationalisation of higher education as one of the cornerstones of developing our higher education system ... Polytechnics have been rewarded by performance-related funding ... Meanwhile we stopped giving performance-related funding to universities on the basis of internationalisation, when we thought that all universities understood that they had to be international by nature, that they couldn't be competitive without it, but we soon realised that this was not the case ... We have now reintroduced the indicator on international activities regarding university funding also.

The inevitable clash between HE setting its own agenda and government countering that with funding measures is clear when Lehikoinen (2004: 47) bluntly states that 'the starting point of this strategy was definitely competition ... This was not seen as a very good starting point by some of our scholars, but we thought the world had changed and we had to react to those changes'.

However, HEIs also have the power to influence education policies in general. Entrance requirements to these institutions are interpreted in a way that results in the imposition of curriculum content and a particular level of assessment at secondary-school level, particularly regarding school exit qualifications. This state of affairs is a reason for frequent conflict with school education authorities as well as national governments, because, by simply viewing certain kinds of secondary education as academic preparation for HE, practitioners in HE run the risk of ignoring the ideological forces that inevitable accompany government-initiated curricula and assessment strategies at school level.

Cases in point
- In the USA, calls for extending a general education into HE is an ongoing debate, traced by Boyer and Levine (1981) and picked up again by Lemann (1999), calling for a 'national curriculum' in reaction to the SATs HE entrance procedures, which consistently exclude students from lower socio-economic groups. Referring to the mutual influence that school and HE exert on each other, Boyer notes, 'The problem is that in recent years, as general education requirements were abandoned by higher education, such requirements were abandoned in the schools' (Boyer & Levine, 1981: 34). Maerhoff (1982: 14), writing in the same time frame as Boyer, berates universities, in particular, for their arrogance: 'Few institutions of higher education bother finding out whether their prescriptions for reform will make good medicine for the high schools'. Maerhoff (1982: 13) is particularly concerned about the fact that, in the USA, the HE requirement for foreign language was dropped in the 1960s, resulting in foreign languages disappearing from high school curricula as well.
- In the recent past, South African school curricula have undergone major changes in response to post-apartheid schooling demands. Opting for an outcomes-based approach to education since 2000, what was previously known as 'subjects' were either merged to form one 'learning area', for example, Geography and History became Social Studies, or re-conceptualised, for example, Biology came to be known as 'Life Sciences' up to the end of compulsory schooling. HEIs never adopted these learning areas. As a result of mounting pressure from academics, parents and teachers, the Ministry of Basic Education spearheaded the development of new curriculum documents in which the term 'subjects' is used again (albeit with one reference to learning areas) and all outcomes-based terminology has been removed (Ministry of Basic Education, 2011).

From these examples, it is clear that the academic autonomy of HE varies depending on the extent of state funding. Even in the case of the Harvards and Cambridges of this world, the presence of national government is obvious in terms of pressure to widen access and particularly in determining the kind of student that HE can expect. Since students exit from a secondary school system that is largely funded and managed by central and/or federal governments, HEIs will need to deal with curriculum changes and innovations that they may not necessarily support. In turn, they exert pressure on schools to provide students with the skills needed at HE level. Schofer and Meyer's (2005: 46) statement that the expansion of HE means that '[t]he university becomes a central, not a specialized, institution' may increasingly move HE into legislative frameworks typical of primary and secondary schooling. However, the real force that results in standardisation and similarity of programmes across HEIs is that of the world of work: in the form of professional councils (e.g. health professions councils) and future employers. The impact of an increasingly globalising world has widened the influence of these 'players' – an issue that will be discussed in more detail in Chapter 3.

Language learning in a step-wise approach to learning

The way in which we look at the development of literacies as one of the outcomes of learning is very narrowly linked to the LoLT. School language is a particular variety of (usually) the national language of a country or region and is deeply embedded in school socialisation: the way we greet the teacher, the way we have to raise our hands to ask for permission to speak, the way we are forced to speak even when we cannot or will not. The process by which educators develop the curriculum, with their focus on what seems valuable, typically inculcates this school language and gradually socialises the learner away from the habits of home language use and in many cases also from the language used at home.

This school discourse differs from the discourses that children learn to use at home, even if education authorities insist that the home language is the *medium of instruction*. Whatever we call this home language, maybe the same as the *medium of instruction*, or a bit further removed, a variety of the *medium of instruction* or, furthest away, quite a different language from the *medium of instruction*, we need to recognise that its use is quite different from that of school language. Like the discourses required at HE levels, this school language requires constant engagement and specialist routines to discover the 'rules of the game' for using it.

Decisions about the use of language in education (i.e. language planning and policy making) are usually in the hands of education administrators, and sometimes language experts, with the result that teachers (and HE lecturers) have little say in the pedagogical relevance or appropriateness of policy decisions to particular contexts (Shohamy, 2006: 78). Policy processes are 'shaped by multiple levels of institutional authority' (Field, 2008: 79) and perceptions of what language is and can do strongly determine the way in which the role of language in education is conceptualised. Perceptions of language as an instrument or a tool are evident in the phrase *medium of instruction,* which posits language as a channel through which knowledge passes more or less unscathed. If you use it well, meaning is revealed, almost like opening an oyster or mining a seam of gold. Using it well is a skill that can be learnt and practised. If misunderstanding arises, so the argument goes, we need to fine tune the receiver (often) or the sender (seldom). The channel is neutral, smooth and singular – any snags can be ironed out by working on the receivers.

At HE level, students are expected to have mastered the LoLT up to a specified level, either indicated by a school exit certificate or tested before entering the HEI. Language support (in the form of specific purposes or academic literacy courses) may be offered for weaker students. (This topic is discussed at length in Chapter 3.) When such support is presented in the shape of a narrowly conceptualised curriculum of foundational (study) skills, the social and affective nature of learning and the complexity of disciplinary language use are denied. A building-block approach that locks language support into first year or foundational courses supports the misconception that 'generic' language support will transfer to disciplinary language use. Larsen-Freeman (2006), writing from a dynamic systems perspective, argues that language learning 'is not discrete and stage-like but more like the waxing and waning of patterns; that, from a target-language perspective, certain aspects of the behavior are progressive, others, regressive; that change can be gradual and it can be sudden; and that the latter notably heralds the emergence of a new order qualitatively different and novel from earlier organizations' (Larsen-Freeman, 2006: 590). What this means is that disciplinary language will probably not develop as the result of a neatly packaged semester module.

The fact that institutes and bureaux of university teaching or academic support are often located outside of academic contexts means that they attempt to facilitate students' membership of their chosen academic field from outside, usually in the form of 'academic literacy' or 'English as a second language' or 'ESL' courses in the first year. As Hyland and Hamp-Lyons (2002: 6) insist, '[i]t is important for EAP [English for Academic Purposes] to ... establish practices that challenge the widely-held assumption that academic conventions are universal and independent of particular disciplines as this undermines our professional expertise and leads learners to believe that they simply need to master a set of transferable rules'. Academic staff, who have to cope with the pressure of their own research, try to carry on in the way they were integrated into the academic community, using a mixture of personal and individual strategies along the lines of, 'I made it – so can they'. This particular stance makes institutions of HE quite a different experience from school and studies of first year students repeatedly report on their perception: you are on your own.

The OECD (2008) claims that only one in three students complete a degree; a result that cannot be ascribed only to language, social class or ethnic minority membership – the reasons often identified for academic failure (see below). So even when we factor out (for argument's sake) minoritised students who do *not* use the language of the institution by focusing, for example, on a middle class, home language speaker of the institutional language, the chances are that this learner will enter HE with good secondary school results and still fail to complete a programme of study.

As will be elaborated upon in Chapter 3, the specialised nature of disciplinary work and the (perceived) idiosyncratic habits of the experts dealing with such work define success in terms of the degree to which students know the 'rules' of these disciplinary 'clubs' where the use of academic language is often tacit yet highly circumscribed. Although the international nature of HE means that disciplinary language is widely acknowledged, the famed autonomy of academics means that scientific paradigms and disciplinary language are often specific to particular universities, faculties and departments, even specific professors. This balancing act between the local and the global constitutes one of the biggest challenges for HEIs not only in teaching and learning but also in terms of research.

Situated in the Local and the Global

A view of the physical placement of schools as opposed to HEIs gives one indication of the way in which society views these different institutions. Primary and secondary schools are often enclosed spaces – either enclosed completely by high walls or by fences; interpreted variously as protective (if you are a parent) or prison-like (if you are an unwilling student). Their physical location echoes their legal status as places where people of a certain age and disposition have to be protected and kept inside and people who want to enter need special permission. The fact that many national and regional education departments require that parents live in the vicinity of the school further attests to its focus on the local with concomitant problems, for example, reserving privilege, since middle-class or wealthy parents who live in the vicinity of the school may improve or add to the school's resources, to the advantage of the learners. Even so-called international schools are reserved (to varying degrees) for the children of embassy staff, foreign professionals in a host country and wealthy parents.

HEIs can be spread over a number of campuses in different cities or buildings and in some cases they are virtual. This relative openness can be interpreted as evidence that *adults* are able to come and go as they please and that the institution serves a wider and, for many centuries, an international population. As Altbach (2004: 64) notes, 'Universities began as global institutions that employed Latin as a common language, enabling them to serve an international clientele of students. Professors, too, came from afar, and the knowledge they imparted reflected the entirety of scholarly learning of that period in the Western world'.

The development of literacy in one or more local languages further attests to the situatedness of primary schools in the local, and additional national or international languages are added as children progress towards secondary schooling. The current term 'additional language learning' is an attempt to move away from subtractive models of language learning, where another, usually dominant language was not merely learnt, but substituted the home or community language. In the 'additive' model, the principle is that children would add to their language repertoire (García, 2009: 52). This terminological sleight of hand has had little effect on actual practice. In Africa, where children may start off their schooling in a home or, more often, a community language, the practice of switching to a colonial language after two or three years persists, leading to the implicit judgement that home or community languages are not good enough for schooling. In view of the fact that HE is available only in colonial languages (with the exception of Tanzania to an extent, and Arab-speaking universities), parents and children would argue that the use of colonial languages in education is obviously the way to go. A more nuanced view of bi-/multilingualism at school and HE level is needed to obviate this either–or choice, as has been argued at length by Alexander (1995) and Banda (2000) in the South African school context and García (2009) in the US school context. The CLIL approach in European schools increasingly includes bilingual education, with English as the main language used alongside local languages.

At HE level, the use of an international language or *lingua franca,* almost inevitably English, is similarly perceived to provide access to more opportunities and better jobs and is seen to facilitate communication among international researchers and students. In the majority of cases, the choice is between English and a national language. The use of a national language at HE level is seen as a problem and obstacle to access and internationalisation (see below for a discussion on internationalisation and globalisation), as is clearly seen in the formulation by Crosier *et al.* (2007: 45, emphasis added) in their overview of HE mobility in Europe:

> The site visits also revealed rapid advancements in the provision of programmes through English, particularly at Master and PhD level. The introduction of these 'Bologna' 2nd and 3rd cycle programmes has certainly boosted the international attractiveness of many universities. However, some systems do not allow the teaching in the first [undergraduate][4] cycle through English, but insist on the national languages. Some universities offer parallel first-cycle programmes through English for international students – but staff and students often do not consider these courses to be of the same quality as the 'national language' programmes. Language *barriers* therefore continue to pose major *obstacles* for mobility, even where programmes are now offered in English.

The use of words such as *obstacle* and *barrier* is testimony to the language-as-a-problem orientation, as identified by Ruiz (1994), but the citation above also shows how attempts to satisfy both the local and the global is not viewed positively by either the institutions or the researchers. A monolingual worldview is evident and pressure to use one language, English, is persistent. The tension that HEIs live with as they manage the demands of local and international students is evident here.

At local level in particular, attempts to wide access have led to the diversification of university populations, which according to Hyland (2006: 16, 17) have led to a move away from the traditional 'white middle class monolingual school leavers in full-time enrolment' to 'working class, mature, ethnic minority and international students'. One of the results of this change, Hyland (2006: 17) points out, is that 'teachers can no longer assume that students' previous learning experiences will provide appropriate schemata and skills to meet course demands, while students themselves bring different identities, understandings and habits of meaning-making to their learning'.

Hyland's assertion underscores the point made earlier that HE has been pressurised to acknowledge a local and diverse student body that has probably existed before calls for internationalisation became louder. This means that HE has to balance the needs of local students against those of international students at different levels:

- Local students may be first-generation HE students with very particular emotional and academic needs.
- They may not have had the advantage of well-resourced schools.
- They may be using a variety of the standard LoLT, which may complicate the introduction of a second language as the main language of learning and teaching.
- The language of secondary schooling may be different from the one used in HE, which would affect particularly the first year performance as well as persistence in the HE system.

The link with secondary schooling is an important consideration if HEIs also need to serve a student body that is mainly local – even if all students eventually want to play on the 'global' stage. In a study on Swedish students, Söderlundh (2008) shows the global and the local in competition when, for example, English is used as the language of teaching. She interviewed students who spoke Swedish in class despite the fact that English was the language of instruction. The reasons mentioned are predictable: a lack of proficiency in English, awkwardness in speaking English to fellow Swedish-speaking students and, most importantly, in this case, 'participants are used to being able to speak Swedish at school' (Söderlundh, 2008: 99).

The dynamic nature of what it means to be 'global' may mean that certain global trends become 'localised'; for example, Haberland and Risager (2008: 43) discuss the role of English at Roskilde University, both for national and for international students:

People do not learn *either* English *or* German *or* French *or* Russian etc., but *first* English and *then* German (*or* Spanish *or* French). They may be better at Spanish than at English, but even those who are good at Spanish will usually still know English. Since this is so for the indigenous student population, the system is self-reinforcing: it attracts foreign students that fit this pattern. In the early years of HIB, e.g. Greek students whose first foreign language was German, or Italian students who were better at French than at English, were not altogether rare at HIB. Now they are.

The diversification of the student population in terms of local and transnational students can be conceptualised as two different movements in HE. The increased enrolment of local students can be seen as vertical, in the sense of non-traditional or minoritised students gaining access to institutions that served, traditionally, mainly middle-class students, a kind of 'upward mobility'. 'Foreign' or 'international' students who gain access to HEIs outside their home country, usually after obtaining a first degree in their home countries, can be seen as a horizontal movement, since they have had access to HE previously, as will be explained below. Compared with schools, where the concern is mainly with vertical mobility, HE has to deal with both, as will be argued next.

Vertical mobility and the construction of minoritised learners and students

Two interrelated themes that emerge from the literature on compulsory schooling are its importance for economic growth and development and the inclusion and performance of minoritised learners. These themes are also important in HE but in a different way. The importance of diversity at school level cannot be underestimated, since the successful management of diversity at that level means that HE will be able to rely on school education to widen participation – an upward or vertical movement – that has led to the rapid expansion of HE. Schofer and Meyer (2005: 39) find in their sociological survey that 'secondary education has a substantial effect on tertiary enrolments'. Widening access to include minoritised students in HE is an issue that brings perceptions of minoritised communities (within a national context) into sharp focus. In the discussion that follows, the role that language plays in the construction of minoritised students will be shown to have serious implications for schools as well as for HEIs when they insist on a single LoLT.

At school level, the argument for widening access to foster national economic growth starts at pre-primary level and can be seen in concerns raised by the general public (in typical 'Why Johnny cannot read' debates) as well as transnational organisations (by launching initiatives to raise literacy levels in developing countries). For example, the Organization for Economic Co-operation and Development (OECD, 2008: 45) reports that too many South African school leavers are functionally illiterate and that improving basic education lies at the heart of accelerated economic growth in South Africa. Except for such nebulous economic advantages, the link between schooling and economic activity is more explicitly demonstrated in research in the USA and UK, where housing costs and primary school performance are correlated positively, with parents moving to areas where 'good' schools are located (Black, 1999; Gibbons & Machin, 2003).

Minoritised groups are categorised as 'minorities' on the basis of several features, for example, ethnicity, home or community language use or immigrant status. Being a member of a particular class (usually working class or low socio-economic status) is taken into account and sometimes a combination of these factors will be taken into consideration (often in terms of gender *and* ethnicity). A quick glance through the table of contents of books on widening access to education illustrates the features that construct certain people as minorities. Cole (2006), for example, treats education, equality and human rights with reference to gender, race, sexuality, disability and class. The word 'disadvantaged' is often linked to children from such communities. For example, in a report on the programme *Aimhigher*, a project launched in Leeds, it is reported that, '[t]here are many areas of serious disadvantage within its borders. Around 11% of the population are from Black and ethnic minority groups with significant numbers of migrant or asylum seeking families' (Muskens, 2009: 27). In a direct reference to the Bernstein idea of lower socioeconomic status (SES) children not having access to an elaborated code that links up more closely to the language of the school, this report traces the history of 'priority education' from the 1970s, where, 'In the UK, The Netherlands, the Scandinavian countries and in other countries too, it was acknowledged that children from lower socio-economic strata and/or children, who were not raised at home in a so-called "elaborated" code, had less chance to attain the highest ranks of education' (Muskens, 2009: 27). Hatcher (2006: 212) links economic status to a particular relationship with knowledge that low SES learners seem to lack and he links this particularly to language: 'Language is not just a medium of communication; it mediates thinking, it enables interior dialogue' (Hatcher, 2006: 215).

Much of the existing literature focuses on the degree to which such learners differ from the 'mainstream', to the extent that the concept of 'mainstream' learners itself becomes problematic. It would be facile to argue merely that this is a process of 'othering' that reproduces power relations in society; the question in a post-modern world should be to re-think the purpose and aim of compulsory schooling. The question is whether we are still seeing schooling from a Deweyan perspective, when he says (Dewey, 1916: 114),

> Accomplishment of this end [providing education for all groups and classes] demands not only adequate administrative provision of school facilities, and such supplementation of family resources as will enable youth to take advantage of them, but also such modification of traditional ideals of culture, traditional subjects of study and traditional methods of teaching and discipline as will retain all the youth under educational influences until they are equipped to be masters of their own economic and social careers.

One can criticise Dewey for his deterministic view of education (among others), but far more striking is the lack of progress, particularly in maintaining bilingual programmes in the USA (see Chapter 3), since these words were written. Just more than 75 years later, DeVillar and Faltis (1994: 1) introduced an edited volume (co-edited with Cummins) on cultural diversity and quality schooling with the statement, 'Schools in the United States are generally characterized by policies and practices that are antithetical to meeting our nation's purported goal of delivering a comparable education to its culturally and racially diverse populace'.

In a 1988 publication, aptly titled *Minority Education: From Shame to Struggle,* Skutnab-Kangas (1988: 32) incisively analysed the process whereby the performance of minority children is always located in a deficit argument:

> The first four phases in the development which most countries seem to be going through are based on *deficit theories.* There is *something wrong with the minority child* (1, L2-related handicap: the child does not know enough of the majority language), *the minority parents* (2, socially conditioned handicap: the parents are working class), *the whole minority group* (3, culturally conditioned handicap: the child's cultural background is 'different'), *or all of these* (4, L1-related handicap: the child does not know her own language and culture properly, and this leaves her without a firm basis for L2-learning, and gives her poor self-confidence). To a small extent there may also be something lacking in majority *individuals* (not systems), peers and teachers who may discriminate, because they have not had enough information.

The complexity of what O'Connor (2001: 160) calls 'intersectionalities' of social identity, which would include the most common categories of race, gender and class cannot, of course, *predict* failure or success, as McGhie (2012) has shown. It would be simplistic to single out language as the main element in success or failure at HE level. However, 'attention to the complexity of how social identity is registered in the social world provides one lens by which we may make sense of how culture, structure, and human agency intersect' (O'Connor, 2001: 161) and when mastery of an academic code consistently emerges across different cultures, races and classes as a significant condition for successfully completing a course of study, the exclusionary nature of such codes needs to be acknowledged, as the following examples show.

Cases in point
- In the case of Ebonics, ethnicity and a particular variety of English led to the request that Ebonics, also known as African American Vernacular English (AAVE) (Talbot *et al.*, 2003: 208), be recognised as the primary language of black learners in the Oakland (USA) school district and that this language be used in classrooms to support their development of Standard American English since their use of Ebonics or AAVE was seen as the main reason for their underachievement and over-representation in special needs classes.

(Continued)

Cases in point (Continued)

• The degree to which low achievement is still located in the child, her language and her culture can also be seen in a recent report on minority children's performance at school by Dustmann *et al.* (2008: 25) where it is noted, 'We find that language spoken at home is an important reason for the low achievement of ethnic minority pupils at the beginning of primary school'. The authors also illustrate how improvement in (presumably English) language ability supports the gains that such children make:

> However, the impact of language on achievement declines as children grow older. Consequently, language helps to explain why ethnic minority pupils make greater progress than white British pupils, and why Black Caribbean pupils make smaller progress than any other ethnic group.

Although the Dustmann *et al.* (2008) article is not always clear on what 'language' may mean in these contexts, the interplay of ethnicity, language and poverty as reasons for failure and excellence is clear. One can only guess that, in the case of black Caribbean pupils, the use of a 'non-standard' variety of English may cause 'smaller progress'. In cases where the use of so-called non-standard languages causes learners and prospective students to struggle with the language of the institution and to 'qualify' for language support, the arbitrary nature of standard languages and school language in particular, is revealed. In their study of modernity, Baumann and Briggs (2003: 9) argue that the construction of particular codes as separate languages is 'at the very core of the process involved in creating language and rendering it a powerful means of social inequality'.

A common and recurring theme in debates around massification and epistemological access concerns students' inability to read and write at appropriate levels, which, in turn, is blamed on low levels of proficiency in the LoLT, typically seen as the responsibility of secondary school teachers or foundational ('academic development') programmes in HE. (The role of academic language development will be discussed in Chapter 3.) Since there are very few completely monolingual communities, our acknowledgement of bi-/multilingualism in schooling seems self-evident. García (2009: 11) argues that 'some form of bilingual education is *good for all education, and therefore good for all children, as well as good for all adult learners*' (italics in the original). This position opens the way for the acknowledgement of bi-/multilingualism in HE, first, because HE is dependent on secondary schooling to deliver students who can manage academic demands, including cognitive academic language use. Second, an explicit acknowledgement that students are multilingual and that this fact is a resource that can be accessed for improved learning goes a long way towards tolerance of linguistic diversity, as García suggests.

Despite Schofer and Meyer's (2005) assertion that, compared with the 19th century, HE has already expanded massively, Egron-Polak (2008: 6),

speaking for the International Association for Universities, states unequivo-
cally that access needs to widen even more and that '[e]quitable access to
and broader participation in HE require active *linkages between higher education and primary and secondary education*' (emphasis in the original). Links to
schools are therefore actively cultivated by so-called outreach programmes
initiated by HEIs, often in an attempt to identify and encourage learners
from minoritised groups to enrol at the HEI.

Cases in point
- Sidney Sussex College at Cambridge University (UK) notes on its
  website:

  > Since the New Year, Sidney's admissions staff have been busy
  > visiting schools, colleges and Higher Education fairs, travelling
  > as far afield as the Channel Islands and Newcastle. We have
  > also welcomed several school groups to the College, to give
  > pupils a taste of student life in Cambridge. (http://www.sid.
  > cam.ac.uk/life/news/newsitem.html?nid=46 on 9 July 2010)

- The so-called Junior University in Porto, Portugal, advertises short
  summer courses for children from 10 to 18 with the express purpose
  of choosing 'their future university course' (http://eucu.net/files/
  Mini-Poster/Junior%20University%20Porto.pdf on 9 July 2010).
- Economic incentives form part of the process of attracting students
  with a particular profile. The University of Oklahoma notes:

  > The K20 Scholars program offers scholarships to high school
  > graduates from the K20 Center's network schools who are
  > entering the University of Oklahoma to pursue degrees in sci-
  > ence, technology, engineering and mathematics. The program
  > provides four-year scholarships and a laptop computer for each
  > student. K20 Scholars also receive additional money to design
  > and implement a service-learning project in their hometown.
  > (http://k20center.publishpath.com/k20-scholars on 9 July 2010)

- In developing countries, these kinds of incentives become very important for students who qualify for HE but do not have the means to
  attend university. In the South African context, the government-
  controlled National Student Financial Aid Scheme of South Africa
  (NSFAS) 'seeks to impact on South Africa's historically skewed student, diplomate and graduate populations by providing a sustainable
  financial aid system that enables academically deserving and financially needy students to meet their own and South Africa's development needs' (NSFAS, 2010). However, the 2009 report raises the
  problem that many HEIs face when they try to address national and
  international needs and widen access: 'Many of the bursaries target
  scarce skills, and finding learners with the required academic subjects
  is a national challenge' (NSFAS Annual Report, 2009: 8).

The outreach programmes described above are important indicators of HEIs' commitment to widening access, which is hoped to lead to increased participation rates in HE in developed as well as developing countries. However, these rates need to be interpreted very carefully. The usual interpretation of participation in HE is that provided by the OECD as the 'proportion of young people who enter HEIs, in each year, in a country' (OECD, 2006: 268). In a 'global' report on HE, Usher and Cervenan (2005: 17) derive scores for the accessibility of education by aggregating different measures to arrive at 'the percentage of the 25–34 year old population [that] has completed a "tertiary type A" (higher education) degree'. This kind of score would obviously be much lower than the population entering HE, but it indicates the importance of persisting and completing a qualification. Once again, social factors may play a role. Shavit *et al*. (2007: 3) point to the many factors that influence the availability of HE and the factors that play a role in choosing HE study in their comparative study of inclusion strategies in HE, 'those raised in middle class homes are less likely to drop out, and are more likely to attend first-tier [research universities] than they are to attend second-tier [vocational or semi-professional] institutions, compared with students from disadvantaged social origins'.

In its wide-ranging review of educational access, the UNESCO Institute for Statistics (2007) compares countries that participated in its World Education Index (WEI) to OECD countries. The WEI includes the Russian Federation, Malaysia, Peru, Chile, Jordan, Brazil, Thailand, Egypt, the Philippines, China, Paraguay, Indonesia, Argentina, Tunisia and India. In this study, the indicator used to compare successful participation in HE across a wide variety of countries is the 'gross graduation ratio, which is interpreted as a proxy for the *share* of the graduation-age population that completes an education programme' (UNESCO Institute for Statistics, 2007: 15). Graduation is defined as the completion of a tertiary type A programme, like Usher and Cervenan (2005). Whereas this definition can be criticised as being just one more formula, the sheer range of countries compared in this way provides a detailed picture of the degree to which countries deliver qualified graduates. The report summarises its findings on participation rates (UNESCO Institute for Statistics, 2007: 18) by pointing out that '[t]he average graduation ratio for tertiary type A programmes in WEI countries is 19.7%, just more than one-half of the OECD average. Yet, with 5.7 million graduates, WEI countries trained more people at this level than all OECD countries combined', which is not surprising when one takes into account that China and India were included in the WEI countries. When Tertiary type B programmes (which have 'a more occupational or practical orientation') are taken into account, the survey shows that '[t]hese programmes play a bigger role in tertiary graduation in WEI countries than in OECD countries' (UNESCO Institute for Statistics, 2007: 18).

Participation rates show the degree to which compulsory education prior to HE consistently fails certain members of a society. When we consider that schools are still struggling to eradicate inequalities and that current trends in terms of migration will probably continue, it is clear that current strategies, of which monolingual education in a national language is one, are not improving participation.

With regard to the South African situation, Bunting *et al.* (2009: 3) make the important point that 'The big equity issue for the university system is not trying to squeeze a few more black students into the institutions, but addressing the inequity in pass rates (success rates), which, it could be argued, *is a problem for both the unequal school system and the universities'* (emphasis added). Vertical mobility therefore remains a problem. Some of the reasons are suggested by Egron-Polak (2009: 5), who notes that the socioeconomic status of potential students as well as their ethnic background remains obstacles to entering HE and university, in particular.

In their review of European HE, Crosier *et al.* (2007: 26) point to the role of HE in vertical mobility: 'Questions of broadening access to higher education and creating a better educated society are also undoubtedly growing, and higher education institutions are at the heart of these crucial societal discussions'. At the same time, they report the puzzling problem that 97% of HEIs agree that they support widening access but that 'only 17% of all European higher education institutions expect socio-economically disadvantaged students to have better opportunity to access higher education in the future' (Crosier *et al.*, 2007: 66). Moreover, 50% of the institutions feel that they are taking enough action on this front. Crosier *et al.* speculate that this may be because HEIs feel that government policy or the school system should take the responsibility for change in this arena. In the USA, debates about widening participation are characterised by extreme opinions, from the initiation of affirmative action programmes to reactions against such policies (Stern & Briggs, 2001). It would seem that, despite their outreach programmes with schools and so-called 'junior' university courses, HEIs perceive their purpose as either advertising the institution or identifying the best students as early as possible and attracting them to the institution with bursaries. As Osborne (2003) notes, 'despite the widening of participation, the relative gains of the under-represented might be limited, as élite institutions preserve their traditional boundaries.'

For the purpose of the current discussion, the relevant point is that a language background that does not provide supposedly seamless access to the LoLT (at secondary and HE levels) forms an important part of the mix of features that constructs a learner/student as from a 'minority' background. The danger for HEIs where internationalisation is high on the institutional agenda could be that concerns about access to HE by minoritised students inside the country are overshadowed by discussions about how to increase access for transnationally mobile students.

Horizontal mobility: Transnational student movements

The term 'horizontal' is used here in more than one sense. It indicates, first, that HEIs provide access to students from *outside* the country to complete mostly postgraduate programmes and, second, that transnationally mobile students attempt to access comparable semesters or modules *within* a particular qualification or a postgraduate qualification that would be compatible with their graduate results at their home institution. Altbach and Knight (2006: 3) indicate that transnational mobility can also act as vertical mobility: '[t]he largest markets are therefore for "demand absorbing" programs that provide access to students who could not otherwise attend a postsecondary institution'. Although the move from graduate to postgraduate studies can also be seen as vertical movement, I want to reserve the term *horizontal* particularly for movements between countries since this in itself is seen as a major factor in the provision of education to linguistically diverse students. This type of movement is actively promoted as the *internationalisation* of HE. Bashir (2007: 9) indicates that there is a proliferation of terms in this area:

> The Organization for Economic Co-operation and Development (OECD) has used the term 'internationalization of higher education' to cover many forms of international exchanges and distinguishes between student, program and institutional mobility to characterize the different forms of this exchange. Others refer to cross-border, transnational, offshore or borderless education.

The purpose of using the term *horizontal* to characterise the movement of transnationally mobile students is to distinguish between access to HE by low-status and minoritised students at a national level and access to HE by international students from outside the country. By contrasting the vertical with the horizontal, a visualisation of the two competing challenges for HE is emphasised.

Reasons for transnational mobility

Varghese (2008: 22) identifies push and pull factors, for transnational mobility, of which increased opportunities for funding support (as a pull factor at postgraduate level) may be linked to limited opportunities in the home country (a push factor). From an institutional perspective, Egron-Polak (2009: 3), mentions eight reasons for HEIs to increase transnational or horizontal mobility: to broaden the choice of programmes, to promote understanding, to learn languages, to further geo-political and economic interests, to improve the quality of programmes, to promote collaborative research, to follow demographic trends and to generate revenue. The fact that language learning is included is significant, particularly when seen as part of the academic advantage of increased mobility.

The official management of transnational student movement is nowhere more evident than in Europe. Within the European Union increased mobility of students is an explicit goal of the Bologna process: 'Increasing the attractiveness of the European Higher Education area for the rest of the world has been the driving force of the Bologna Process since its inception'

(Crosier *et al.*, 2007: 46). There are many bigger and smaller reasons why there should be such a strong push to increase the attractiveness of European HE. Nastansky (2004: 49) notes that internationalisation is driven by various forces, of which globalisation and the developing European community and particularly the Bologna process are the two most important forces. Lehikoinen (2004: 41), from a Finnish perspective, adds that the first reason for internationalisation in her country was to enhance the quality of local HE by offering local students a wider selection of courses (by sending them to foreign universities) and, after a while, also attracting foreign students and staff to Finnish universities.

Lofty ideals about increasing intellectual exchange are, however, overshadowed by the much more concrete motivation of financial gains. In their review, Crosser *et al.* (2007) report that, '[a]s well as furthering academic and research links with other regions of the world, these students provide an independent funding stream for the institution, which is in some cases used to make up part of the shortfall in national funding to meet the full economic cost of EU students'. In the United Kingdom, enrolling foreign students is a lucrative business as a direct result of the Thatcher era, when expensive study fees were introduced for foreign students. As Schumann (2008: 15) points out, at this stage, high study fees had already been introduced at American (presumably the USA), Australian and Canadian universities.[5]

This practice is continued in the UK today because the number of local enrolments was capped by the Labour government of Tony Blair and foreign students constitute a welcome source of income (Altbach & Knight, 2006: 2). As Marginson and Van der Wende (2007: 5) point out, '[f]or certain institutions, especially in the English-speaking world, international operations have become the primary mode of development'. In Europe, where HE is (at least to some extent) free, countries had to make the decision whether they would have a different fee structure for foreign students. The view of education as a 'common good' and, therefore, free (to varying extents) is strong in Europe and is seen as an obstacle to 'handing over the development of higher education to the free market' (Bashir, 2007: 70). However, Coleman (2006: 5) notes a year earlier, that in Europe too '[t]he phrase 'international students' increasingly means not the 'organized mobility' of mutual exchanges but the 'spontaneous mobility' of fee-paying individuals'. Varghese (2008: 22) indicates that Australia, Canada, New Zealand, the UK and the USA levy fees that are higher for international students than for domestic students; France, Greece, Hungary, Italy and Japan do not distinguish between foreign and domestic students while Denmark, Finland, Norway and Sweden do not levy fees on foreign students.

Internationalisation and globalisation

The risks of international mobility should not be ignored, as Egron-Polak (2009: 13) points out '[t]oo much focus on revenue generation and commercialization/commodification of HE' as one of the risks. This warning seems to be too late when one reads Bashir's statement (2007: 7) that '[h]igher education has today become a tradable service, which although not yet on the same scale, is similar to the trade of telecommunication or financial services'. With reference to private universities, Varghese (2008: 15) points out that, 'the emergence of the private sector, cross-border institutional linkages and full pricing of educational services contributed to bringing education under trade laws (GATS)'. Contrasting the income of transnational student mobility to income generated in the more traditional form of fellowships and research agreements, Bashir (2007: 4) claims

> In 2005, the annual exports from five leading exporters of higher education, exceeded by 10 times the annual commitments of multilateral and bilateral aid for higher education. Simultaneously, in importing countries, the annual value of higher education imports was large relative to their domestic public expenditure on higher education.

The definition of globalisation as 'the widening, deepening and speeding up of worldwide interconnectedness' (Held et al., 1999: 2) and its elaboration by Beerkens (2004) as 'a process in which basic social arrangements within and around the university become disembedded from their national context due to the intensification of transnational flows of people, information and resources' seem optimistic at best and, at its worst, deeply naive when compared with the assertion by Bashir (2007: 53, produced by the Education Unit at the World Bank (HDNED)) that 'liberalization of trade in HE is also being pursued in the context of bilateral and regional trade agreements' as countries in the developing world are pressurised to accept further expansion of GATS agreements.

The perspectives of Held and Beerkens on the one hand and Bashir on the other typify two opposing viewpoints: one concerned with (higher) education as a public good, with a focus on social development (which would include transnational students) and an increase in quality or increased quality assurance in research, teaching and community involvement. On the opposite side is the view of (higher) education as a financial enterprise with developed nations setting the agenda. Marginson and Van der Wende (2007: 5) put it mildly when they say that the playing fields in globalised HE are not level for all players (as a 'liberalised' HE would suggest):

> Nations, and institutions, have space in which to pilot their own global engagement. But this self-determination operates within limits that constrain some nations and institutions more than others, and complete abstention by national systems of higher education is no longer a strategic choice.

It is, for example, far more difficult for HEIs from developing countries to compete for international funding on an equal footing with HEIs from Europe or the USA. The fact that students from Africa are the least mobile, says as much about the low participation rate in African HE as it does about the financial constraints facing such students. In fact, developing countries are subsidising HE in developed countries, as Varghese (2008: 26) points out with reference to the UK, 'the foreign students not only mobilize funds but also help subsidize the domestic students'.

Views on the differences between globalisation and internationalisation have also become less idealistic. Twelve years ago, Scott (2000: 4) explicitly distinguished between globalisation (with its focus on economic markets and competitiveness) and internationalisation (with its focus on nation states and formal diplomatic ties) by arguing that the former is not merely a more intensive form of the latter but that globalisation actively works against national borders 'as national boundaries are rendered obsolete by the transgressive tendencies of high technology and mass culture'. However, national boundaries and national structures are not that easily dismissed. Marginson and Van der Wende (2007: 5) view globalisation from the perspective of national borders: 'In many nations *international mobility*; global comparison, bench-marking and ranking; and the *internationalisation* of institutions and system; are key policy themes; and *governments* and university leaders are preoccupied by strategies of *cross-border* cooperation and competition' (emphasis added to demonstrate their nation-state perspective).

Scott's view that national boundaries are rendered obsolete seems premature, particularly when one views the results of surveys on the global movement of students and the problems of finding comparable curricula or qualifications and, at least in Europe, the struggle to establish a credit transfer system (Crosier *et al.*, 2007: 36ff.). The acceptance of a new qualification structure is also pointed out as a problem, for example, in Italy where employability is related to state-issued qualifications in some fields. Since a bachelor's qualification is not familiar to employers, these graduates struggle to find employment (Crosier *et al.*, 2007: 25). In 2010, which was the due date for the achievement of the Bachelor–Master distinction in European universities (in terms of the Bologna agreement), news agencies in Germany reported that a growing number of HEIs are 'returning to the diploma as an exit qualification in engineering subjects'.[6] The way in which HEIs are embedded and grow from their regional and national contexts may be changing, but it can only change as much as the society (not necessarily even the government) is prepared to allow such a change. A simplistic interpretation of what is required for an HEI to take its place on the global stage would at best run the risk of developing policies and practices that only work in the short term and, at worst, alienate a potential student population as well as future employers. Knight (2005: 15) offers wise words when she notes (in the context of Latin American HE and internationalisation) that,

> It is important not to place values in opposition to one another. Seldom is there a black and white discussion or an either/or statement of values. More often, values form a continuum. For example, cooperation and competition are neither mutually exclusive nor opposed to each other.

Transnational movements worldwide

At supra-national level, in Europe, the push for internationalisation (particularly movements among European countries) has led to the imposition of curriculum change in terms of modularisation (for ease of substitution), assessment (from a final examination to credit accumulation) and quality assurance (to ensure that 'foreign' modules adhere to the standards set by the home institution). Bekhradnia (2004: 3) criticises the 'increasingly bureaucratic structures' that this process involves and the *Trends V* report on European HEIs (Crosier *et al.*, 2007) confirms the problem. Despite the majority (66%) of HEIs reporting that they use the European Credit Transfer System (ECTS), there are significant exceptions: the UK, Sweden, Spain, Greece and Russia being among them. Even more problematic is the fact that 47% of the institutions polled report that some of their transnationally mobile students struggle to have their courses or modules recognised when they return to their home institutions.

On the worldwide stage, the USA is the most popular destination for transnationally mobile students, although this lead shrunk during the Bush era (Varghese, 2008). Although this fact may appear interesting, the percentage of transnationally mobile students relative to domestic students is smaller than in the other countries.

In their review of HE in 45 countries, Crosier *et al.* (2007) report that countries in the EU cite Europe as the most desirable destination for transnational student mobility, 'by a margin of 25%' (2007: 46) and they list other regions in descending order:

(1)   Eastern Europe
(2)   Asia
(3)   North America
(4)   Latin America
(5)   Australia
(6)   The Arab world
(7)   Africa

One of the supra-national programmes to increase student mobility is the Erasmus Mundus project, which aims to increase mobility of students from Africa, Asia and the Americas to Europe. At the 2008 conference *EU–Africa cooperation in higher education through mobility* (Brussels, 4–5 December 2008) the number of students who move from these regions to Europe is detailed as follows: '[t]he overall total of 866 students places Africa third behind Asia (3431) and the Americas (1230)' (Conference Report, 2008: 3). Reporting on the success of the programme, it is noted that (Conference Report, 2008: 3):

> the success rate among African applicants is the lowest of any world region, at around 8%, the average success rate among all applicants being around 15%... A repeated refrain was the need to revitalise

and reform Higher Education and to do so in cooperation across national boundaries, to establish compatible structures and systems, which would facilitate mobility within Africa as well as between Africa and Europe and other parts of the world.

The problem of women being under-represented rears its head in this context too, with the conference reporting that only 24% of the African students were female. It notes that the '[m]obility of EU students to Africa is low' (Conference Report, 2008: 3).

The UNESCO Institute for Statistics (2007: 62) compares OECD countries with WEI countries and provides a reason for the fact that WEI and OECD countries do not differ much in terms of their expenditure on HE:

> Higher education markets are much more international in character with a significant share of students, teachers and researchers looking beyond their home countries for the best education and work opportunities. This forces governments to enable their higher education institutions to compete internationally and to offer attractive reputations, facilities and financial supports for both staff and students.

Significantly, the report points out that '[r]elative to national wealth, WEI countries tend to spend less on primary and secondary education than OECD countries. However, they invest considerably more per tertiary student' (UNESCO Institute for Statistics, 2007: 63).

In Africa, transnational student movements at postgraduate level are largely regional and towards universities that are perceived as offering better opportunities (in the form of bursaries, support or incentives) than those in the home country. In sub-Saharan Africa, these transnational movements are determined by regional cooperation agreements.[7] For example, in South Africa, as the only country in sub-Saharan Africa to attract 'substantial numbers of foreign students' (Altbach & Knight, 2006: 5; Higher Education Monitor, 2009: 15) 7% of all HE students in 2007 were transnationals (a total of 53,738) and 5% of these came from SADC (Southern African Development Community) countries as part of a planned strategy by the Ministry of Education (Higher Education Monitor, 2009: 26).

Despite the enormous expansion of policy and bureaucratic energy expended on transnationally mobile students, the number of such students worldwide remains quite small. Altbach and Knight (2006: 9) quote evidence from Australian researchers who 'argue that perhaps 15 million students will study abroad by 2025 – up from the current two million', but caution that this number may be optimistic, since a decline in numbers has been recorded in the USA, the leading host country.

The implications of mobility for multilingual higher education

From the above, it must be clear that vertical mobility, in the sense of providing successful access to so-called minority groups, is a concern at all levels of education. What makes HE special is the danger that its focus on widening access to local students can be diverted to advantaging relatively small numbers of transnational students, either for financial reasons or to foreground internationalisation goals. Stevenson and Willott (2010: 195) note, for example, that 'few UK universities undertake activities to increase the number of refugees studying with them, failing to recognise them as a specific "widening participation" target group'. The impression that transnationally mobile students require more institutional support than domestic students (from any group) is clear from Stevenson and Willot's (2010: 195, emphasis added) statements that

> they [refugees] find they have the same social, psychological and practical support needs as international students but, as refugees, are classed as *domestic* students. Thus they do not have access to the *extensive support* mechanisms put in place for other international students.

In the current economic climate, where governments cut funding to HE it stands to reason that institutions will feel the need to look for funding elsewhere, and in some countries transnationally mobile students constitute a lucrative option. The fact that government spending per capita on HE may still be higher than their funding of primary and secondary levels places an added burden on institutions to show a good return on this investment. For the purposes of this chapter, it is important to consider what mobility implies for HE that would set it apart from school education in terms of multilingual teaching and learning.

Proficiency in the LoLT is noted by Varghese (2008: 23) as a reason for 'inter-regional flows' of students and he notes that 'language familiarity may explain the increasing flow of cross-border students to English-speaking countries such as Australia, the UK and the USA'. Jones and Caruana (2010: xix) highlight the limitations that 'language difficulties' may place on the integration of transnationally mobile students in the host HEI. They warn that 'considerations of language mask much deeper cultural difficulties such as conflicting values' (Jones & Caruana, 2010: xix).

The view that English is *the* LoLT in HE, and therefore the key to internationalisation, is well documented. HE can escape neither internationalisation, as Marginson and Van der Wende (2007: 5) note, nor the use of English. It is an essential competence that Graddol (2006: 71) compares with computer literacy: 'learning English has become just as important in basic education as learning how to use applications such as word processors, spreadsheets and internet browsers'. This is indeed the reason why English is the main target for the European model of integrating language and content teaching (CLIL) at school level. Whittaker *et al.* (2011: 344) note that, '[in] Madrid, for example, in the last five years, about 250 primary schools have introduced CLIL through English in an ambitious bilingual program, and, as these students move into secondary school, new schools are incorporating CLIL into their curricula at this level (over 30 new schools in the academic year

2010–11)'. Therefore, although the locality of schooling and the focus on its direct surroundings may place the emphasis in school education in the local, the inclusion of English at primary and secondary school level shows the influence of internationalisation drives at HE level.

Conclusion: Finding a Place for Higher Education in Multilingual Education

Is there a particular reason why multilingual HE should be approached and treated differently from bi-/multilingual education at primary- and secondary-level schooling? This chapter showed how the legislative frameworks and mobility of students (vertical and horizontal) make HE different from the situation at schools, but that views of learning and language learning are essentially the same. However, the relative academic freedom of HE practitioners, coupled with increasingly diverse classrooms that can change from one semester to the next, imply a qualitative change to the way in which language (broadly speaking) is used in HE. On the one hand, compulsory pre-primary, primary and secondary levels of schooling deliver the students who gain entry to HE. What happens at these levels in terms of widening access is crucial for HE. In their cross-country survey of the way in which equity is achieved in education in OECD countries, Causa and Chapuis's (2009: 30) highlight 'the importance of early intervention policy for attenuating intergenerational socio-economic inequalities in educational opportunities', concluding that 'childcare and early intervention policies could be effective to reach this objective'.

On the other hand, the prestigious nature of HE means that it has an effect on the structuring of secondary and primary schooling. The result could be that a monolingual focus in HE will legitimise monolingual approaches at primary and secondary school level, as is indeed happening in various parts of the world, for example, in Africa (where African languages are seldom used officially beyond the first three or four grades of primary school, see, for example, Kimizi (2009) and Qorro (2009)) as well as in urban centres in India, where elites are able to place children in schools where English is used as the LoLT (Amritavalli & Jayaseelan, 2007). In Europe, secondary schools increasingly introduce English alongside local languages, a move that is not necessarily supportive of multilingual education, as Chapter 5 will argue. Hoffmann (2000: 13) traces European policy decisions to include compulsory English language courses at primary school level. Coleman (2006: 5) points out with reference to CLIL,

> But if CLIL has demonstrated benefits at secondary level, and is firmly harnessed to European ideals of multilingualism and the MT + 2 formula (mother tongue and two additional languages for all citizens including school pupils), in reality the target language adopted as the medium of teaching can often be English.

While children need to develop school language proficiencies from a fairly low base to engage and make meaning of academic texts and materials, HE students need to have developed proficiency in a particular LoLT to a high level to gain access to HEIs. The assumptions of teachers and lecturers are radically different: not many lecturers would identify the development of academic language proficiency as part of their job. In fact, Airey (2009: 96) found in his study that Physics students at a Swedish university did not see studying in a second language as a problem (despite the fact that they experienced problems) and that language goals were not necessarily mentioned as part of a particular science syllabus. The perception remains that language is a transparent medium that needs to be mastered before attending HE, and if additional support is required, this should happen outside a student's chosen discipline in a separate (usually first-year) module. Such a 'step wise' approach means that language is seen as foundational, something that needs to be mastered before a particular course of study is tackled. As Northedge (2002: 256) notes, university lecturers often do not fully appreciate.

> [...] the sociocultural groundings of meaning. Their thoughts are so deeply rooted in specialist discourse that they are unaware that meanings they take for granted are simply not construable from outside the discourse.

The implementation of CLIL at primary and secondary school level is starting to have an impact on teacher practice in terms of managing the academic language demands of various subjects. A 2011 US textbook for teachers on 'content area literacy', as it is called by the authors Antonacci and O'Callaghan (2011: xix) starts with the sentence, 'There is increasing concern for middle and high school students who do not or simply cannot read and write the required range of texts needed for academic achievement'. The various strategies include using other languages as resources in developing subject-specific vocabulary, reading and writing fluency. It remains to be seen to what extent HE lecturers are willing and/or able to support the disciplinary socialisation of local students who do not 'automatically' master the language and content of their chosen disciplines or transnationally mobile students who struggle to 'translate' academic content from one LoLT to another.

For HEIs, the situation is doubly complex and vertical access can be seen as in direct competition with horizontal access, which means that institutions may have to choose between providing a supportive context for minority or low-status national languages/varieties or very powerful international languages. HEIs and students themselves may prefer to use a powerful international language rather than one that they perceive as having no 'marketable' advantage. Many African institutions are struggling with the position of, for example, Pidgin English (Bobda, 2006), Swahili (Blommaert, 2006) and Southern African languages (Van der Walt, 2004a). However, the situation is not limited to former colonies. At the University of Luxemburg, for example, a commitment to the use of Luxemburgish as an academic language is in direct competition with the increased use of English, alongside French and German. At the trilingual University of Bolzano, Ladin is similarly in competition with English; alongside German and Italian (see Chapter 3 for more detail).

Managing the (often) conflicting demands of widening access locally and 'internationalising' institutions by, among others, increasing the enrolment of transnationally mobile students means that HE needs to balance demands (not to mention budgets) locally and globally. The following two examples illustrate how institutions differ in their management of local and international demands. The erstwhile Rector of Maastricht University, Ritzen (2004: 37) typifies the interplay between the local and the global when he identifies the actors in decisions about 'internationalising' institutions of HE: the students, who will include local students from local (often monolingual) schools, the academic staff, who may be recruited from all over the world and who would mostly be multilingual, the administrative staff who are often recruited locally (and who may be monolingual too) and the local and international stakeholders who release funds and impose policies. Ritzen (2004: 38) implies that the solution is to move towards English-medium education, with 'qualifications in at least two other foreign languages'. At the University of Bozen/Bolzano, the importance of local languages plus English has recently been underlined by increasing the proficiency requirements for English, Italian and German (Prior, 2012). The context and managerial agendas within which these statements are made are crucial and show the relative importance of 'global' and 'economic' pressures: in the case of the University of Maastricht, internationalisation is understood to demand an English-medium approach; in the case of the University of Bozen/Bolzano, global and local pressures demand active use of more languages *for learning and teaching* as well as the workplace. The different local contexts also create a different perspective on language needs: in the example from the Netherlands, the assumption is that students would move towards one operational language with language *qualifications*; and in the Bozen/Bolzano example, it is almost self-evident that students and lecturers would actively use up to three languages for teaching, learning and research.

Both these approaches can be reconciled with multilingualism in education since both are situated in multilingual contexts. However, the prevalence of a monolingual perspective on education tends to edge out the value of other languages, particularly when managers in HE construct language as a problem. As was pointed out at the start of this chapter, language needs to be seen as a resource, not only for teaching and learning but also for research and community interaction. This perspective within the sometimes-conflicting demands of the local and the global is encapsulated by Scott (2000: 7, emphasis added), who discusses two new paradigms of knowledge production as part of the globalisation challenge that HE needs to face in the 21st century:

> The first is the crucial importance of context, not simply in terms of the end uses of science; not only in terms of helping to define scientific problems and to select appropriate methodologies; *but by redefining reliable knowledge as knowledge that is socially robust*. The second is the proliferation of research communities: not only have advances in communication and information technologies enabled research collaboration to take place on a global scale, but these new communities also embrace *socially distributed* researchers.

The emphasis on a social perspective implies a local embeddedness and a global connectedness, for which a monolingual view of education and learning is both inefficient and insufficient. One example of how academics manage this process is mentioned in the Lillis and Curry (2010: 126, 127) study on academic publishing, where research participants indicate how they make decisions to publish some research in English and other in local languages. Although the view of what the most appropriate choice would be will differ, the view of themselves as situated in different communities for whom different languages need to be used is one example of how languages act as scientific resources. The argument put forward in subsequent chapters builds on the fact that languages are central to processes of presenting globally and locally based research.

In their criticism of current work on the way in which globalisation shapes HE, Marginson and Rhoades (2002: 285) notes that '[a] further conceptual shortcoming of the literature is that it fails to adequately address the local dimension' and language, not only in the sense of a particular language but also in the sense of academic language at HE level, is inevitably local. This is the case for English as well as for Xhosa. Dealing with this localised entry to full HE membership is overwhelmingly a language issue, as Chapter 5 will argue.

Scott's (2000: 7) view points to the dimension of responsible and responsive science. HE is multilingual and a pretence at monolingual teaching and research results in risky teaching and learning practices (because the multiplicity of languages brought into the classroom is not acknowledged) and in unresponsive and superficial research (because the context and materials available in other languages are not acknowledged). This point of view does not deny the usefulness and depth of cognitive expressiveness of global languages – that would be to deny the very existence of this book. It does, however, call for recognition of the reality on every HE campus and for the need 'to reshape our concept of bilingualism and bilingual individuals in order to fit the communicative exigencies of the bilingual languaging needed in today's interdependent and technologically enriched world' (García, 2009: 55).

Notes

(1) There is still a dispute about the name of the former capital and for that reason and in the interests of multilingual tolerance, I will use both names.

(2) 'Elite closure' is 'a strategy by which those persons in power maintain their power and privileges via language choices' (Myers-Scotton, 1990: 25).

(3) Support must be understood in the widest sense here. Achoka *et al.* (2007) mention poverty, gender imbalances, problematic policy frameworks and the HIV/AIDS pandemic as problems affecting the provision of basic education in Kenya. With the possible exception of gender imbalances, where parents choose not to send girls to school, the other problems can all be tackled, should sufficient funding and welfare measures be made available by the state.

(4) 'Undergraduate' is used in the widest possible sense here, merely to clarify the term 'first cycle'. The first cycle in Bologna terms indicate study that would in Anglo-Saxon terms be thought of as the first, or Bachelor's degree; the system which European universities are (supposedly) moving towards. The use of 'undergraduate' in this system is problematic, since students' first degree may already be at Masters level.

(5) In the original, 'Margaret Thatcher führte im Jahre 1980 konstendeckende Studiengebühren für ausländische Studierende ein; an den amerikanischen, australischen und kanadischen Universitäten gab es bereits vorher hohe Gebühren für ausländische Studierende' (Schumann, 2008: 15).

(6) 'Führende Technische Hochschulen in Deutschland kehren in den Ingenieurfächern wieder zum Diplom-Abschluss zurück. Neben den Universitäten in Berlin, Braunschweig, Darmstadt, Dresden, Hannover, Karlsruhe, München und Stuttgart zählt dazu auch die RWTH Aachen'.

Bundesbildungsministerin Schavan sagte, der Diplom-Ingenieur habe einen sehr guten Ruf. 'Es ist deshalb ein Zeichen von Selbstbewusstsein, neben dem internationalen Master-Abschluss auch diesen Titel zu vergeben.' At http://www.wdr.de/themen/kurzmeldungen/2010/08/02/der_diplom-ingenieur_kommt_wieder_.jhtml on 2 August 2010.

(7) See Ogachi (2009) for a discussion of the degree to which regionalisation and internationalisation compete in East Africa.

2 Linguistic Diversity in Higher Education: Official and Unofficial Multilingual Settings

Introduction: Language in Higher Education Institutions

In the previous chapter, a case was made for seeing higher education (HE) as a very specific case in bi-/multilingual education discussions that will require particular approaches and practices. In this chapter, a closer look at HE institutions (HEIs) worldwide is provided to elaborate on the points raised in Chapter 1. The purpose in this chapter is

- to provide a snapshot of HE worldwide and its increasingly multilingual nature;
- to describe officially and explicitly bi-/multilingual HEIs and the contexts from which they grew; and
- to invoke the concept of *ecology* as a conceptual lever to destabilise monolingual orientations to language planning, policy and practices in HE.

The snapshot of multilingualism in regions around the world is not meant to provide an exhaustive description but to provide a sense of the ubiquity of multilingualism in HE contexts. The discussion focuses on tensions at regional level and the effect of transnational mobility on HEIs.

When providing an overview of this nature, some kind of organising principle is necessary and I considered a variety of approaches: from formal (in terms of their legislative frameworks) to informal bi-/multilingual institutions; from bilingual to multilingual institutions; or from a historical and developmental perspective, which would have meant a history of the various countries. The realisation that an account of all these aspects would require a separate book led to my decision to start from my own context and continent and then simply move west. Since a thorough overview of countries and their language policies is currently being undertaken in the *Language Planning and Policy* series edited by Robert B. Kaplan and Richard B. Baldauf (published by Multilingual Matters) and, from a different perspective, the series *Language and National Identity* edited by Andrew Simpson (Oxford University Press), this chapter homes in on the aspect of multilingual HE in particular regional and institutional contexts.

The discussion that follows will start with the obvious fact that HEIs are situated in, supported (in terms of providing students, goods and services) and closely watched by the local community where the physical institution finds itself. As was pointed out in Chapter 1, HE is dependent on public funding (to varying degrees) and even designated private institutions have to take cognizance of government policies and have to manage the learning of students from government-funded schools. At the same time, the global trend seems to be that public funding for HE is shrinking with an increase in the contribution expected from parents and the students themselves. Bain (2001: 59) observes that in countries as dissimilar as China, Germany and the UK, 'students and their parents are increasingly viewed as able to carry a larger share of costs through tuition and other expenses'. Even the famed free education in Europe is under pressure so that at least a means test is used in some cases to distinguish students whose parents can afford to support their HE studies from those who need more assistance from the state. Increasingly too, pressure is put on students to complete their studies in as short a time as possible, and this pressure is relayed to the HEIs themselves, particularly in the form of debates about 'improving throughput rates'.

Although education is generally seen as a public good (particularly in arguments that link participation rates to the economic growth and vitality of countries), governments are using various techniques to spread the economic burden of HE: emphasising the importance of collaboration with industry, requiring contributions by families and future employers as well as requiring strict (and often restrictive) governance of institutions along business principles. The marketisation of education is a critical debate for multilingual HE too, since multilingualism is seen from the language-as-a-problem perspective, where costs of, for example, translating materials and providing academic development for students who do not have sufficient control over the dominant language of learning and teaching (LoLT) are seen as an immediate liability, with scant attention to the costs of monolingualism when, for example, students graduate and need to function in multilingual professional contexts, as Chapter 4 will argue.

In their overview of the expansion in universities in particular, Frank and Meyer (2007: 290) provide a detailed analysis of the role and function of universities in society, arguing that the increase in institutions and student numbers 'imply denser linkages between the university and society' and increasing calls for 'relevant' research and teaching. Such a public role for HEIs may not be to the taste of all academics but as Frank and Meyer (2007: 290) show, the university (and one can support this claim for all HEIs) also has a profound effect on society in terms of certification and; '[i]n short, vis-à-vis all sorts of public and private matters, the authority of the university speaks to the widest range of decision makers'.

The pressure to enter HE, as the case below shows, results from the conviction that a strong HE section is vital to the success of a country as a force in the globalising world. Universities, in the radical sense of the word *university*, 'exhibit the intensifying interpenetration of the global and

---

A case in point

At the University of Johannesburg, more than a thousand students attempted to register for undergraduate studies at the start of the 2012 academic year (see http://www.nytimes.com/2012/01/11/world/africa/stampede-highlights-crisis-at-south-african-universities.html?_r=1). This university is one of the few that still allow late registrations and students who were not sure whether their school-exit certificates would be good enough for university entrance delayed their applications. On 10 January 2012, students who wanted to register surged forward to enter the premises of the University and a mother who accompanied her child was trampled to death. In the wake of the tragic events, the Minister of Education, Dr Blade Nzimande (2012), addressed the problem of perceptions that university study is the only viable option for HE. The Education Department is making efforts to support ailing and severely under-resourced vocational or technical colleges and other post-secondary institutions to meet South Africa's demand for skilled labour. Previous attempts met with resistance because of the perception that authorities want to direct black South Africans to 'lower level' HEIs (Nzimande, 2012).

---

universal with the local and particular' (Frank & Meyer, 2007: 289). The implication of such interpenetration is that a local and national population will, by necessity, demand an institution that provides education in national languages, or in a national language, while international concerns will pressurise institutions to use a 'global' language, usually English. These conflicting demands are part of HE life and reflect its enormous sphere of influence: to prepare a country's professionals (and thereby confer status on local languages) and to provide a gateway to a global stage.

Recent publications on the experiences of transnationally mobile students, for example, Jones (2010) and the special edition of the *Journal of Studies in International Education* in 2010 (number 5), focus increasingly on students' experiences, motivations and challenges when studying abroad. These movements also open up new avenues of investigation, such as global citizenship, the possible nature of international classrooms and curricula, adequate support systems for students participating in these programmes and, inevitably, their language competence. The perception that an international lingua franca, English, is a solution to the 'problem' of transnational mobility is belied by the flood of literature on problems with not only language competence, but also the academic practices of institutions (Leask, 2011: 9):

> Barriers [to successful academic integration in host institutions] included perceptions of the English language competence of international students, high levels of risk associated with task failure, the limited amount of time available in class to build the communicative skills required to produce a high quality outcome and the substantial effort required to work across cultural and linguistic borders.

Despite the obvious multilingual nature of communities and 'internationalised' HE, the official acknowledgement thereof in the form of bi-/multilingual programmes are few and far between. Officially, bi-/multilingual HEIs differ widely in size, purpose and nature. The most prestigious ones belong to a network of comprehensive, research-oriented bi-/multilingual universities, mostly in Europe and Canada. The section that follows presents an overview of both *de facto* and *de iure* instances of multilingual HE, followed by a focused discussion of the contexts of *de iure* multilingual institutions.

Africa

According to Gadelii (2004: 7), there are only five African countries that are regarded as monolingual: Burundi, Madagascar, Rwanda, Lesotho and Somalia. He reports that although African languages are used in education, this is limited to kindergarten and primary school levels, where 30% of education takes place in non-African languages (which includes Afrikaans). This percentage jumps to 75% at secondary school level and to 95% at HE level (Gadelii, 2004: 28–30). However, the picture may not be entirely accurate, since, as Muthwii and Kioko (2004: 3) point out, the so-called mother tongue policies are often subverted and colonial languages are used instead. Directly after independence, the use of former colonial languages in education was seen as an easy solution to problems of education and training by providing 'adequate literacy materials for use in the schools' and as a way to promote unity (Muthwii & Kioko, 2004: 2). In some countries, colonial languages offer a solution to a multilingual context that makes the choice of one or two local languages impossible. In Cameroon, for example, where there are 279 living languages (according to Ethnologue.com), English and French are seen as solutions to very complex language demographics. In South Africa, where Afrikaans was used as a LoLT at what are known as historically Afrikaans universities (HAUs), this language is seen as *preventing* access to the majority of South Africa students whose LoLT at secondary school level was English. Other local or regional languages are marginally part of the HE picture, despite national policies that exhort institutions to develop them as scientific, academic languages. At most South African universities, access and placement tests assess students' English language proficiency with a view to providing academic language support. In some cases, study materials are also developed in Afrikaans, Sotho, Xhosa and Zulu to support learning; for example, bilingual terminology lists or 'study notes' that are meant to explain the prescribed, English, text.

The history of colonisation makes it relatively simple to paint a picture of a continent in which the LoLT in HE reflects the nationality of the colonisers. Creating a list of HEIs would supposedly show that HEIs use Portuguese in Mozambique and Angola; German in Namibia; Italian in Ethiopia; English in South Africa, Botswana, Zambia, Zimbabwe and other Anglophone countries; and French in the Democratic Republic of the Congo, in Algeria, Morocco and other Francophone countries. The picture is obviously far from being this simple mainly as a result of political changes during colonisation as well as post-colonial developments. Whereas Portuguese is indeed used in Mozambique and Angola, Namibia uses English and in Francophone Africa, universities are increasingly using English alongside French. HE in Cameroon, for example, is based on the French model but many institutions are French–English bilingual. The Agence Universitaire de la Francophonie (AUF), an umbrella organisation that fosters university training in French (organised from the Université Senghor in Alexandria, Egypt) claims representation on all continents, in 90 countries, with most members concentrated in France, Vietnam, Algeria and Canada (AUF website).

The problem with identifying one language as a LoLT in a particular country or institution in Africa is that official policy seldom reflects the reality of teaching and learning. Dzahene-Quarshie (2010: 67) reports that in Tanzania, where Swahili is particularly strong in education, the media and in government, '[t]he pressure of English is so strong that it has led to the government's inability to implement the long-standing proposed Swahili medium policy in secondary education, (using Swahili as the medium of instruction) although the agencies charged with preparation and implementation have long completed the task'. Blommaert (1992) describes the use of Campus Kiswahili by academic staff at the University of Dar es Salaam, where switching to and from English is common practice. It is self-evident in cases where the LoLT is not a home or community language that lecturers and students will code switch to a home or community language that they have in common. Bobda (2006) reports on the Anglophone part of Cameroon where Pidgin English is increasingly learnt as a home language and where authorities at the University of Buea try unsuccessfully to ban 'Pidgin' from the campus with posters that proclaim, 'The medium of studies at UB [University of Buea] is English, not Pidgin' (Bobda, 2006: 58). Code switching in classrooms starts at primary school level (Dzahene-Quarshie, 2010; Setati et al., 2002, Van der Walt, 2009) and clearly continues up to HE. This means that HE in Africa is de facto bi-/multilingual because home and community languages are used alongside the official LoLT to mediate academic material and the day-to-day business of academic life.

Are there possibilities for other languages to compete officially with the high-status, former colonial LoLTs in HE? Although there is a number of possibilities, it would be difficult to claim that they are all 'indigenous' or that their history is untainted by some form of imperialism. Arabisation in Algeria illustrates a process of language planning that attempted to create a 'non-colonial' identity. The effort was meant to create unity among people who use a language that is perceived to be indigenous to North Africa. However, Arabic itself was imposed on an indigenous population. Djité (1992) describes the process whereby the Berber population was forced to start using Arabic in the 9th century. The subsequent colonisation by France in 1830 meant that French replaced Arabic. After independence, French was replaced by Arabic as the LoLT from 1962 onwards as part of the Arabisation process of which the purpose was 'to restore to Arabic – the very expression of the cultural values of our country – its dignity and its efficacy as a language of civilisation' (extract from the Tripoli Programme, Benrabah, 2007: 72). The educational system remains French, however, requiring, for example, a baccalaureate for entrance to HE studies. The Arabisation ideal was ratified only in 1990, with the law of Arabisation requiring that the administration be 'totally arabised by July 5 1992, and tertiary education by 1997' (Djité, 1992: 15). Teachers from Syria and Iraq were imported to fill the gap left by monolingual French teachers. The date for implementation at HE level was pushed back to the year 2000, and in 2001 the plan was suspended altogether (Benrabah, 2007: 76). Abdelaziz Bouteflika, the influential president of the country at that time, expressed concern at what he perceived to be the low standard of Algerian HE degrees, attributing the problem to the monolingual (Arabic) education system. Since then, both French and English have been re-introduced at primary and secondary school level. French never really disappeared from HE classrooms. Benrabah (2007: 99) claims that no study has been conducted on language use in university classes in Algeria, and he speculates that '[i]t is most likely that the results reported for Jordan in the 1990s ... are applicable to Algerian universities as well', where the majority of the interaction would be Arabic–English code switching – in Algeria this would be Arabic–French – making such universities (and probably other institutions of HE as well) *de facto* bilingual.

As can be seen from the Benrabah quote above, the use of Arabic creates a bond with countries outside of Africa. However, the perception that there is one, unitary Arabic is one of the problems in education. In this regard, Benrabah (2007: 56) distinguishes between 'arabicisation' and 'arabisation', where the former is a feature mostly of the Arab Middle East, Libya and Egypt and the latter of Algeria, Morocco and Tunisia. 'Arabicisation', according to Benrabah (2007: 56), refers to a linguistic process whereby Arab replaces a colonial language and is enriched by 'newly borrowed or derived/revived words' and 'arabisation' has a cultural dimension with the purpose of creating a national identity with strong religious links to Muslim countries, as can be witnessed in attempts by the Congress of Ba'th to set up a Pan-Arab community with its own constitution (Benrabah, 2007: 59). In this context, local varieties of Arabic are regarded as inferior, which means that even Arabic-speaking children will struggle to manage the school language, which is based on standardised, written Arabic. (See Benrabah, 2007: 68–69 for more information on this topic.)

Kiswahili is another possible contender in HE and Blommaert (2006) critically analyses the way in which it has been constructed as a 'pure' Bantu language, showing that Kiswahili was spread by the former colonial powers for practical purposes and has been imposed on inland groups in a very purposeful manner. Momanyi (2009: 128) takes a more positive view and sees a significant role for the language 'because it is non-ethnic'. Although she refers to the role of Kiswahili in HE mainly as a subject to be studied (rather than a LoLT), her view of the importance of the language as a lingua franca in the Kenyan community means that graduates will probably need it for professional purposes, which can increase its status at HE level. In Tanzania, Legère (2006: 177) shows how the Ministry of Education failed to support terminology development (which is crucial for the use of a language in academic domains) and then bemoaned the fact that Kiswahili was not yet sufficiently developed. Legère (2006: 182) blames the Tanzanian government for not supporting the development of Kiswahili and concludes, 'The recent corpus development teaches also SW [Kiswahili] antagonists a lesson – although it is possible to block the introduction of SW as the medium of instruction and learning beyond primary schools, it is impossible to stop its advance in domains which are not controlled by the state apparatus'.

In the apartheid era, the Afrikaans language developed and grew in Namibia and South Africa at the expense of African languages, and in South Africa it is used officially at former Afrikaans HEIs as a LoLT alongside English. The most prominent of such institutions are the universities of Pretoria, Johannesburg, the Potchefstroom campus of the North-west University, the University of the Orange Free State and Stellenbosch University. However, all South African institutions of HE are required, through the national Language Policy for Higher Education policy (2002), to foster academic language use of one African language, which means that monolingual English institutions also develop materials, glossaries and other forms of teaching support in African languages. It would be difficult at this stage to generalise about the degree to which bilingual HE can be said to be entrenched at monolingual, English institutions of HE in South Africa.

In a continent marked by poverty and strife, Maseko and Kaschula (2009: 132) see a very specific role for HE to reflect and support the multilingualism that characterises all African HE contexts:

> Through multilingual learning and teaching universities can promote transformation, linguistic tolerance and cultural sensitivity in higher education. This responsibility is appropriate to universities mainly because of their principal function as centres of research, enquiry and development. As vocational training institutions, they can also influence the employment market by using the linguistic ability of their graduates as a selling tool.

This is an imperative that the HE section in Africa can hardly ignore. Pillay (2008: 134) notes the dismal participation rates in sub-Saharan Africa, which 'are substantially lower than the average for both developing countries and industrialised/developed countries … In addition, the median participation rate for Sub-Saharan Africa is 2.5% compared to the developing country median of 13% and the industrialised country median of 58%'. This situation is hardly surprising, since the drop-out rate from primary school is unacceptably high in some African countries and, even in cases where a high percentage of learners progress to secondary education, their levels of literacy and numeracy may not enable them to be successful at that or subsequent levels (Spaull, 2011: 24). As Muthwii and Kioko (2004: 5) point out, '[t]he issue of school drop out is closely associated with that of language of instruction', and more worryingly, 'where an international language is the preferred language of instruction, as is the case in Kenya, Uganda and Zimbabwe, it is not necessarily the case that using it is successful in enabling school children to achieve useful levels of literacy'. Unless the resources that potential students have at their disposal can be acknowledged and enhanced, participation rates at primary, secondary and HE levels in Africa will not rise.

Latin America and the Caribbean

Reports on HE in this region focus on recent improvements in participation rates, as Aponte-Hernández *et al.* (2008: 123) note, '[t]he rate of increase of access to Higher Education surpasses the population growth of the region, pointing to unprecedented progress in most countries'. Holm-Nielsen *et al.* (2005: 40) single out Argentina, Uruguay and Chile as the regional leaders, with a 30% enrolment rate. However, true massification in terms of providing access to minoritised groups is not evident, and 'countries with the greatest participation at the level of Higher Education also reflect the largest inequalities between the quintiles of this sector' (Aponte-Hernández *et al.*, 2008: 122). The reason for an increase in HE participation by higher-income groups could be the marketisation of HE, since private institutions account for 40% of enrolments in HE, and Holm-Nielsen *et al.* (2005: 70) claim that '[h]igher education in Latin America remains largely elitist, with the majority of students coming from the wealthier segments of society'.

Access to HE by minoritised groups seems to be hampered not only by a lack of finances, but also by what Morrow (1993, see Chapter 1) calls *epistemological access.* The role played by language cannot be underestimated, since 'poor students from rural areas score 20 points fewer [sic] in language compared with students from families with higher incomes' (Aponte-Hernández *et al.*, 2008: 121). Although legislation on the use of indigenous languages for schooling purposes has been introduced, Hidalgo (2008: 345) notes that such legislation is 'not necessarily favourable or attuned with the reality of indigenous cultures'. The complexity of the situation is described by Hornberger (2007: 178), who notes that, in Bolivia, parents are concerned that their children are not learning enough Spanish, experiencing a bilingual education model as monolingual, indigenous teaching. When HE is also perceived as 'hampered by weak learning outcomes in primary and secondary education' (Holm-Nielsen *et al.*, 2005: 48), it is clear that Latin American institutions have problems similar to those experienced in Africa. Aponte-Hernández *et al.* (2008: 135) clearly indicate the complexity of the situation:

> In spite of the progress in intercultural-bilingual education in education systems that serve this population in the region, the lack of resources and low relative quality of the public institution serving these groups are not sufficient to be able to overcome the lack of progress, exclusion, and poverty of these groups.

In a report on internationalisation, Gacel-Ávila (2007: 403) notes that the region has the lowest rate of student mobility in the world and that it attracts very few transnational students. Reasons include problems with the transferability of credits (Lopez et al., 2011: 209ff.), a national rather than an international focus (Gacel-Ávila, 2007: 400) as well as '[i]nsufficient proficiency in foreign languages' (Gacel-Ávila, 2007: 404). Although many authors echo this sentiment, the solution is invariably to increase English language proficiency. In their conclusion to a volume dedicated to Latin America, Gacel-Ávila et al. (2005: 348) note:

> Most of the country studies identify the lack of proficiency in foreign languages among students, faculty, and staff. This has a negative impact on the international competencies of Latin American students and scholars and on their ability to take advantage of opportunities for international cooperation. For this reason, the teaching of English as a second language is key. Many programs have been launched in recent years to improve the level of English.

The way in which English language proficiency is fostered differs across the region. In Colombia, for example, where a form of Spanish–English bilingual teaching and learning exists, Jaramillo (2005: 200) indicates that, in the 32 universities polled, '[a]lmost 60 percent of students prepare a few subjects in English, while 91 percent develop modules supported by a bibliography in English'. With regard to Mexico, Gacel-Ávila (2005: 256) notes:

> Half of private institutions and just 13 percent of public ones expect students to have a command of English before commencing studies. [...] But only 9 percent of public and 28 percent of private universities demand a higher level of proficiency upon graduation than at matriculation, suggesting that the language requirement is probably more of an administrative requirement than a genuine policy to promote the learning of foreign languages.

In Chile, the effect of HE expectations for language proficiency is clear in initiatives for primary and secondary school (Sanchez, 2005: 166, emphasis added) 'Forty-five percent of traditional universities report that their faculty do not have spoken or written mastery of a foreign language. [...] The government has initiated a plan at the primary and secondary level to make *bilingualism* a core strategy in the next few years'. The fact that a lack of proficiency in English is not mentioned specifically and that the focus is on bilingualism may be an indication that local languages and regional interests remain important considerations.

Double or joint-degree programmes, where degrees are partially offered by partner HEIs, also imply the use of more than one language. Although such programmes can be followed at a regional level, the fact that most of these programmes are followed outside Latin America and the Caribbean

(Miranda, 2008: 207) means that the languages involved will be mostly Spanish and English, since the majority of transnationally mobile students from Latin America and the Caribbean attend institutions in English-speaking countries (Gacel-Ávila, 2005: 360).

Landinelli (2008: 163), as well as Miranda (2008: 227), focuses on the shared multi-culturality of the region and its impact on HE, with the former referring to increasing numbers of graduates emerging from 'intercultural HE' and bilingual education contexts, while the latter mentions the various (majority) languages and their role in future cooperation among HEIs:

> In the world today, more than 400 million people speak Spanish, and more than 200 million speak Portuguese. This means that 600 million people can speak to each other within the Ibero-American cultural area. In this sense, the example of the creation of International Certification System of Spanish as a Foreign Language (SICELE), made it possible to unify criteria and methods of assessment for the granting of certificates of the mastery of Spanish as a second language for Spanish speakers, and established a common seal of quality. One should also note the decision by Brazil which has for several years established Spanish as required subject in public and private secondary schools as a favourable step toward Latin American integration. The sentiment of confidence in our languages will undoubtedly strengthen their use in the world, and will result in increasing prestige for our education projects and our culture which is so varied and at the same time so shared.

Latin America and the Caribbean are often discussed together and seem to share problems of exclusion, high poverty rates and low expenditure on HE (Gazzola & Didriksson, 2008). Didriksson (2008: 22) claims that, 'Within the framework of gaps and asymmetries of the current international division of knowledge, technological innovation, and the revolution in science and its applications, the Latin American and Caribbean region finds itself excluded'. Although the region can be said to face similar problems (Aponte-Hernandez et al., 2008: 118), the fact that English is a national language in parts of the Caribbean has implications for HE. Aponte-Hernandez et al. (2008: 130) indicate that '[t]he high per capita incomes of a large number of English-speaking Caribbean countries have afforded conditions for a growth in agreements between existing institutions (Barbados, Jamaica, Trinidad and Tobago, US Virgin Islands, among others) and England, the United States, and Canada that include graduate programs, medicine, veterinary medicine, and business administration'. They also point to the variation in participation rates, contrasting relatively low rates in Central America to favourable gains in the Caribbean (Aponte-Hernandez et al., 2008: 130).

Miranda (2008: 156) is concerned that a lack of 'effective regionalisation' prevents the Caribbean from making the most of its multi-cultural context, noting that three of the UN languages are used as national languages in the region. Recommendations for supporting regional cooperation, and in that way strengthening HE as a public good, include '[s]ystematizing the study of the three international languages, introducing the study of different histories into the curriculum of all universities of the area, fostering regional experiences and exchange for students, making possible collaboration on themes of absolute priority such as respectable tourism or the protection of fragile ecosystems are only some of the advantages that could be derived from such activities' (Miranda, 2008: 156). In terms of transnational mobility worldwide, intra-regional cooperation is more common than inter-regional cooperation (Varghese, 2008: 15) and the impulse will probably be strengthened when close neighbours feel that they have something in common, mostly in terms of language use and budgetary challenges.

There are similarities with African countries; in the sense that participation in HE increases for those who are able to pay for HE and effectively manage the dominant languages of HE. Without trivialising the differences between Africa, Latin America and the Caribbean, it seems as if a focus on strengthening the local is a prerequisite for participating in transnational exchanges and international HE. However, a view towards the future means that international LoLTs are seen as necessary additions to local, multilingual contexts.

Northern America

Although a 'continental' perspective is taken in this discussion, Canada is discussed separately in the case of Northern America because of its bilingual nature and the existence of officially bilingual institutions.

Canada

The Ontario Ministry of Training, Colleges and Universities (at http://www.edu.gov.on.ca/eng/general/list/frenchlanguage.html#universities) in Canada lists five HEIs in Ontario that offer French–English bilingual HE:

- University of Ottawa
- Laurentian University
- Federated St Paul University
- Sudbury University
- York University (Glendon Campus)

In the province of Nunavut, the Nunavut Arctic College[1] (3 campuses and 24 Community Learning Centres) is an English–Inuktitut bilingual institution, the only post-secondary institution in the Nunavut province.

The distribution of language options differs widely, from institutions offering many programmes in both languages (University of Ottawa) to those offering a choice of languages at a satellite campus (such as the Glendon Campus of York University) and others (such as McGill University) that offers programmes mainly in English, but where students are allowed to submit their work in either English or French. There are also institutions that offer specific programmes in French and English, for example, the Master of Public Service at the University of Waterloo, for those students 'who would like to concurrently complete the Canadian Public Service Commission's bilingual requirement for federal employees' (on their website at http://www.mps.uwaterloo.ca/BilingualOption.html). Offering advice to prospective MBA students, the website *Canada's Higher Education & Career Guide* notes (emphasis added):

> Currently, HEC Montreal is the only school in Canada that affords its program entirely in either English or French and even offers some classes in Spanish. However, the School has no specific requirement stating that a student must take his/her degree entirely in one language or another. On the other hand, the Schulich School of Business at York University in cooperation with Faculté des Sciences de l'Administration de l'Université Laval in Quebec City offers a joint York/Laval University whose goal 'is to graduate bilingual and bicultural managers with a superior understanding of the realities and conditions of the Canadian business environment'. *If you want a bilingual education then you will be restricted to a limited number of schools in central Canada.*[2]

In terms of the context of bilingual institutions, it makes sense that the majority of the bilingual HEIs are situated in the east, and mainly in Ontario, which borders on the French-speaking province, Quebec. The University of Ottawa is probably the most well-known bilingual HEI in Ontario and it will be discussed in more detail below.

The USA

Although bilingual school programmes are available in the USA, they have come under fire since the 'No child left behind' movement in the 1990s, to the extent that García notes that the term 'bilingual' has all but disappeared from public discourse (García, 2009: 10). In an article aptly titled 'Hard sell: Why is bilingual education so unpopular with the American public?', Crawford (2007: 145) claims that bilingual education has been controversial since the 1970s but that 'the bottom dropped out' in 1998. The reason was Proposition 227, which called for the exclusive use of English as a LoLT and which was overwhelmingly accepted by Californian voters, leading to similar actions in other states. García (2009: 194) notes:

> The United States is caught in a double bind. On the one hand, at the national level, anti-bilingual sentiment is running high, tied to anti-immigrant efforts. But on the other hand, informed parents are looking beyond our borders and seeing the world through new eyes and languages. To these parents, it is clear that their children must become competent bilinguals.

The important point about bilingual education in the USA is that it is located primarily in schools. This does not mean that appeals for bilingual HE have not been made; they just seem to be incomprehensible or impossible. If bilingual *school* education is problematic, surely HE cannot even be on the agenda! In an article on the possibility of multilingual teaching practices in HE, Friedenberg (2002: 219) recounts how an anonymous reviewer of an opinion piece she wrote on the topic rejected as simply 'far fetched', the idea of university professors *translating* their notes for language minority students.

St Augustine College in Chicago and Boricua College (New York, New York) are two of a few bilingual HE colleges in the United States. They are privately funded and offer bilingual (dual-language) programmes.[3] However, this is only evident when one reads the mission statement and history page of the college website. On the website, College View (which has the purpose of helping prospective students find a suitable college)[4] the *Facts and Figures for St Augustine*[5] page describes the 'Primary language of tuition' as English and the 'Enrolment concentration' as 'non-traditional', which refers to students who are mainly older and probably studying part-time. For Boricua College, no information is provided (on the website College View) about the primary language of instruction and it is only when one looks at information showing the diversity of the campus that it becomes clear that 83% of the student population is 'Hispanic'[6] and that Spanish would be used on campus.

Although Spanish and English do not constitute the only bilingual combination in the United States at school level, it is the dominant combination at HE level. Spanish–English bilingual HEIs constitute only 10% of all HEIs in the USA, although more than two-thirds of all Spanish-speaking students are educated at such institutions, according to the website of *The Hispanic Association of Colleges and Universities*[7] (HACU). This association represents 'Hispanic-serving institutions' as full members when at least 25% of the student body speaks Spanish. This, of course, does not mean that the institutions are officially and explicitly bilingual[8] in terms of instruction and educational materials.

Claiming that their post-secondary degree is the 'first-ever discipline-based, dual-language postsecondary degree program'[9] is a Puerto Rican-based university with campuses and partnerships in the USA: the Sistema Universitario Ana G. Méndez branched out into Miami and Orlando under the auspices of Regis University in Denver. The focus of their programme offerings is on working adults over the age of 23 (probably also described as 'non-traditional') and most classes are conducted in the late afternoon and evening. Although the first motivation was to provide programmes for mainly Spanish-speaking adults without competing with existing English-speaking educational providers, the students need to use both English and Spanish, and the explicit aim is for English students to learn Spanish and Spanish students to learn English.

From a more comprehensive basis, the Inter-American University of Puerto Rico offers education in Spanish and English after having 'vacillated

several times between Spanish and English before wisely settling for both'
as Purser (2000: 452) notes. The most important reason, according to Purser
(2000: 455), is that '[i]ts bilingual policy promotes an improved academic,
social, and economic outlook for Puerto Rico as a whole, with enhanced possibilities for exchange and co-operation with partners in both Latin and
North America'. From the database of the International Association of
Universities (World Higher Education Database, 2010) it does seem, however, that only the School of Law in San Juan uses both English and
Spanish.

One of the most well-known and unique bilingual universities is
Gallaudet University in Washington DC. It was founded in 1864 (granted
university status in 1986) and describes itself as 'a bilingual, diverse, multicultural institution of HE that ensures the intellectual and professional
advancement of deaf and hard of hearing individuals through American
Sign Language and English' in the mission statement on its website
(www.gallaudet.edu). The status of a particular sign language as a separate
and independent language, as well as the view that people who use both
sign language and an oral language are bilingual, is a view that is often lost
in studies of bilingual education. Grosjean (n.d.: 2) defends the right of deaf
and hard-of-hearing children to learn sign language and feels the need to
emphasise that sign language 'is a natural, full-fledged language that ensures
full and complete communication'. He also emphasises the importance of
learning this language as a first language and of becoming bilingual by
pointing out that (Grosjean, n.d.: 3):

> Despite considerable effort on the part of deaf children and of the
> professionals that surround them, and despite the use of various
> technological aids, it is a fact that many deaf children have great dif-
> ficulties producing and perceiving an oral language in its spoken
> modality. Having to wait several years to reach a satisfactory level
> that might never be attained, and in the meantime denying the deaf
> child access to a language that meets his/her immediate needs (sign
> language), is basically taking the risk that the child will fall behind in
> his/her development, be it linguistic, cognitive, social or personal.

It is indicative of HE administrators' view of sign language that provision for deaf or hard-of-hearing students would normally be seen as part of
their services to 'disadvantaged' or 'handicapped' students, rather than
bilingual education. The University of Kansas, for example, proudly reported
on 2 May 2010 on Kim Bates, who coordinates interpreters (and who does
interpreting herself) to translate lectures and classroom discussions for deaf
and hard-of-hearing students using sign language, yet the university does
not describe the programmes that such students follow as bilingual HE.[10]

Although the USA may not be known for its bi-/trilingual HEIs, it is
generally reported to be the country with the highest share of transnationally mobile students, that is, 69.43% in 2004 (Varghese, 2008: 17). Since it is

the preferred destination for Latin American students, one would expect a higher incidence of bilingual HEIs. Although the number of transnational students relative to domestic students is small, less than 3.4% of the total number of students in HE (Varghese, 2008: 18), the students are probably concentrated in particular institutions, which may open up the possibility of bi-/multilingual teaching and learning practices such as suggested by Michael-Luna and Canagarajah (2007 – see Chapter 4).

Asia

In his overview of language and identity in Asia, Simpson (2007: 7) notes that '[t]he linguistic interference in the development of national languages in much of Asia from the presence of a colonial language entrenched in government bureaucracy, legal systems, and education is something which has not been experienced in a parallel way in the emergence of national languages in western Europe, and continues to be an important challenge to the full acceptance of national languages in a number of national states'. HE in certain countries in Asia is also influenced in various ways by the fact that compulsory education at primary and secondary education levels has not been achieved. As Chudgar and Shafiq (2010: n.p.) note, '[i]t is clear, however, that without tremendous efforts by families, communities, and policymakers, Afghanistan, Burma, and Pakistan will not reach universal primary education by 2015 ... It also remains unclear when Bangladesh, India, Nepal, and Sri Lanka will attain universal secondary education'.

Britain, the USA and Australia have opened branch HE campuses in Asia (as in Europe and Africa), capitalising on the hard currency of higher degrees earned in English at English institutions. However, they are dependent on local administrators and lecturers who probably do not use only English for learning and teaching. For example, Graddol (2006: 80) mentions that 'the fastest growth for UK universities now appears to be in transnational students studying for a UK degree in branch campuses or joint ventures established in Asian countries'. Such institutions would most certainly require a certain level of proficiency in English to enrol for their programmes, but English may not be the primary and certainly not the only language of most students and lecturers.

Although there are countries like Japan, Korea and Bangladesh, where a national language is also spoken as a home language by the majority of the population, it is more common to find the choice of one national language based on the home language of a dominant majority (e.g. Thailand and Myanmar), or the home language of a high-status and powerful minority (e.g. Malaysia and Sri Lanka) or a language that is not spoken as a home language by any of the groups (e.g. Indonesia, Pakistan and the Philippines (Simpson, 2007: 6)).

The study of language policy and attempts to support non-colonial languages are varied across Asia but what seems to be a common trend is that HE, and universities in particular, would choose the colonial language (in previously colonised countries) as the LoLT. When local languages are used, English is often presented as the language of opportunity: a chance to study or find a job 'abroad'. In the discussion that follows, I will focus on three countries in Asia as instances of three distinct scenarios: India as a multilingual, post-colonial country managing a variety of languages in education; Japan as a relatively monolingual country where Japanese is used from primary through to tertiary education level; and Malaysia, as a multilingual country where an indigenous language is widespread in education. My discussion of these cases shows the range of options and the range of language policy decisions that can be taken.

India

An overview of the role of language in the Indian educational system runs the risk of being so general that it is useless, or of becoming the subject of an entire chapter by itself. The focus here will be on HE, but it must be seen in the context of a multilingual country where public primary and secondary education is mostly conducted in local languages. As is the case in Africa, the 'pervasive multilingualism' (Amritavalli & Jayaseelan, 2007: 79) in India makes the description of language use in terms of 'mother tongue' or 'home language' problematic, although Amritavalli and Jayaseelan (2007: 78) claim that English bilingualism (i.e. English plus a 'mother tongue') 'is outstripping other types of bilingualism' and that the pattern for non-Hindi speakers is 'first, bilinguality in Hindi; and second, trilinguality in English' (Amritavalli & Jayaseelan, 2007: 80). This point is endorsed by Mohanty (2012: 143).

Status planning for local languages in India is governed by an appendix to the Constitution, called the Eighth Schedule, which, according to Amritavalli and Jayaseelan (2007: 61), is now the 'sole constitutional acknowledgement of certain linguistic groups as Indian'. Despite criticism that it has led to a hierarchy of languages, with Hindi at the top, linguistic groups continue to lobby for inclusion in the Schedule. Amritavalli and Jayaseelan (2007: 61) doubt whether any real advantages can flow from inclusion in the Schedule. In fact, Mohanty (2012: 139) points out that 'the marginalisation and educational neglect of Indigenous, tribal and minority (ITM) languages lead to educational failure, capability deprivation and poverty of the minority language groups'.

In schools, home and regional languages are used for instruction at primary and secondary levels, although, as in Africa, private schools in urban centres offer English as a LoLT from the first grade onwards, with predictable results: 'the language of schooling is now the visible symbol of the divide between education for the "masses" and education for the "classes"' (Amritavalli & Jayaseelan, 2007: 78). In the 1960s, attempts were made to include local languages at HE level as well but the Department of Education had to acknowledge that 'Indian language medium courses are generally not popular among the students because of lack of professional comparability and poor employment potential' (Amritavalli & Jayaseelan, 2007: 79).

Japan

In Japan the LoLT of HE is Japanese, despite North American universities setting up branch campuses in Japan, since Japanese parents prefer sending their children to institutions that use Japanese as a LoLT and children then spend years abroad, presumably to also develop proficiency in other languages (De Mejia, 2002: 191). The exception is the Christian University of Tokyo, which is the only bilingual university in Japan, according to De Mejia (2002: 191). The university identifies three 'commitments', of which the third is to be an international institution, 'embracing a supranational perspective', which is explicitly linked to the use of Japanese *as well as* English (The three commitments of ICU, 2012):

> To promote mutual understanding and exchange in the international community, language ability is vital. ICU provides a bilingual education in English and Japanese.

The *commitment* concludes that ICU sees itself as 'a bridge both to and from Japan'. The institution seems to draw on the Christian University High School for many of its students and according to the statistics on its website, 7.4% of the student enrolment forms the 'international' (i.e. non-Japanese) component of the student body.

Malaysia

The back-and-forth history of a local language taking on a powerful international language, in this case English, is nowhere more graphically illustrated than in the case of Bahasa Melayu. As Gill (2004) recounts, Bahasa Melayu was legislated and successfully elaborated and instituted as the language of education, including HE since the 1960s. This was done to empower the largely rural Malay population in particular. However, in order to compete internationally, the government decided in 2002 that science and mathematics would be taught in English from primary school level up to HE level. As Gill (2004: 121) notes of the introduction of English in 2003, 'the same factor of economic inequity rears its head again to stimulate a reversal of the language policy'. Each change is characterised by a transition period of bilingual education, first in the 1960s with arts taught in Bahasa Melayu and science and technology in English. With reference to the Universiti Kebangsaan Malaysia, which was founded with the express purpose of enhancing the status and use of Bahasa Melayu at university level, Gill (2004: 122) reports that it, too, is using a transitional bilingual model, despite its strategic plan to continue promoting the language.

Since 2003, a number of changes have taken place (Hashim, 2009) with the government changing back to the use of Bahasa Melayu for science and mathematics at school level from 2012. Deputy Prime Minister Tan Sri Muhyiddin Yassin announced on 8 July 2009 (*The Star Online* of 8 July 2009[11]) that, 'Beginning 2012, students in Year One and Year Four in primary schools, and Form One and Form Four in secondary schools, will learn Math and Science in Bahasa Malaysia... The two subjects will be taught in two languages until 2014 for other students'. The bilingual option is seen as a temporary solution to bridge the gap between the statement and the implementation of the policy. Acknowledging the multilingual nature of the country, Omar (2007: 359) recounts the policy-making process by pointing out that

> Socio-economic developments in the country and processes of globalisation especially in the area of education and technology subsequently motivated a change in mindset and it came to be believed that the national language, Malay, could maintain its critical position as the single most important symbolic embodiment of national identity, even if certain linguistic space was ceded to another language for use in various official and formal domains, notably English.

As in the case of other countries with a recent history of colonisation, the national and local languages are widely used outside the classroom. In the case of Bahasa Melayu, the language was also used inside the classroom, and a switch to English will invariably mean the use of both languages to mediate complex, cognitive materials.

China

In a UNESCO report on *World Education Indicators* (WEI) in 2007, it is reported that '[a]s a consequence of strong growth in tertiary education, China became the country with the most tertiary graduates in the world – 2.4 million in 2006' (UNESCO Institute for Statistics, 2007: 18). This is a result of 'massification' efforts in the 1970s, significantly called the 'booming phase' by Brandenburg and Zhou (2007: 16), when examination-based entrance requirements were set and the qualification framework followed the UK and USA models. These changes formed part of a deliberate strategy to launch China on the global stage (Brandenburg & Zhou, 2007: 17). Despite these changes, the WEI report (2007) also shows that the countries covered in it 'are still far behind OECD countries, three-quarters of which have graduation ratios greater than 30%'.

As part of the globalisation process, China joined the World Trade Organisation in 2001 and the *China Education and Research Network* (CERN, 2010) announced that '[c]olleges and universities across China will launch bilingual education to meet the need for bilingual personnel after the country's accession to the World Trade Organization'. The language used alongside Putonghua would be English and the report notes that, to solve the problem of teachers' English language proficiency, 'the Ministry of Education will send more Chinese teachers to receive training overseas'. In 2003, the Ministry of Education once again urged institutions of HE to ensure that English–Chinese bilingual education programmes 'achieve 5–10% of the total courses taken for undergraduates in higher education institutes in China' (Li & Wang, 2010: 353).

The kind of bilingual education that is envisaged is similar to the CLIL concept that is mooted in Europe and subjects like Science, Mathematics, Business Studies and Computer Studies seem the ones most often followed in English. What this seems to imply is that students would take some of their courses entirely in English and others in Chinese. Li and Wang (2010: 355) discuss problems with appropriate materials and make the comment that English textbooks do not always fit the Chinese circumstances but that 'the textbook in Chinese does not satisfy the purpose of bilingual education', clearly indicating that the concept of bilingual education means immersion in English.

The call from the government for bilingual education obviously fell on fertile ground because Hu (2007: 94) talks about the 'juggernaut of English–Chinese bilingual education' and claims that 'within a space of 5 years, this form of bilingual education [content teaching in English] has gained tremendous publicity and momentum and is sweeping across a country that has until recently taken great pride in its culture and indigenous languages dating back 5000 years' (Hu, 2007: 95).

Because of the competition among universities to be seen as prestigious and as 'key' HEIs (Jiazhen, 2007: 201), most students and academic staff compete to attend them and the impression is created that the success of bilingual education at 'non-key' institutions is compromised because of the lack of English language proficiency. Language proficiency is also the main problem noted by Li and Wang (2010) in a case study of bilingual programmes at Northeast Forestry University, Harbin, Heilongjiang Province.

It is worth mentioning HEIs in Hong Kong separately since they have a long tradition of teaching in English. The Chinese University of Hong Kong markets itself as the oldest university in Hong Kong and calls itself a bilingual and multicultural institution (http://www.cuhk.edu.hk/english/aboutus/mission.html). Even in Hong Kong, institutions where English is regarded as the only LoLT and where English-speaking members of staff form the majority of the teaching and research staff, code switching to Cantonese and the use of Cantonese by the students is widely noted. Yang and Lau (2003: 109) note in their language attitude survey that 'lecturers believed that it was more important to deliver content matter than to use English in class'.

The Russian Federation and Eastern Europe

The use of more than one language in HE is not unusual in multilingual Europe. However, the expansion of Russia as the Soviet Union and the split between west and east in the aftermath of World War II have resulted in marked differences between what was known pre-1990 as 'western Europe' and 'eastern Europe'. For that reason, this division will be made in full acknowledgement of the fact that it is not relevant anymore. However, it helps to explain the existence of formally bi-/multilingual HE in the west as opposed to the east. A testimony to recent changes is the newly established Europa University Viadrina on the border between Germany and Poland; an example of how bilingualism has been managed at regional levels since 1990.

The recent history of Eastern European states is reflected in their language in education policies, where Russian was either used alongside a local language in schools or was the only LoLT. With the collapse of the Soviet Union, many states returned to the use of local languages at school and HE level and Hrycak (2006: 78) argues that this is because people are used to the idea of a national identity being grounded in a national language: previously Russian and now Ukranian or Kazakstani. Countries that have joined the European Union are pressured into teaching in English because of international students. However, the situation is not a matter of simply using English for international students. In the Czech Republic, 60% of the foreign student intake consists of Slovak students who follow programmes offered in the Czech language (Crosier *et al.*, 2007: 188). Coleman (2006: 7) notes,

> The need for an international *lingua franca* arising from the demise of the Soviet Union and integration into global markets led more than half of school pupils across Central and Eastern Europe to learn (rather than study) English, and the percentage of Hungarian students learning English rose from below 20% to over 50%.

Authors such as Enyedi and Medgyes (1998: 4) as well as Dörnyei and Csizér (2002) document the decline in students studying Russian in Eastern European countries, although German seems to have retained its position. In terms of attracting transnationally mobile students, Varghese (2008: 16) reports that, although North America and Europe attract the biggest percentage of these students, the Russian Federation and 'other Eastern European countries' attract most of the transnationally mobile students from Central Asia. With reference to the Baltic countries, Coleman (2006: 8) reports that they form an 'honourable exception' to the general move to programmes offered in English, but he adds that 'even there English-language HEIs can be found'.

Western Europe

In the discussion that follows, the term 'Western Europe' is used to refer to the 24 member states of the European Union. The focus is on bi-/multilingual institutions and gives an indication of the role that English plays in multilingual contexts.

In 2003, the first conference on bi- and multilingual universities was held in Fribourg (Switzerland), followed by the second conference in 2005 (Helsinki, Finland), the third in 2007 (Bolzano, Italy) and the fourth in 2010

(Luxembourg). It is clear (as can be seen on the conference websites[12]) that the Bologna Declaration and European concerns with 'plurilingualism' (as a term used particularly in Europe to refer to individual multilingualism) are the main drivers of such conferences.

Without taking into account HEIs such as colleges or academies that train translators and interpreters, the following list provides an indication of the spread of prestigious, bi-/multilingual universities in Europe:

- In Ireland and Wales, using English alongside Irish and Welsh
  - The University of Wales Trinity Saint David[13]
  - National University of Ireland (Galway[14])
- In Finland, using Finnish, Swedish and increasingly English
  - The University of Helsinki
  - Åbo Akademi
- Purser (2000: 452) reports a new addition to the bilingual university landscape in Germany, on the border with Poland, where German and Polish and increasingly English are used
  - The Europa University Viadrina
- In Spain, in Catalonia (using Catalan and Castilian) and in the Basque region (using Basque and Castilian)
  - The University of Barcelona
  - University of Lleida
  - University of the Basque Country
- In Switzerland, using German and French and increasingly English
  - The University of Fribourg
- In Italy, using Italian, German and English
  - The Free University of Bozen/Bolzano (Italy)
- In Luxembourg, using French, German and Luxemburgisch
  - The University of Luxemburg

The context within which these institutions developed is discussed next, but it is important to note right from the start that they are increasingly including English as a LoLT alongside national languages. The introduction and use of English is welcomed by university administrators because of its power to 'internationalise' institutions (Ritzen, 2004) thereby allowing European universities in particular to compete with USA and British institutions. The Academic Cooperation Association (ACA) organised a conference on the role of English in Higher Education in 2001 (Maiworm & Wächter, 2002) and initiated an investigation into the prevalence of English-Language-Taught Degree Programmes (abbreviated ELTDPs) in Europe. The ACA finds that such programmes are relatively rare and their key recommendation is 'the appeal to governments and universities and colleges to substantially increase the offer of ELTDPs, in order to provide a (continental) European alternative to study in the USA, Australia or Canada' (ACA). Graddol (2006: 74) notes that in 2003–2004, 1500 master's programmes were taught in English in European countries that do not use English as a home language.

In the report *Progress in Higher Education Reform across Europe* (2008), the offering of courses in English is linked to student mobility, and increased student mobility is seen as a sign of progress. What is interesting in the report is the way in which other languages are positioned in relation to English. In a series of case studies, universities that do not offer programmes in English are constructed as not progressing well:

- Universities in Cyprus show 'some improvement' in terms of student mobility because private universities are able to offer programmes in English. The report states, '[t]herefore, students from other countries now have the option of studying at university level in Cyprus without having to learn the Greek language' (*Progress in Higher Education Reform across Europe*, 2008: 176).

- In the Czech Republic, student mobility has also increased because 'the capacity of Czech HE institutions to offer courses in English has improved'. However, such progress must be qualified because 'of the fact that Slovak students (studying in the free courses delivered in the Czech language) are looked upon as foreign students' (*Progress in Higher Education Reform across Europe*, 2008: 188). The fact that foreign students profit from their knowledge of a language in the same language family seems to be evaluated negatively, rather than positively! The tendency of mobility to be strong when languages are closely related or where students live in border areas where they may be familiar with another national language is also mentioned in the case of the Netherlands regarding students coming in from German border towns and Dutch students going to Belgian institutions (*Progress in Higher Education Reform across Europe*, 2008: 428).

- In Denmark, the report notes approvingly that there are increased offerings in English at Danish institutions, but again laments the fact that some programmes are offered in both English and Danish: 'In this way, increased internationalisation is not always resulting in an integrated international study environment' (*Progress in Higher Education Reform across Europe*, 2008: 205).

- Estonia, Latvia, the Netherlands, Norway and Slovenia are praised for increasing their academic offerings in English.

- In Slovenia, at the University of Ljubljana, the progress of the University is seen and judged from the perspective of its English programmes: 'Next to international programmes like ERASMUS, the university, with support of external stakeholders, initiated special funds to attract students from former Yugoslav republics and invested its own resources to offer courses and programmes in foreign languages. However the number of English taught programmes is still very limited' (*Progress in Higher Education Reform across Europe*, 2008: 552). The University of Maribor is criticised as follows: 'It is remarkable that mobility strategies are focused on students from ex-Yugoslavia instead of investing in English taught programmes for a wider audience' (*Progress in Higher Education Reform across Europe*, 2008: 563).

- One remarkable exception is the lament in the report about the way legislation in Latvia prevents universities from offering programmes in Russian, 'although the interest from Russian students are considerably (*sic*)' (*Progress in Higher Education Reform across Europe*, 2008: 370).

These descriptions are striking for two reasons: first, it is remarkable that local or regional languages are seen as a hindrance to transnational student mobility because such a view denies the possibility that institutions may decide or may be under pressure to attend to local and regional demands for education first. A feeling of 'neighbourliness' or 'charity begins at home' may be at the heart of HEIs' language decisions, especially where close cooperation with neighbouring countries may be more important than a few students from far-flung countries. This situation is similar to the one in Latin America, where language similarities support mobility in the region. Second, *not* using a local or regional language, as in the case of Latvia, probably has its roots in the recent past; much like sentiments against the use of Afrikaans in South Africa.

The opening of borders in Europe has led to increasing mobility of the HE student population. The ERASMUS programme accelerates the growth of this phenomenon in Europe and Graddol (2006: 76) indicates that 'between 2 and 3 million students each year travel to another country to study'. Van Leeuwen (2007: 3) notes that:

> a university degree therefore implies a certain degree of 'international competence': students must be equipped with adequate linguistic and intercultural skills to function effectively in an international and multicultural context and to enable them to participate in the international labour market.

As was pointed out in the Introduction, publications on student experiences, global citizenship and 'internationalised' curricula have increased in the past three years, bearing testimony to the importance of intercultural awareness and a socially responsive attitude. As Bourn (2010) reports, the students in his study favoured the social justice element of global citizenship above an orientation towards the market (as Van Leeuwen proposes above), a conclusion supported by Ben-Tsur (2012) on student mobility towards conflict zones. As Bourn points out, it is a challenge for universities 'to ensure this interest becomes the dominant voice in promoting their international outlook rather than as a subsidiary to one based on market share and economic need' (Bourn, 2010: 27). Although these are small studies and a social justice orientation can quickly become a patronising 'do good' orientation, an engagement with social issues beyond the borders of one's own country presupposes more than a good command of English.

The Middle East

The term Middle East is used here to cover a geographic area that is widely divergent: from Turkey in the east, where HE systems approximate those of Western Europe, to Saudi Arabia in the west, where HE needs to juggle demands for internationalisation in a theocratic government (Cheng & Beigi, 2012). Findlow's (2006: 23) description of the United Arab Emirates is true to an extent of the whole region when she describes the context as 'one where the country itself is changing, people (especially young people at university) are exposed to "otherness" in a way that their parents were not, local heritage is steeped in political struggle, official discourse endeavours to be eclectic and reconcile (*sic*)'. The way in which a convergence of culture, language and religion influences decisions about attending HE is described by Arar and Haj-Yehia (2010) who present a striking example of the tensions and challenges experienced in this region. Palestinian women living in Israel choose to attend HE in Jordan because it is seen as 'a place that maintains Muslim women's norms of behaviour' and 'the geographical proximity to their homes in Israel enables continuation of the family patriarchal supervision' (Arar & Haj-Yehia, 2010: 375). Although Arabic (the language that these students would have used at secondary-school level) is the LoLT, English is becoming more important in Jordanian HE. Hamdan and Abu Hatab (2009) indicate that the 'Ministry of HE [in Jordan] has recently required that all postgraduate students should obtain a score of 213 on the computer-based TOEFL (Test of English as a Foreign Language) or 5 on the IELTS (International English Language Testing System) exams as the admission requirement in scientific faculties and as graduation requirement in the humanities and social sciences'.

The division between state and private education at primary and secondary levels is echoed in a language division between Arabic (for state-funded institutions) and English or French (for private institutions) in some areas. Findlow (2006) describes the situation in the UAE, where (at that stage) a functional division was made at HE level between cultural and social studies and humanities in Arabic and technology and commerce-related subjects in English. A similar division can be seen at other universities in the region, for example, Hamade (2007) reports on two colleges at Kuwait University where the College of Science uses English and the College of Social Sciences uses Arabic. Four years later, Gallagher (2011: 66) claims that English is so dominant in HEIs of the region that it is almost impossible to study at that level through Arabic. Findlow (2006: 32) emphasises students' conflicting identities that result from the use of these two languages, noting that code switching could be 'a way in which the UAE's linguistic-cultural dualism can be seen as inevitable, even enabling, in such transitional times: a strategy for dealing with the essential dualistic nature of consciousness and society, and for laying claim to two identities and "cultures" at once'.

In contrast, Elyas and Picard (2010: 137) link the use of English to an uncritical acceptance of Western curricula and teaching practices in the majority of Gulf countries. The underpreparedness of students to manage HE study in English is a concern in Saudi Arabia and other countries in the Gulf region (Ghaith & Diab, 2008) and solutions tend to focus on improving English language proficiency and in separating the languages. The use of both languages in one classroom does not seem to be considered.

The HE system in Turkey has expanded recently, and Grossman, Sands and Brittingham (2010: 103) note that the system has grown from 18 established institutions in 1992 to 94 state and 9 private universities in 2009, of which some are English-medium universities. Doğançay-Aktuna and Kiziltepe (2005: 254) claim that '[t]he most significant function of English in Turkey is its instrumental use within public and private educational institutions that also act as the main agent of language spread'. By their count in 2005, there are 21 private institutions, which are all English medium and one Turkish–English institution, and of the 53 public institutions, 23 are English medium and 11 are Turkish–English bilingual. However, since the remaining institutions offer instruction in English for students who scored high enough in university entrance tests, particularly in disciplines such as medicine and economic and management sciences, it seems safe to infer that most institutions use some kind of bilingual education model.

In Turkey, since the introduction of a 2001–2002 policy for HE that compels students to follow a foreign language course up to the sixth semester, Doğançay-Aktuna and Kiziltepe (2005: 255) speculate that '[t]hough the policy does not specify the particular foreign language to be taught, given the emphasis placed on English in Turkey at the expense of other languages, the lack of trained teachers to teach other languages, the role of English in global communication, and the attitudes of the Ministry of Education thus far, this will most probably be English'.

In the region, generally, HEIs face the challenge of internationalisation and the perception of English as an instrument of upward mobility, which creates a demand for its use in professional training, particularly at HE level. Findlow (2006: 20) concludes that '[i]n the Middle East, in Israel as well as Arab countries, descriptions [of language use in HE] have concentrated on the ways in which the native language has become symbolic of nostalgia and authenticity, with the colonial language (English or French) increasingly associated with "status" in a modern, internationally oriented sense'. The Middle East is no different from the rest of the world in this regard.

The Role of English[15]

As is clear from the foregoing, much has been written about the role of English and particularly of the increased use of English as an indicator of the degree to which HEIs are 'internationalised' and the purpose of this section is not to repeat the obvious. In the discussion above on HE in Europe, a lack of English language programmes is seen as a lack of progress (in the report *Progress in Higher Education Reform across Europe,* 2008).

In his overview of global population demographics, Graddol (2006: 20) claims:

> An 'English factor' is found in virtually every key macro trend: whether it is business process outsourcing (BPO), the rise of urban middle classes around the world, the development of new communications technology such as the internet, the global redistribution of poverty, the changing nature and control of news media, or the reform of education in universities and schools.

As a language, English carries a heavy symbolic burden. The use of English at HE levels is constructed as (among others):

- building a bridge between the local and the global, with English being the instrument to internationalise HE (Ritzen, 2004);
- progressive, as evidenced by the reports on universities' ability to present programmes in English (*Progress in Higher Education Reform across Europe*, 2008);
- inevitable, as Brink and Van der Walt (2005) note in describing the inclusion of English in officially multilingual HEIs;
- 'the first foreign language in almost all educational systems' (Beacco & Byram, 2003: 52);
- providing a competitive edge, as seen by governments that plan for the introduction of English at primary school level;
- empowering, by giving disadvantaged groups the opportunity to enter HE, as in Malaysia;
- uniting heterogeneous communities, where English is seen as instrumental to nation-building, as in a number of Anglophone African countries;
- providing evidence of national ambition, as in Singapore (Simpson, 2007) and personal ambition, as argued by Montgomery (2004: 1334); and
- providing opportunities that would otherwise not exist, as in Japan (see above).

This means that the presence of English is accompanied by expectations to the extent that just using English well is often regarded as sufficient qualification for a job, particularly as a teacher of English (Bobda, 2006; MacKay, 2002).

Internationally, the academic context is directed towards and by English: most academic publications appear in English and student textbooks are also increasingly published in English, leading Lillis and Curry (2010: 1) to report that it is seen as 'the default language of Science and academic research and dissemination' by academics as well as translators and editors. Even academic language journals dedicated to the teaching of languages other than English publish articles mainly in English (Heffernan, 2003).

The status and spread of English is such that educational language planning is primarily concerned with planning for the position of local languages vis-à-vis English. Coleman (2006: 2) indicates the importance of language use in HE as a high-status domain, and in his overview of the spread of English in European HE states that, 'in diglossic societies, the formal and prestigious functions are the first to be lost: hence the importance of higher education'. In institutions where English becomes the language of communication among academic staff and students because of recruitment patterns and internationalisation drives, the institution itself can be characterised as diglossic to an extent, with students using home or local languages among themselves and with staff members who share their languages, reserving English for classroom and formal academic contexts, like conferences.

It may not be immediately obvious from the literature on internationalisation or at conferences on English-medium universities, but, based on the increasing use of English as a LoLT, most (prestigious) HEIs (nationally and internationally) now offer bi-/multilingual education. In her summary of papers at an international conference on *Multilingualism in Society, the World of Work, and Politics* (presented by the Sprachlehr Institut at the University of Freiburg, Germany), Lauridsen (2012) concludes in her summary of a parallel session on university teaching in a foreign language:

> Most HEIs used to be monolingual, but are now in different stages of moving toward being bi-trilingual, i.e. offering programmes and modules in one or two additional languages. The vast majority are moving towards EMI [English Medium of Instruction].

> A smaller number of universities are defined as bi-/trilingual universities because they are located in bi-/trilingual countries or border areas.

> Fascinating to see how much we have in common.

Even if we do not want to acknowledge that a *de facto* bilingual educational setting prevails at most modern HEIs, it is true that most of them offer language support for students who struggle with a particular LoLT. Entrance tests of language proficiency and academic support programmes serve as an acknowledgement that the student population is increasingly linguistically diverse and that this fact complicates learning and teaching. With this in mind, there seems to be a continuum of HEIs with two clear groupings of institutions at either end. In all cases, a linguistically diverse student population affects the language landscape of teaching and learning.

On the one hand, there are HEIs in countries such as the USA and the UK, where the language used outside and inside the classroom is mainly English, a situation that may support the English language development of 'foreign' students. Although the classrooms and campus life may appear to be dominantly monolingual, it only takes a stroll on the campus grounds to realise that a multiplicity of languages and varieties of English are used to mediate study in English. When the government of the time placed a cap on study fees for British citizens (introduced in response to the Dearing Report (1998)) HEIs actively recruited transnationally mobile students because there was no cap on their study fees and such students proved a very lucrative proposition. The UK Council for International Student Affairs (UKCISA, 2010b) claims that up to 30% of universities' income is derived from transnationally mobile (non-EU) students (since EU students pay the same amount as UK students). Because of their reputation, HEIs such as Cambridge and Oxford are very popular with transnationally mobile students and the limited places available ensure that such institutions can select only the very best. This is noticeable at postgraduate level in particular. The organisation UK Council for International Student Affairs publishes the following statistics on its website (UKCISA, 2010a):

In UK HE in 2008–2009, transnationally mobile students made up:

- **13%** of full-time first degree students and **11%** of all first degree students
- **68%** of full-time taught postgraduates and **43%** of all taught postgraduates
- **50%** of full-time research degree students and **43%** of all research postgraduates

These numbers have to be treated with caution, since UKCISA (2010b) states that '[t]he precise number of international students in the UK is not known as no central statistics are kept of all those in both public and private sector institutions'.

UKCOSA: The Council for International Education (2007: 10, 11) reports on the kinds of services offered to such students of which language courses, study skills courses and cultural events form a major part. Students are usually informed of English language requirements before they travel to the host institution and are offered additional English language support (mostly free of charge) throughout their course of study (UKCOSA: The Council for International Education, 2007: 11). Such support is clearly a central issue since learning English is the only topic of discussion under the heading *Study issues* although a 'buddy' or 'mentoring' system (offered by 29%) and 'tandem learning' (offered by 20% of the institutions polled) are listed under the heading *Student support and advice*. Satisfactory performance on the IELTS, developed at the University of Cambridge and managed by University of Cambridge ESOL Examinations, the British Council and IDP Education Pty Ltd., is generally required for admission to UK, Australia, New Zealand and many African universities.

Data about transnationally mobile students in the USA are provided by the Institute for International Education (at http://www.iie.org/opendoors), which states on its website that it receives support from the Bureau of

Educational and Cultural Affairs of the US Department of State. According to this organisation, 3.5% of the total student population in the USA constitute transnationally mobile students, fairly equally divided between undergraduate and graduate students. The requirements for international students vary but English language proficiency in the form of satisfactory results on the TOEFL or IELTS are compulsory for transnational students for full admission to US HEIs.

At the other end of the continuum are universities and colleges that use more than one language for learning and teaching: the officially bi-/multilingual institutions mentioned in the first part of this chapter. Such institutions generally require that students provide proof of language proficiency in their main language (or preferred language of study) and often in other regional or international languages as well. The way in which students demonstrate their proficiency is by means of the Common European Framework of Reference for Language (Council of Europe, 2001) and the European Language Passport. At the University of Fribourg (Switzerland), for example, students have to demonstrate proficiency in either German or French and the expectation is that they will become bilingual in the course of their study. An added motivational factor is the *Lizentiat/Diplom mit Zweisprachigkeits-Zusatz*, something like a degree with an endorsement that the student completed her or his studies using both languages.

Somewhere in between these two ends of the continuum are institutions where a dominant LoLT is used by students and staff who share other languages that are not used at all or that are used only partially for instructional purposes. In such communities, a local language may be used for learning and teaching, as in, for example, Europe, in some South African, mainly Afrikaans communities, in institutions where Arabic is used or in China. In some instances, English is used mainly as a LoLT to accommodate international students and to prepare students for professional contexts where English might be the language of the workplace. In such cases, academic language support may be offered but quite often students and lecturers are assumed to be proficient in English, especially at postgraduate level. Students may have access to study material in their home languages and have the advantage of sharing a home language with their lecturers. This is increasingly the case in South Africa where study materials are being developed in African languages and where more home-language speakers of these languages are appointed in academic positions. In these cases, the teaching and learning situation is *de facto* if not *de officio* moving towards bilingual education.

Universities in South Africa may find that their campuses are similar to institutions in the USA and Britain (in the case of English universities) or to European universities (in the case of HAUs). However, the location of South African universities is always multilingual. It would be rare for a student to encounter only one language outside or even inside the classroom.

The continuum can be summarised as follows:

| Hypothetically purely monolingual in teaching and learning practice. | Language proficiency entrance tests, academic language support in English. | Language proficiency entry requirements, academic language support for some students, learning material support in home/community languages, most lecturers know English plus home/community languages of majority of the students. | Bi-/multilingual language policies govern teaching and learning practices. |

The discussions on the role of English in HE are reflected in the diagram, indicating that bi-/multilingualism does not necessarily imply knowledge of *any* number of languages: it means *English plus* other languages. As noted in Chapter 1, this perception is implicit in Graddol's (2006: 100) statement that knowledge and use of English will be seen as a basic skill in future:

> In an increasing number of countries, English is now regarded as a component of basic education, rather than as part of the foreign languages curriculum. *A surprising number of countries now aspire to bilingualism.* (Emphasis added.)

Jenkins (2003: 141) indicates that *English-knowing bilinguals* are 'regarded as aberrations by English mother-tongue speakers in the UK and US, [but] are the *de facto* norm throughout the rest of the world'. The term *English-knowing bilingualism* is increasingly used to indicate HE settings where the knowledge of English is required alongside other languages to mediate academic texts and widen access to HE. However, as Van Leeuwen (2007: 5) points out, it is not enough for European students to have a good command of English because it is also important 'to have the ability to express themselves at an academic level in their own language or in the language or languages of the country in which they take their degree, if only because they will often pursue their profession in this language'. It is self-evident then that universities that claim to be 'internationalising' (by using English) need to follow some kind of English-plus bilingual education model. The use of various entry requirements for English as well as other languages is evident in the assessment industry, where tests like the IELTS, TOEFL and, in Europe, increasingly TLP (which is aligned with the CEFR) underline the importance of European languages alongside English.

Although publications and conferences focus on the role of English and the problems of 'English-medium' HE, it is clear that English is one element in a complex and multilingual context that demands more than 'English language support'. Spolsky (2005: 2153) points out: 'A host of non-linguistic factors (political, demographic, social, religious, cultural, psychological, bureaucratic, and so on) regularly account for any attempt of persons or groups to intervene in the language practices and the beliefs of other persons or groups, and for the subsequent changes that do or do not occur.' For that reason, any attempt by HE administrators and managers to create policies for the introduction or management of languages in education will do well to heed Ferguson's (1977: 9) caveat that, '[a]ll language planning activities take place in particular sociolinguistic settings, and the nature and scope of the planning can only be fully understood in relation to the settings'. A study of the context and settings of officially bi-/multilingual HEIs provide a glimpse into the organic way in which languages co-exist.

The Sociolinguistic Setting of Bi-/Multilingual Higher Education Institutions

In this section, a theoretical analysis that has emerged from studies of bilingual school education is applied to explicitly multilingual HE to show that bi-/multilingual HE is determined and conditioned by the same factors that apply for bilingual education in general: historical, socio-structural, cultural, ideological and social psychological factors (Hamers & Blanc, 2000: 323). The term *condition* is understood to indicate those contextual factors that *determine* the development and form the sociolinguistic setting of bi-/multilingual education settings. Bi-/multilingual HEIs in South Africa and Europe are used as examples of contrasting settings to highlight their complexity.

Spolsky (2005: 2154) indicates that 'sociolinguistic setting' should be interpreted to include anything that affects language practices and beliefs or that leads to efforts at intervention.' The conditioning factors identified by Hamers and Blanc can be used as a tool to systematically study the setting (in the form of the history, development and current responses to challenges) of HEIs that explicitly declare themselves bi-/multilingual.

The section that follows will deal with each of these factors to show that the way in which they are realised can create a 'habitat' that determines the way in which languages interact and live alongside each other. Although the factors will be dealt with separately below, they are obviously intricately and tightly interwoven.

Background to bi-/multilingual higher education institutions

Research on the integration of English language teaching into so-called content subjects in HE has only recently gained currency in the form of international conferences on *Content and Language Integrated Learning* (CLIL), starting at the then Peninsula Technikon in Cape Town in 2002 and continuing at Maastricht University in 2004, 2006 and later. The main concern seems to be the English language proficiency of students and academic staff and the best way to structure learning and teaching of content subjects in a language (English) that is not the students' school language. The Bologna Process, which encourages mobility and greater competitiveness in European HE, can be seen as the official driver behind the increased use of

English alongside local and/or national languages, particularly at postgraduate level, although student expectations for employment opportunities and mobility also play their role (identified as 'push' and 'pull' factors in Chapter 1). Of course, these problems are not new for HEIs in Africa and India, where former colonial languages are, at least *de iure,* the only LoLT.

The use of a language for HE teaching and learning implies standardisation first and status and corpus planning procedures subsequently; that is, such a language must be seen to be used in the media and in educational materials (status planning) and must have the necessary lexical and discourse resources to mediate and constitute learning and teaching at HE level (corpus planning).

In South Africa, many universities that used Afrikaans as a medium of instruction have started implementing dual or parallel-medium instruction, using English alongside Afrikaans, while developing study materials in regional African languages for study support. Universities that have traditionally been seen as English speaking have also introduced regional languages as instructional tools. Research on the effects of translation, interpretation and code switching is starting to emerge and a special edition of the *South African Linguistics and Applied Language Studies* journal (*SALALS* 26(3)) pays attention, in particular, to South African research on these kinds of practices.

In European universities that are not explicitly bi-/multilingual, the model of bilingual education, referred to as CLIL above, is in its infancy as far as research at HE level is concerned. Darn (2006) thinks that,

> Most current CLIL programmes are experimental. There are few sound research-based empirical studies, while CLIL-type bilingual programmes are mainly seen to be marketable products in the private sector.

In the UK, such programmes focus mainly on learners in the age range 7–16 (Darn, 2006). European Union-funded research on CLIL in European HE started in 2002 (CLIL Compendium), most notably in Finland and the Netherlands. Both these countries are also known as leaders in the field of programme offerings in English. As was argued in Chapter 1, research in the area of multilingual HE is in its infancy, and, by describing the context of bilingualism in HE (in the next two sections), it becomes possible to understand the importance of acknowledging and building on local (multilingual) contexts.

Historical factors

The history of a region and the university situated within it can create a context where bi-/multilingualism seems self-evident and obvious. This is the case in many European and North American border regions. In these cases *border* can be understood in the sense of administrative borders between regions and provinces and such borders are often drawn because of the political paradigm whereby people who speak the same language are thought to belong together. Because of cross-border contact, people use more than one language to differing degrees of competence. The strategic positioning of a university, which is an expensive enterprise, could seek to serve both communities, as is the case with the University of Fribourg, situated between the south-west French-speaking part of Switzerland, and the north-east German-speaking part. The University of Ottawa is similarly situated on the border between mostly English Ontario and mostly French Quebec.

Quite another situation exists in the case of the Universities of Helsinki (Finland) and Barcelona (Spain) where the 'border' is more linguistic than physical. The social histories of these universities provide a mandate for them to support minority languages by using them for teaching and learning purposes alongside other official languages. In Finland, which was a province of Sweden for a long time, Swedish is a minority, high-status language and the University of Helsinki is under state obligation to produce graduates in Swedish. Since Finnish is spoken by 94% of the population, it is used alongside Swedish as a LoLT. In Spain, Spanish or Castilian is a majority, high-status language, but the University of Barcelona is situated in Catalonia where Catalan is the majority language. As a result of its long history of oppression, the University of Barcelona is mandated by the Parliament of Catalonia to foster and maintain Catalan by using it as a LoLT alongside Spanish. In this case, as in the case of Helsinki and Ottawa, financial support is provided by the regional authorities so that universities can carry out this mandate. The fact that these languages may not always live together peacefully is evident in the photo of English graffiti on a wall in the town of Figueres, next to the Salvador Dali museum, where many tourists are bound to see this slogan for the Catalonia is not Spain movement.

Graffiti outside Barcelona. (Photo: Author)

The histories of South African universities that are currently using explicitly bilingual models of education are, obviously, closely linked to the recent history of apartheid and the suppression of local people and their languages, a position from which Afrikaans benefited. The historical borders were (and still are) racial ones. HAUs were founded in areas where Afrikaans speakers were concentrated and where well-resourced schools produced the students for these institutions. The HAUs use English increasingly as a LoLT but there are also attempts to maintain Afrikaans and to develop indigenous languages as academic languages. Although one can argue for the maintenance of Afrikaans in the light of the national language policy for HE, it must always be seen in the perspective of its racist legacy.

At some South African institutions, bilingual education practices are being developed in the form of study materials in African languages and African language requirements for staff. These are, however, recent developments that have yet to be woven into the fabric that constitutes an institutional 'history'. The social and historical contexts within which these universities operate are multilingual but home language speakers of English are generally a minority. The situation is similar to that in European universities where English is used increasingly as part of an internationalisation strategy: the majority of students and staff use English as an additional language and it is not spoken much outside the classroom.

Socio-structural factors

Social structures in this case refer to the relative status of languages in bi-/multilingual communities, where high status is a reflection of the degree to which one language is seen to give access to power. When one studies the context within which bilingual universities function, one has to take socio-structural factors into account because the students carry the values and prestige that communities attach to languages into the classrooms.

In bilingual institutions, it is seldom the case that both languages have equal status. When English is one of the LoLTs, it is usually valued very highly and people generally fear that its high status may eventually push out the lower-status language. At the University of Ottawa, the status of English and the fact that the majority of students are English speaking have led to entrance tests for French and English being abandoned, since very few English-speaking students are fluent enough in French to be able to study through it. At the HAUs in South Africa, the status of English and the lure of jobs overseas mean that many Afrikaans students themselves clamour for English instruction.

If bilingual teaching can be seen as a socio-structural balancing of the status of two languages, the high status 'weight' of English as a world language can be balanced to some extent by the activism for and vitality of low status or minority languages. In such cases, the status of English is counterbalanced by a vocal and militant group that clamours for the right to instruction in French in the case of Ottawa and Afrikaans in the case of some

HAUs. As Hamers and Blanc (2000: 329) point out, no language group wants to lose its speakers and, therefore, 'tends to minimise the risks of assimilation and subtraction in education'. The lower-status language group may therefore emphasise or even exaggerate the distinguishing features and 'otherness' of the group to maintain a separate identity.[16]

Another kind of balance is achieved at Fribourg, Barcelona and the Christian University of Tokyo. The University of Fribourg is situated in the bilingual canton of Fribourg. Only 30% of the students are French and 50% are German, but the town of Fribourg is mainly French, which may once more act as a balancing factor to prevent one language from dominating. Furthermore, students are encouraged to *become* bilingual graduates and the University uses this as a marketing strategy (Langner, 2003). Both languages are accorded equal status in this way. The University of Barcelona is located similarly, with Spanish being the majority, high-status language for the country, but Catalan the majority language in Catalonia with an active support base and financial incentives for Catalan education from the regional government. Although the Christian University of Tokyo uses English as a LoLT, the students and the environment are overwhelmingly Japanese speaking.

The balance between Finnish and Swedish is maintained at the University of Helsinki because of the status of Swedish speakers and the fact that Swedish is also spoken outside the country. This means that the 5% Swedish speakers, who are also materially privileged, can support a university despite the fact that Finnish speakers form the majority of the university population.

In all these contexts, a power balance is achieved by the necessity to use a local language alongside English, resulting in bilingualism for local students. The extent to which transnational students become bi-/multilingual may depend on individual students, the official support offered by the host institution as well as the degree to which such students are integrated into everyday academic life. As their study of transnational students' experiences shows, such students are often avoided because of a perceived lack of language proficiency, as Leask (2011) found in her study of transnationally mobile students' experiences in Australia.

Cultural and ideological factors

As has been discussed above, bilingual universities generally support the idea of bilingualism and are situated in bi-/multilingual environments. Even in populations where citizens are monolingual, the multilingual nature of their environment will appear to be an everyday phenomenon, as in Switzerland and parts of Canada. Bi-/multilingualism would be seen as normal and even normative. A bilingual education system that develops in such an environment is 'natural' or is a natural extension of contexts where languages have co-existed for many years. The prevailing institutional and regional culture derives much of its colour and peculiar rituals and even speech patterns from the day-to-day contact of people from different language backgrounds.

It seems as if bilingualism is so commonplace in some contexts that universities in such locations can assume their students to have sufficient control over their 'second' language (meant in this case to indicate a 'weaker' language rather than a language learnt after the home language). At institutions such as the Universities of Ottawa, Helsinki, Fribourg and Barcelona, programmes and modules may be offered in both languages but the universities do not guarantee such provision, which means that students may find they suddenly have to follow a module in a language different from the rest of their course. In these cases, bilingualism can be seen as 'cultural capital' (after Bourdieu, 1986) supported by an institutional ideology that validates bilingualism.

The Universities of Luxemburg and of Bozen/Bolzano are two of a small number of HEIs that also attempt to raise the status of languages that are not generally used at HE level: Luxembourgish (a variety of German) and Ladin, a so-called Romansch language. In both the cases, these institutions also manage teaching in three other languages, which means that their resources are strained.

Although South African communities are multilingual and the national government places much emphasis on multilingualism, the prestige and status of English and, to a lesser extent, Afrikaans is such that most educational institutions are using it as the only LoLT, even at pre-primary levels. As Bamgbose (2004) indicates, conferences on the use of African languages in education are still debating *whether* to use African languages as media of instruction rather than *how* to use them (Bamgbose, 2004: 18).

In this context, the role of Afrikaans is ambiguous and still seen by many as belonging to an ideology of racial separation, despite substantial numbers of Black home language speakers of Afrikaans. HAUs are struggling to navigate this perception: the University of Pretoria is deliberately moving towards English because 40% of its students are Black and use English as a LoLT (Brink & Van der Walt, 2005). The movement is resisted publicly by a right-wing Afrikaans group that insists on home language instruction. North-West University was created when the University of Potchefstroom (Afrikaans) merged with Bophuthatswana University 50 km away, which means that black and white students are effectively separated by distance. It hopes to solve its language problems by using mainly Afrikaans at the Potchefstroom campus, English at the Bophuthatswana campus and both at the Vaal Triangle campus. Stellenbosch University has a bilingual policy but pressure is building for the increased use of English.

All three universities are located in contexts with substantial numbers of Afrikaans home language speakers who may *not* wholeheartedly support the use of Afrikaans in education. Many Afrikaans parents send their children to English schools and can support their children's learning because they can buy additional materials and help. In these cases, the language in the home remains Afrikaans so that, even if the children should decide to attend an HAU, they would not necessarily struggle with the LoLT. Although the specialised nature of academic language cannot be trivialised, Afrikaans speakers generally need not struggle much with English because of the fact that Afrikaans and English are close cousins in the Germanic language family. The culture in South Africa is still heavily marked by the apartheid past: students who study together do not necessarily live or socialise together, especially on rural campuses. For example, in a study commissioned by the Stellenbosch University management in 2001, an investigation into student life showed that white and black Afrikaans students still experienced two separate 'cultures' on campus (Mouton & Hunter, 2002). The situation may have improved since, with bigger numbers of black students on campus.

It is often said that the use of African languages in education is neglected by the speakers themselves, something that is increasingly said of Afrikaans speakers as well. Ideology and history converge in perceptions, voiced by Mazrui and Mazrui (1998: 8), that racial dignity is more important to Africans than linguistic aspirations. (He excludes Afrikaans speakers in this case.) However, the fact that dignity is sought through (among others) a high-status language such as English or French illustrates the close link between personal power and dignity and language use. It is the development or maintenance of power and dignity that fuels the desire to use or avoid a language in high-status enterprises. For African languages, this means that language planners and linguists may encourage the use of these languages in high-status domains whereas the ordinary speakers, including high-ranking politicians and businessmen, may want to rather use English to confirm their standing. The circularity of the process ensures that low-status languages remain essentially low status. Most South African universities have started to increase the status of African languages by introducing their use in study materials and by encouraging staff members to learn a regional African language. At the University of Kwa-Zulu Natal, according to a news bulletin on its website, 'UKZN's Language Policy seeks to elevate isiZulu to the status of an academic language and a language of instruction and research as well as of general communication' (UKZN Academics Lead the Way in Language Policy, 2012). In terms of the Language Policy, lectures in isiZulu were introduced in specific programmes in 2008. Four years later, they have to admit that students are not willing to attend lectures presented in Zulu only because they prefer English (Visser, personal communication). Although Zulu is used extensively in South Africa – it has the highest number of speakers of all the national languages – it is not regarded as useful for HE learning and teaching. This conviction must be traced back to primary and secondary school perceptions and practices, where English is supposed to be the LoLT.

Social psychological factors

Social psychological factors refer to the vitality and extent to which languages are used in communities. The variety of domains in which languages are used is indicative of their vitality, and if local or low-status languages are seen to be used in high-status enterprises such as the media, public platforms and university education, their use inside and outside the university is validated. In bi-/multilingual communities, students encounter and use a variety of languages on the street, in shops and marketplaces, and with friends and family.

All of the bilingual universities mentioned above depend on a vital language community, solid primary and secondary school grounding in at least one of the LoLTs, familiarity with print materials in both languages and continuous interaction with friends, family and lecturers in the 'lower' status languages. Ensuring the vitality of low-status languages is dependent on maintaining the diversity of domains within which they are used. As Hamers and Blanc (2000: 286) point out, 'At a psychological level, this use is dependent, on the one hand, on the language competence of the members and their desire to use their language; on the other, on the opportunities to use their language in a variety of contexts'. University education, as a high-status enterprise, is a powerful domain, which lends prestige by means of scholarly lectures, papers, articles and books in the low-status language.

However, the vitality of a language, as evidenced by its use in the media and the fact that it is used throughout the country, does not guarantee its position as a language that can be used in secondary school and HE. Ironically, and perhaps predictably, Djite's (1992: 26) warning that 'there is nothing more contrary to the interests of the people and to equal rights than to impose a linguistic variety known only by the elite as necessary for full participation in the nation-building process' has to be elaborated in the light of the University of Kwa-Zulu Natal's effort to use Zulu as a LoLT at HE level. We will have to consider not only the imposition of a high-status language, but also that of a local language that is not *recognised* as useful by HE students. In contrast, a bilingual qualification offered at the University of Limpopo in which English and SeSotho sa Leboa are used as LoLTs (see Chapter 4) has grown in popularity every year since its inception in 2003. Maybe the message for African languages and for English lies in the fact that bilingualism seems to be valued above the domination of one language.

Conclusion

The conditioning factors identified by Hamers and Blanc (2000: 321) were formulated for school-based education, but it is clear that they are realised in very specific ways at the institutions mentioned above. *Sociolinguistic setting* refers to the geographic location (in terms of the history and ideology of an institution) as well as the institutional culture (including the socio-structural and social psychological factors) within which bi- or multilingualism is seen to be an everyday phenomenon. By using the conditioning factors as a starting point, we can describe the 'habitat' of bilingual institutions, which makes it possible to determine the *ecology of language* in each. This very rich metaphor forms the basis for Hornberger's *continua of biliteracy model* (Hornberger, 2007: 182), which allows us to move from setting to implementation, from macro (policy and planning issues) to micro (teaching and learning) matters (as elaborated further in Chapter 4). These factors provide guidelines for thinking about the possible place and role of English (in the constellation of local and institutional languages) by considering the context of each individual institution.

English-plus Multilingualism: What the Sociolinguistic Setting at Bi-/Multilingual Higher Education Institutions Means for the Inclusion of English

When we look at the European and Canadian contexts, we see bilingual institutions using high-status languages with a long record of standardisation. They receive students from established, well-resourced schools. In this context, the introduction or increased use of English takes place against a solid schooling background. In South Africa, as in the rest of Africa, students come from backgrounds that can vary from few or no resources and limited academic literacy development in home/community languages or in a former colonial language to situations similar to European schools.

In terms of language ecology, English does not share much of a history of bilingualism (in the sense described above) with many languages in continental Europe. Its shared history with French in Canada is turbulent and the common accusation is usually that French speakers are expected to learn English, but not the other way round.

When one extends the metaphor of a *historical border* to the increasing use of English, it is clear that the shared history of local languages and English is a fairly recent one compared with the centuries of co-existence (peaceful and otherwise) of German and French or Catalan and Spanish, to name only two. If one can identify a 'border' of some kind across which English is used alongside other languages, it will be a generational one. In most cases, if the younger generation is taught English at school, it has more opportunities to travel to English-speaking countries and consumes popular culture in English. Rather than a historical basis, we can say that English is the beckoning future for the younger generation.

In Africa, there is a difference as far as a shared history is concerned, where former colonial languages have always lived alongside local languages as both coloniser and liberator (when one looks at struggle literature, for example) as well as languages of opportunity and access to HE. Currently, as pointed out above, the history of particularly English seems less important and the bright future it promises is the main motivation for using it in education. In this context, literacy is seldom developed in a minority language, and where it is, the 'switch' to English is usually made as soon as possible.

Socio-structural factors

Socio-structural factors that reflect the status of a particular language are closely linked to power and upward mobility. As has been stated before, the use of a language in HE settings is in itself indicative of its status. In European HE, English is perceived as the language of opportunity, particularly in view of Europe's open borders, and transnational mobility is supported because '[a]n opportunity to study abroad is at the same time seen as better preparing domestic students for international careers' (Coleman, 2006: 5). Opportunities to study abroad abound, particularly at postgraduate level, and are supported at least partially by HEIs and national governments. Examples that spring to mind immediately are Fulbright Scholarships to the USA, DAAD Fellowships to Germany, the ERASMUS and SOCRATES programmes within Europe and Commonwealth scholarships, to name only a few. Guides to funding opportunities are published every year and websites such as UNESCO's Study Abroad guide (http://portal.unesco.org/ education/en/ev.php-URL_ID=21997&URL_DO=DO_TOPIC&URL_ SECTION=201.html) alert students to funding opportunities. When English is seen as either facilitating successful applications or as a prerequisite for such opportunities, particularly when supported by HEIs themselves, the status of English runs parallel to the status of HE qualifications, irrespective of whether the language is used in the community. This status is reinforced by the overwhelming number of scientific publications and textbooks in English. As Hamel (2010: 17) notes, reversing the shift towards scientific monolingualism 'would certainly have to challenge existing power relations in academia'.

The forerunners in this shift are HEIs in countries where languages are not spoken widely outside their borders. Marsh and Laitinen (2005), in their survey of undergraduate mobility in Europe, point out that such countries are accelerating the process of *Englishisation* without any gains in multilingualism. If the prevailing institutional discourse encourages the use of English to attract students from other countries, its own students can hardly be expected to stay put and use only the local language. However, since the local language still remains necessary for employment opportunities, the pressure to obtain good results on exit tests and examinations may swing the balance back in favour of the local language, particularly when it is also used as a LoLT at secondary school level. This conflict between local and cross-border concerns plays itself out in student attitudes towards transnationally mobile students, with local students concerned that they may cause offence, but at the same time concerned about work needing to be done well, as students in Osmond and Roed's (2010: 120) study report: 'We have got modules and we have to do presentations and three international students who are working with me are quite nervous about standing up in front of people'.

This situation is, in essence, no different from that experienced by bi-/ multilingual HEIs that have to manage students' expectations to gain access to jobs not only in the region (e.g. Catalonia) but also more widely (in this case, in Spain). The solution offered by HEIs such as the University of Fribourg (Switzerland), which aims to support students to become bilingual in the course of their studies, indicates institutional commitment to bilingualism rather than a narrow focus on English proficiency as an access mechanism.

In post-colonial countries where access needs to be widened and throughput improved, the acknowledgement of bi-/multilingualism can mitigate the effect that a lack of English language proficiency has on entrance to HE. In most African countries, proficiency in the LoLT of an HEI needs to be at a specific level for entry into HE. Analysing the effect of using performance on school-exit English examinations as *the* entry requirement into HE in Lesotho, Seelen (2002) shows that performance in English is not as good a predictor of success as school performance overall. Seelen (2002: 229) concludes that 'the current emphasis on English as an entry requirement actually works to keep more talented students outside the walls of the university'.

The question remains as to how Hornberger's (2007: 186) recommendation that attention be paid to '"learners" first language, oral, and receptive language skills development' can be implemented. In Europe, the entry requirements for university study include a specific level of performance in certain languages, as evidenced by the language portfolio and language passport (CiLT, 2006). Requirements for a specific level of performance in a local language as a prerequisite for university entrance in South Africa (and the rest of Africa) are not even a vague possibility. Yet, a high level of proficiency in a local or home language may in fact be a powerful predictor of the successful development of academic biliteracy. As an exit requirement, a local language will enhance the employability of graduates. The focus in such cases is not only on proficiency in the powerful languages, notably English, but also on the degree to which all languages that the student has at his or her disposal can mediate academic content and develop biliteracy.

On the basis that home language proficiency may give an indication of a student's potential to transfer skills to a dominant language, it seems a relatively simple step for HEIs to develop tests of language proficiency for regional languages. The proposal is not that all home language speakers of these languages should take the test but that the performance of those students who studied the language up to grade 12 level may be indicative of their chances of success at developing academic biliteracy. As an exit requirement, particularly for students in education, health sciences and the law, knowledge of local languages for professional purposes will confirm the importance of such languages. Once more, the proposal is not that all students be forced to comply with a language requirement, but to reward those who do by awarding a degree with a language endorsement. This type of system is used as a marketing tool to attract students to the University of Fribourg (Switzerland) where they can graduate with certification that they are fully bilingual. Similar to the situation at the University of Bozen/Bolzano, it is compulsory for those students who do not have the proficiency to complete a degree in two languages to show a minimum of competence in the 'second' language so that they are awarded a qualification with a 'second language endorsement' (*Lizentiat/Diplom mit Zweisprachige Zusatz*) (Langner, 2003: 60, 61). In this way, students are encouraged to make use of a unique opportunity to develop bilingual proficiency. I believe that this is an example that can, and should be, followed in cases where local languages are presented as subjects for school exit examinations.

Cultural and ideological factors

As has been shown above in the example of the University of Kwa-Zulu Natal, 'home languages' or regional languages may be varieties that are not deemed suitable for educational purposes. Lecturers may despise 'street language' or, as described by Bobda (2006), lecturers may ban Pidgin English from the university campus. It is clear that perceptions of what may be used in the classroom extend not only to local languages but also to varieties of high-status languages.

With reference particularly to educational institutions where there is a big difference in status between local languages and the powerful written and literary language, Hornberger (2007: 186) responds that 'what is needed is attention to oral, multilingual interaction at the micro level of context and to learners' first language, oral, and receptive language skills development (that is, to the traditionally less powerful ends of the continua'.

The introduction of English may draw attention away from local, minoritised languages, as stated in Chapter 1, but a bi-/trilingual focus opens up the opportunity for students' voices to be heard, even when the language in question does not have a history of academic use and is used mainly for exploratory or social talk (Setati *et al.*, 2002; Moate, 2011).

A multilingual perspective does not expect students to be 'multiple monolinguals' (Jessner, 2008: 15) who need to have mirror competencies in all languages before they can be used in education. Prior (2012) indicates that the workplace demands for students who complete their studies at the University of Bozen/Bolzano and who are employed by international companies in the region seem to focus on receptive skills in English, rather than the full range of English proficiency. What this means for HE where English is introduced as a LoLT is fairly obvious: English cannot substitute the local language; nor can the local language be banished from the class. Former monolingual HEIs need to learn to tolerate the existence of more than one language in the classroom. The hegemonic power of English needs to be mitigated by acknowledging the multilingual nature of classrooms. Transnational students (who are, by and large, bi-/multilinguals themselves) need to be accommodated in English without losing the unique perspective and intercultural experiences that their mobility is supposed to facilitate. Coleman (2006: 11) puts it succinctly:

The distinctive approaches to lecturing in Italian, Spanish or German universities are currently part of the benefit of student exchanges, making young people question the narrowly ethnocentric, monocultural perspectives which too many of them take abroad, and a key element in developing their intercultural competence, their recognition that cultural norms are relative and not absolute, socially constructed and not given. How will they learn to look at their own culture in a new light if Anglo-American norms dominate a newly homogenized European academic discourse? If the only language on the PowerPoint slides is English?

Social psychological factors

Much of the current debate on the introduction of English in HE focuses on the threat that it is perceived to pose for local languages. Hamers and Blanc (2000: 346) point out that the biggest threat to bilingualism is when the family network is invaded; 'of all domains it is the family network that most resists the penetration of the dominant language'. Quoting research on language shift in the USA, Canada, Western Europe, Scotland and West Africa, Hamers and Blanc (2000: 296–298) document the way in which societal factors result in communities assimilating with a dominant culture.

Of course, the situation is quite different in an educational context where the 'dominant culture' is not represented by its speakers, as much as by its print and electronic presence, as a language of global access. In such cases, there is very little reason why the 'subordinate community' would stop using their language in and outside the home and in classrooms. Using electronic media and print-on-demand services to support learning in languages other than English sidesteps the inevitable objection that small print runs in local languages are not financially viable. The universities of Fribourg and Barcelona (among others) offer the opportunity to improve proficiency in any of the languages of the institution through self-access and electronic courses developed at the institutions.

The strong position of home languages may change in Europe with the increased use of English in primary and secondary schools, particularly in private schools. Unless the introduction of English is oriented towards bi-/multilingualism, language shift and elite closure may be some of the consequences. In Africa, the indigenous languages are in a weak position vis-à-vis English and, as Finlayson and Slabbert (2004: 13) indicate with reference to school education, 'Political will, leadership and innovative educational solutions (e.g. multilingual software that gives learners free choice) are needed to make a difference'. The importance of multilingual education starts at school level, as Gajo (2007: 3) points out, 'the school constitutes a symbolic (as the institutional image) and practical (as the pedagogic contract) framework to legitimise, develop and stimulate bi- and multilingualism'.[17]

Conclusion

Hamers and Blanc's (2000: 321) conditioning factors can, to some extent, be said to predict the success of a multilingual language policy. The context within which these factors are realised show that local languages have to be very strong to *continue* living alongside English. The inevitability of English tends to mask the complexities of learning and teaching and it often seems the easiest route to go 'straight for English' as many schools in South Africa have done. Graddol (2006: 117) points out that,

> There are, however, a number of problems which the rush to English tends to ignore. First, bilingualism needs to be better recognised as a normal, rather than a special, condition. This makes the debate about the virtues of mother-tongue education more complex.

The proponents of home language instruction (at all levels of education) may unwittingly sabotage their own case, as Banda (2000) implies when he cautions against confronting parents with a choice between the home language and English. Using the home language while developing English offers the possibility of quality learning and teaching opportunities as well as increased employability.

By looking at the context (ecology) of English-knowing bi-/multilingualism, we can find spaces for local languages by acknowledging their presence in the classroom, as Chapter 4 will show. In Van der Walt (2004a), I criticised the South African Language Policy for Higher Education (2002) for being too vague and mealy-mouthed in its professed support of multilingualism, thereby giving HE the possibility to avoid this responsibility. I point out that (Van der Walt, 2004a: 147):

> Beyond arguments of financial constraints, it is important that higher education institutions pay attention to and support and/or develop biliteracy because of the enhanced potential of home languages to successfully mediate cognitively demanding tasks and improve throughput rates.

The domains in which local languages are used may be constrained by forces outside the university gates. In Europe, as much as in Latin America, globalisation is driving the use of English in various domains. Internationally, there is a boom in Business English courses, and when companies move production sites outside their countries, the language of negotiation is usually English. International peace-keeping forces have to find a *lingua franca*, which is usually English (see Woods (2006) in this regard). Air traffic control is done in English. In HE, as Graddol (1997: 45) notes, English can be seen as the main driver of language shift. Within African countries, decisions for the use of English are also made to ensure 'effective' communication inside and outside the country. English is reserved for high-status domains, like the government, the courts and the armed forces. These decisions restrict the use of local languages to the home and the street, which would reinforce the hegemony of English as the only language capable of performing 'high' functions.

If HEIs are committed to the maintenance of English-knowing bilingualism they will have to validate such bilingualism and make it a marketable attribute for their graduates. Such a decision in itself will demonstrate the social and psychological value of local languages alongside English.

Notes

(1) See http://www.arcticcollege.ca/about/Default_eng.aspx
(2) http://www.canadian-universities.net/MBA/MBA_Criteria_Language.html
(3) See their mission statement and history at http://www.staugustine.edu/index. php?src=gendocs&ref=ABOUT_missionstatement
(4) At http://www.collegeview.com/index.jsp
(5) At http://www.collegeview.com/schools/st_augustine_college/figures
(6) This term is used as it appears on the website. I am aware that this label is not the one that all speakers of Spanish prefer.
(7) See http://www.hacu.net/hacu/HACU_101_EN.asp?SnID=491448998
(8) For the full list of institutions, see http://www.hacu.net/assnfe/Company Directory.asp?STYLE=2&COMPANY_TYPE=1,5&SEARCH_TYPE=0
(9) http://www.insidehighered.com/news/2010/04/08/agmus
(10) http://www.kansan.com/news/2010/may/02/matter-interpretation/ (accessed 28 September 2010).
(11) http://thestar.com.my/news/story.asp?file=/2009/7/8/nation/20090708144354& sec=nation (accessed 18 November)
(12) See   http://www.unibz.it/en/public/research/languagestudies/events/eventbimu. html for the 2007 conference in Bolzano/Bozen and http://www.palmenia.helsinki. fi/congress/bilingual2005/ for the 2005 conference in Helsinki.
(13) See at http://www.wales.ac.uk/en/NewsandEvents/News/General/Thecreationofa newUniversityinWales.aspx
(14) See http://www.nuigalway.ie/about-us/who-we-are/how-we-are-unique.html
(15) This section of the chapter is a revised version of a section of an article that appeared under my name in *Language Learning Journal* 38 (3), 253–272.
(16) One example of such an attempt is the current profusion of cultural festivals and particularly Afrikaans festivals in South Africa, where activities that are supposed to demonstrate the culture of Afrikaans-speaking people are promoted.
(17) My translation of: L'école constitue un cadre symbolique (image institutionnelle) et pratique (contrat didactique) de légitimation, de construction et de stimulation de ce bi-plurilinguisme.

3 Managing the Consequences of English-plus Multilingualism: The Development of Multiliteracies

Introduction

The previous chapters provided a snapshot of the challenges faced by multilingual higher education (HE) in terms of widening access and increasingly managing the demands of transregionally and transnationally mobile students. The focus in this chapter is particularly on the way in which HE has responded to the demand for language support to be offered in English. The field of English for Specific Purposes (ESP) and, in later developments, English for Academic Purposes (EAP) has been prominent in this regard. However, the chapter will go beyond these endeavours by discussing the development of students' academic literacies and the potential to exploit not only other languages in general but also full-blown academic literacies that students may have developed in other languages at school or undergraduate level.

The chapter starts off by looking at generic language teaching assumptions, particularly in the Communicative Language Teaching approach, moving to the development of specific purposes courses, particularly English for academic purposes. Within the context of transnational student mobility as well as widening access, the chapter considers the potential of existing literacies to improve academic performance by fostering bi-/multiliteracies in HE, applying Hornberger's (2007) concept of the *continua of biliteracy*. Throughout the chapter, the focus is on the social embeddedness of learning, which has specific implications for the development of academic literacies. The complexity of language, and, more specifically, academic literacy demands in multilingual HE, is therefore discussed from a learning and teaching perspective, rather than a managerial or policy perspective, thus positioning the field of academic literacies in the broader context of literacy studies and sociocultural theories of learning.

Language Learning and Teaching Paradigms and Their Influence on Academic Literacy Acquisition

As stated in Chapter 1, the theoretical lens for the arguments put forward here is that learning is a social practice embedded in local routines and methods, which in turn are influenced by wider regional, national and international paradigms and practices (see Section 'Context' in Chapter 1). This sociocultural perspective is not immediately evident in dominant thinking about languages of learning and teaching (LoLT), which has been criticised for not paying sufficient attention to such wider debates. Canagarajah (1999: 20), as well as Pennycook, laments 'the severe lack of critical sociologies of language classrooms' (Pennycook, 2001: 115).

As the dominant language teaching paradigm, Communicative Language Teaching (CLT) has not been implemented successfully, despite its learner-centredness and attempts to turn the classroom into a social space where learners and teachers interact in meaningful and authentic ways (in the target language) (Jacobs & Farrell, 2003). The main reason is that assessment practices tend to pull in the opposite direction, towards individual achievement on discrete-point, pen-and-paper tests.

However, the problem is more fundamental than fine-tuning various aspects of CLT. In learning and teaching languages, the fundamental assumption is still that native-speaker proficiency *in a native-speaker environment* should be the target for language learners. The most obvious consequence of this orientation is a perception that the purpose of language teaching is to acculturate learners to a particular language community, irrespective of whether the language is used for social or academic purposes. In terms of that assumption, courses focus on communicative activities embedded in national cultures within national borders. Whether textbook or web-based, a learner in a French language course will meet Vivette and César from Fos-sur-Mer in a chapter on the people of the Midi (Gaston & Bruézière, 1974: 74) or in an online course, learners will learn how to use the Metro in Lyon and listen to *Sous le ciel de Paris* as sung by Yves Montand (Français Interactif). In a German language course, the learner will meet Erich buying beer, bread and ham (Griesbach & Schulz, 1976: 126) and in the Goethe Institute's intensive courses for (among others) students, they are promised not only German, but also lessons about Germany and its people'[1] (Goethe Institute). Similarly, the learner of Sotho will learn how to form the negative by transforming the sentence 'The oxen drank water' (Groenewald, 1990: 51). Although such an orientation may not seem problematical at first glance, the implications for academic language proficiency become clear when we consider:

- the particular language and its spread as an academic language;
- the role of explicit cultural elements in language learning and teaching; and
- the domains in which international HE students will be using an additional language.

The abovementioned examples can be criticised for their essentialist (and in the case of Northern-Sotho even racist) view of culture but in the case of French (and English, of course) language learners' purpose may not primarily be to join the speech community presented in these language courses. French is used in Francophone Africa to gain access to education, often from primary school levels upwards. However, the language(s) used outside the classroom may be any of a number of local languages and varieties of French (or any other colonial language). In the South African context, Coetzee-van Rooy (2006: 447) blames this view of language learning for denying the existence of varieties of English, through 'the assumption that the learner's identity develops from that of a monolingual first-language speaker, through an interim bilingual phase, towards the stable final state of a monolingual second language or (at its most complex) a bilingual speaker'. One of the consequences of this approach can be seen in students' reaction to it, described by Canagarajah (1999: 91) (with reference to Sri Lanka) as 'an oppositional attitude towards the course' because the presentation of material has little or no link to students' lived experiences or their cultural values. Whether Vivette and César have to give up their livelihood because of pollution in the Mediterranean or Sophie and Jacques are considering moving to a rural community to escape the busy streets of Paris is immaterial when one has to negotiate the intricacies of Organic Chemistry at the University of Algiers. As Canagarajah's (1999: 91) analysis of student glosses (in the kinds of language textbooks mentioned above) show, 'they [the student glosses] symbolize the counter-discourses the students use to detach themselves from the ideologies of the textbook, forestall cultural reproduction, and construct for themselves more favourable subjectivities and identities'.

There seem to be two major assumptions underlying the design of language learning courses that aim to teach communication for purposes of being integrated into an L1 speech community:

- The first assumption is that language is taught mainly for interpersonal communication. The dominance of the Communicative Approach to language learning and teaching means that oral communication and 'functional' writing (in the form of letters, newspaper reports and advertisements) as well as writing based on oral communication modes, such as dialogues, feature prominently in local adaptations of this approach. The orientation seems to be that the generic or universal 'method' or 'approach' can be filled with local content, but this seems to happen with little regard for the purpose of teaching that particular language in a particular context.

In South African English language textbooks, the communicational aspect dominates in the form of language functions and structures that emphasise interpersonal and even private language use, again following the assumption that the learner will use the language like a native speaker: for service encounters, to invite family members to birthday parties, to write letters to local newspapers and even to write personal diary entries.

- The second assumption has been called a monolingual bias (Ortega, 2010) because the courses seem to be designed primarily for monolinguals who need to move from one (home) language and culture to a second language and culture, rather than for multilinguals who are elaborating their repertoire of domain-specific language use across various languages.

In post-colonial societies, these assumptions result in language development courses with a wide and diffuse aim that are often wasteful in terms of time as well as in terms of prescribed texts and tasks. Instead of studying academic or non-fiction texts and engaging in academic meaning-making activities, learners read, for example, Shakespeare or Jane Austen, practise writing diary entries as fictional characters and write narrative essays on 'Suddenly a shot rang out...'. These activities need to be adapted to include texts and activities that develop similar language skills but with an academic slant: e.g. reading extracts from textbooks, writing a diary entry as Isaac Newton on the day he formulated his theory about the force of gravity (and explaining what that is!) and writing a narrative essay as a French nobleman describing his escape from Madame Guillotine, capturing the context of and main reasons for the French Revolution. Canagarajah (1999: 97) paints a picture of Tamil students' language needs just as Resnik (1993) does of Puerto Ricans in the USA, and this picture is very similar to that of (South) African societies:

> Only formal English is required for strictly institutional and educational purposes, so their needs are grammar or code-focused. They [students] are looking for a form of functional curriculum which would use L1 as a significant medium of classroom interaction, since in the social milieu English and the vernacular function in a mixed and integrated manner, as a multi-vocal or hybrid medium of communication.

The introduction of Content and Language Integrated Learning (CLIL) at school level in Europe is meant to support learners by developing language proficiency (mostly in English, see Section 'The Sociolinguistic Setting of Bi-/Multilingual Higher Education Institutions' in the previous chapter) in academic subjects. As has been stated earlier, much more research needs to be done on the success of this approach. A longitudinal study on secondary school learners' ability to master academic register in English (Whittaker et al., 2011) provides an indication of the long road ahead for researchers who want to make claims about the possible success of a CLIL approach. Reporting on the development of coherence in academic writing over four years, they conclude that 'there is some development towards the academic register required for successful writing in the disciplines at school' (Whittaker et al., 2011: 357).

When English (or French or Spanish) is taught at secondary school level in a way that does not acknowledge the multilingual nature of learners and prepare them for academic language use, the pressure is on HE institutions (HEIs) to develop courses for students who need to improve their *academic language proficiency*, mostly in the form of *academic literacy* courses. In the wake of transnational student mobility initiatives, transnational students similarly need to develop *academic literacy*, usually in English. However, depending on the country in which they will be studying, students may also need to develop interpersonal communication skills in English or in the local language. In North America, England, Australia and New Zealand, a transnational student will need the full range of language competencies and will therefore need to learn English for academic as well as social purposes. However, a French student following a programme offered in English in Germany will need to develop academic literacy in English and some interpersonal communication ability in German.

A case in point

In a case study of transnational students' experience of their studies at the University of Siegen, Schumann (2008) describes students' feelings of alienation and a lack of interaction with German students. There is a perception that programme offerings in English will solve both academic and social problems. However, a Chinese student's comments show that the use of English may not solve this problem. She laments the fact that her German is still at a very basic level because she does not have enough opportunity to use German. As she notes, 'the lectures are only 90 minutes ... afterwards everybody disappears ... I simply don't have the opportunity to speak to German students' (Schumann, 2008: 38). A lack of contact with local students will, in all probability, not be solved by developing academic literacy in English.

English as the language of science

The status of English as the main and most popular language of science sometimes obscures the fact that other languages are widely used in HE and for scientific publications. German and French may seem obvious choices to mention but Spanish, Chinese, Russian and Arabic are widespread. However, Davis (2003) estimates that by 2010, the estimated percentage of the global economy represented by particular languages would result in the top ten ranking shown in Table 3.1.

The sudden drop from the second-ranked to the third and further down is marked but not remarkable since the global acceptance of English and the size of the Chinese population would account for their positions. When one compares these numbers to one of the few quantifiable phenomena in

Table 3.1 Top ten languages ranked by their percentage of the global economy

Ranking	Language	Estimated percentage of GDP
1	English	28.2
2	Chinese	22.8
3	Japanese	5.6
4	Spanish	5.2
5	German	4.9
6	French	4.2
7	Portuguese	3.4
8	Italian	2.9
9	Russian	2.1
10	Arabic	2

academic environments, which is the language of academic publication, it is clear that there is no competition for English. In Table 3.2, derived from an analysis by Lillis and Curry (2010: 10), based on Ulrich's Periodicals Directory (2001), the number of academic journals in English is compared with academic journals in other languages. Category B journals (Table 3.2) are those with 'some English', described by Lillis and Curry as including 'anything from the abstracts/keywords to the entire journal' (2010: 10).

Although 'some English' is a very diffuse criterion, it shows the power and status of English as an academic language and, even if only keywords appear in English, this is an acknowledgement of that power and status. The percentage of academic journals that excludes English is 9.2% of the total number of publications. When this admittedly rough measure is compared with the projected GDP rankings above, it is clear that English has a global, academic 'market share' of just more than 90%.

Textbooks at undergraduate level may still be published in local languages, but the option of publishing in English and thus having a bigger market (from the perspective of the publishers) or the option of preparing

Table 3.2 Category B journals

Number of refereed, academic journals in all languages	25,864
Number of refereed, academic journals with 'some English' (see Lillis and Curry's explanation in the text)	22,910
Number of refereed, academic journals that include the following languages: Mandarin Chinese, Hindi/Urdu, Spanish, Arabic, Russian, Portuguese, Bengali, French, Japanese, German. According to Lillis and Curry, often with 'some English'.	7110
Number of refereed, academic journals in Spanish, French, German, Portuguese and Chinese: *excluding* English.	2383

students for postgraduate studies in English (from the perspective of HE practitioners) becomes very attractive. Liu (2009: 96) reports that in 2001 the Chinese Ministry for Education suggested that, in order to improve the quality of undergraduate education, 10% of all curricula should be offered bilingually, that is, in Chinese and English. To this end, English textbooks were imported, as Liu (2009: 96) reports:

> Consequently, for example, about ten of the most famous universities in China decided to buy and use almost all of the textbooks being used in Harvard University, Stanford University and MIT in 2002. The list of materials concerns natural science, engineering and medicine as well as law, economy and management. In particular, Fudan University has bought 7600 kinds of textbooks from Harvard University; among the 1440 curricular [sic] in Tsinghua University, there are about 500 using original English textbooks from Western countries.

Based on reports by other scholars, Liu claims that this practice is not limited to the top universities that he identifies above. In addition, as Ellis (2003: 332) points out, '[c]learly, the content of many of the tasks that figure in both research and language teaching materials implicitly espouse the cultural values and norms of the Western English-speaking world'.

Small wonder then that language learning courses for academic purposes focus overwhelmingly on English. As was indicated in Chapter 2, English, as a language that symbolises mobility and access to global job markets, has a special status that accounts for the growth in publications on English for specific and academic purposes. In a new edition of *Academic writing: A handbook for international students* (Bailey, 2011), the advance book announcement (http://tandf.msgfocus.com/q/18AGkaOruqmVTYZ/wv) declares, 'Most international students need to write essays and reports for exams and coursework. Yet writing good academic English is a demanding task' – a clear indication of the perceived importance of English in HE.

The growth of English for Specific Purposes and English for Academic Purposes

The development of language courses for specific purposes can be traced back to the emergence of specialist English courses in the 1960s (Howatt, 2004: 340–343) and a proliferation of language courses for business people, engineers, lawyers and doctors. This particular branch of language teaching emerged as a direct result of (the) communicative approach(es) to language learning, with an emphasis on learners' language needs, measured against the demands of a particular professional domain of language use. The popularity of such courses is rendered starkly by Yang (2001: 353), who notes that, in China, 'In 1995, the long-standing English Language and Literature program could not be found in any admission bulletin of Guangdong universities, except for Guangzhou University of Foreign Studies. Instead,

English for Business, English for Foreign Trade and English for International Legal Studies, among others, were established to attract students'. The same trend is observed by Kolesnikov (2012) in Russia, where students prefer a focus on the analysis of language use in professional contexts to the more traditional philology courses.

While initial specific purposes courses focused on professional contexts, it soon emerged that HE students face very different language demands in the course of their studies towards these professions. The academic environment, although it prepares students for their professional lives, requires a particular engagement with academic language use that does not necessarily overlap with that of the professional environment. By the early 1980s, English courses for academic purposes were already firmly established as an area of investigation (Hyland, 2006: 2). In the first article of the *Journal of English for Academic Purposes*, Hyland and Hamp-Lyons (2002) trace the development of the field of EAP, linking it to growth in the field of ESP. In their discussion of the definition of English for Academic Purposes, they note, 'such definitions conceal as much as they reveal, including not only study-skills teaching but also a great deal of what might be seen as general English as well' (Hyland & Hamp-Lyons, 2002: 2).

Hyland (2006: 16–23) traces the development of English for Academic Purposes (hereafter EAP) as moving from a study skills-based approach, through disciplinary socialisation to an academic literacies approach. To a

---

A case in point

(1)   At the University of Auckland in New Zealand, the Department of Language Studies and Linguistics offer a skills-based programme that Basturkmen (2012: 62) describes as having 'an EGAP [English for Generic Academic Purposes] orientation and aims to teach a generic set of skills and language competencies to students across a range of disciplines'. An initial course is followed by an advanced skills course, which students typically take in the first and second years of undergraduate study.

(2)   The table of contents of a new handbook on academic writing referred to earlier (Bailey, 2011) shows how study skills and general proficiency in English are intertwined. The first section of the book deals with reading and comprehension, including 'Reading: finding suitable sources' and 'From Understanding Titles to Planning'. The third section of the book deals with *Accuracy in writing* (http://tandf.msgfocus.com/q/18AGkaOruqmVTYZ/wv):

   3.1 Abbreviations 3.2 Academic Vocabulary 3.3 Articles 3.4 Caution 3.5 Conjunctions 3.6 Nouns and Adjectives 3.7 Prefixes and Suffixes 3.8 Prepositions 3.9 Punctuation 3.10 Singular or Plural? 3.11 Synonyms 3.12 Time Words 3.13 Verbs – Passives 3.14 Verbs of Reference 3.15 Verbs – Tenses.

certain extent, this movement follows the shift in language teaching from a focus on discrete skills to a task-based[2] curriculum that integrates skills.

The aim of this book is not to analyse the usefulness of task-based curricula but rather to accept the meaning making and motivational potential of 'real-time communicative tasks' (Ellis, 2003: 1) above sentence level for the development of EAP. However, the approach to academic language development, similar to language development generally, has changed as insights into language learning changed over time, as I argue later.

In EAP, the goal of specificity, as indicated in English for *Specific* Purposes (ESP), may not be that easy to achieve, for two reasons. In the first place, it may be easy to identify subject jargon (called *academic vocabulary* in the preceding example) but it is difficult to separate knowledge about, for example, the syntax of English from discipline-specific syntactic elements; some knowledge of 'general English' is obviously part of 'specific English'. Second, and linked to the first reason, is that the levels and abilities in a particular class may differ widely so that no assumptions can be made about 'general' language ability. Moreover, the composition of the transnational student population for a given semester is not fixed, and this fluidity has resulted in student exchange programmes making predictions about possible language proficiency problems and subsequent course design; obviously a complicated business.

Although EAP is now an established field within ESP, its application in teaching and learning at *undergraduate level* runs into further problems. The first problem is that the development of academic language proficiency may not always appear relevant to students, who are motivated to develop proficiencies for their profession. For example, teaching EAP to law students will touch on areas that overlap with ESP, such as reading a case and statutes, but other areas will focus on developing particular academic strategies, like answering a typical legal problem question and writing a research paper, which are required for academic success. As Hyland (2006: 23) points out, '[f]or most students university is a temporary experience of acquiring knowledge, more or less firmly bracketed off from other domains of life and the more urgent workplace priorities of earning a living and building a career'. The majority of students are studying in a particular field to enter its profession rather than the field of academic endeavour. The time spent on academic preparation is, after all, so very little compared with the rest of their lives practising as a doctor or politician or translator. Furthermore, as Basturkmen (2012: 67) notes, the area of language teaching for specific purposes requires extensive research to demonstrate that certain proficiencies are actually developed in such courses: 'Researchers might consider investigating different models of integration of EAP programs and disciplines across settings to identify language teachers' and students' perceptions of the benefits and language teachers' and subject teachers' perceptions of difficulties in implementing the different options'.

A second problem is encountered with the transferability of competencies: for example, writing for academic law purposes is different from lawyerly writing. Even the reading of cases, which, at first glance, must seem immediately relevant to both academic and professional contexts, may require particular scanning techniques that depend on whether the reader wants to derive information for an academic assignment or needs to find support for a particular argument that will be presented in court the next day. The demand by employers for relevant, workplace-related communication skills have resulted in Australia in, what Basturkmen (2012: 63) calls, the 'new vocationalism', whereby academic literacy concerns are replaced by workplace requirements. In other cases, EAP courses are presented in the first or second years of study, moving on to ESP courses in the final year of an academic programme. The professions themselves may introduce courses that develop professional proficiency as part of an induction programme.

From English for Academic Purposes to critical academic literacy

The assumption that students in HE need to have a specific level of language proficiency is evident in entrance requirements and tests of language proficiency (see Chapter 2). In terms of the European Framework of Reference for Languages (Council of Europe, 2001), level C1 is generally seen as appropriate for HE studies. In the USA and the UK, specific levels of achievement are required on tests such as the Test of English as a Foreign Language (TOEFL) and International English Language Testing System (IELTS). Depending on the point at which transnational students want to enter a particular programme, requirements may be more specific. For example, law schools in the USA may require a specific level of performance on the Law School Admission Test (LSAT) designed to assess graduate students' ability 'to understand concepts and make decisions in a quick manner' (Graduate School Tips website). In light of the rationale for EAP, the entrance tests are only the starting point because students require (and may even demand) an engagement with tasks that show a direct connection with their academic studies and preferably their chosen professional direction as well.

EAP courses can be approached from different theoretical positions and the field has gone through a variety of developments, from skills transfer through disciplinary socialisation to critical academic literacy (see Hyland, 2006: 16–23 for an overview). Hyland and Hamp-Lyons (2002: 5) claim that the academic literacy perspective emerged from 'educational marxism and critical linguistics/critical education, and so it argues from very different premises than traditional EAP'. However, it must be clear that EAP cannot be isolated from discussions about learning as social practice in general and critical pedagogy in particular. It would be difficult for an enterprise like English language teaching and EAP to remain impervious to debates about critical pedagogy, critical academic literacy and critical language awareness. Canagarajah (1999: 20) states that critical pedagogy 'has evoked much hostility' in English language teaching circles and writers such as Pennycook (1998, 2001) would certainly agree with him. Rather than seeing EAP as something separate from disciplinary socialisation and academic literacy, as Hyland (2006) presents them, I prefer to focus on the ways in which language support programmes, including EAP, need to merge aspects of these orientations. Although this may be criticised for being eclectic, it is certainly not revolutionary to argue that 'language support' in the broadest sense of the term needs to be sensitive to the context in which it unfolds for optimum learning to take place, as Basturkmen (2012) also argues.

Some 'merging' is already evident in Street's interpretation of literacy acquisition and practices, which he calls the 'ideological model': 'what the particular practices and concepts of reading and writing are for a given society depends on the context: that they are already embedded in an ideology and cannot be isolated or treated as "neutral" or merely "technical"' (Street, 1984). The ideological model is distinct from the 'autonomous model' of literacy (in general), where literacy is seen as a 'neutral technology' that must simply be applied irrespective of the social context from which it originated. Basing his argument on the work by sociologists and sociolinguists, Street (2011: 61) points out that, 'the ways in which teachers or facilitators and their students interact is already a social practice that affects the nature of the literacy being learned and the ideas about literacy held by the participants, especially the new learners and their position in relations of power'. This point of view resonates with Lave and Wenger's (1991) situatedness, which provides the conceptual framework for a very specific perspective on academic literacy development.

The Possibilities of Situated Learning for Academic Literacy Development

As was argued in Chapter 1, a focus on language use as a function of a specific social setting is seen, for the purposes of multilingual HE in particular, in the context of Lave and Wenger's (1991: 31) theory of situated learning. Such a view supports an understanding of the demands of academic language use in terms of which increasingly fine-grained specificity is required: from language use for specific purposes to language use for academic purposes to language use in particular academic specialisms. Lave and Wenger (1991: 36) are adamant that the complexity of moving from the periphery (e.g. as a student) to 'full participation' (e.g. as a successful PhD student or an academic) is not a linear process; nor is it a movement from the periphery to 'a centre'. In fact, they resist 'attributing a prescriptive value to the concept of peripheral participation and from proposing ways of "implementing" or "operationalising" it for educational purposes' (Lave & Wenger, 1991: 41). However, their ideas have been seized upon in attempts to explain progress in learning as well as to structure learning and teaching. The linear structure of progress in education (from one semester and academic year to the next) forces a similar structuring of teaching and, supposedly, learning. It is worthwhile to return to Lave and Wenger's original thoughts on the concept of peripheral participation to see how problematic it is to 'translate' a theory of learning into a theory of teaching or instruction.

In their discussion of situated learning, Lave and Wenger (1991: 35) describe their view of learning by saying that 'learning is not merely situated in practice – as if it were some independently reifiable process that just happened to be located somewhere; learning is an integral part of generative social practice in the lived-in world'. To conceptualise learning, they use the phrase 'legitimate peripheral participation', whereby students (in this case) participate as novices in the discourse of particular disciplines and sub-disciplines. For Lave and Wenger (1991: 35), students' position as legitimate peripheral participants characterises the learning situation, whereby 'peripherality, when it is enabled, suggests an opening, a way of gaining access to sources for understanding through growing involvement'. The word *growing* as a present participle suggests development and increasing mastery of knowledge, skills, values and practices.

Becoming an acknowledged participant in a particular academic field is seen as a process of 'disciplinary socialisation' (Hyland, 2006: 19), which invokes to a certain extent the idea that learning is socially situated, or, from an HE perspective, what Ramsden (1997: 214) calls 'a model of student learning in context'. Both in terms of 'general' teaching and learning concerns and in terms of the role of language or English specifically, the embeddedness of learning dominates and directs discussions on these topics, as can be seen in recent work done by Barton (2007), Hornberger and Street (2008) and Gee (2008).

To become a reflective, proficient user and developer of texts, as a (novice) insider in a particular disciplinary area in a particular institutional context, means that cognitive academic language proficiency requires more than the ability to become academically and critically literate. 'Language' (as interaction, not as a single language) is embedded in a context that requires not only a particular way of speaking but also of *doing*: initially attending lectures and seminars and later also conferences. The PhD student and aspiring academic will be involved in teaching courses and attending meetings. Limiting this process to a particular language course is inadequate, not only because learning takes place outside the classroom as well but because communication in multilingual contexts is not limited to one language. As such, any language course can only 'suggest an opening' or provide the starting point for 'growing involvement' (Lave & Wenger, 1991: 35). As a stand-alone course taught by language practitioners from outside the discipline, academic language proficiency is essentially seen as divorced from disciplinary content and context. Even when language practitioners integrate texts and practices from the discipline, their position in academic units as well as the timing and accreditation of courses may result in a view of academic literacy that approximates Street's (1984) autonomous approach to literacy development: an orientation that sees academic literacy as neutral. As Street (2011: 61) argues, it is not valid to suggest that 'literacy' can be 'given' neutrally and then its 'social' affects only experienced or 'added on' afterwards. In fact, as Heller (2008: 65) points out when she links the New Literacy Studies to a Bourdieusian perspective, literacy education must be seen 'not simply as practice, but as practice embedded in the interested construction and legitimation of social difference and social inequality'. As pointed out in Chapter 1 schooling and, by extension, HE act as sites where social inequality can be (and to a large extent is) reproduced, exactly at the point where social inequality is constituted as an intersection of low socio-economic status, multilingualism and minoritised ethnic or race status. Without a critical perspective, the education of HE students as professionals, either in their chosen professions or as academics, can be seen as the ultimate process of reproduction whereby students collude in the process of duplicating existing power relations. However, working from a critical perspective that challenges existing power structures can quickly result in accusations that power is being withheld from those who need it the most. In other words, being critical about the ways in which dominant languages uphold power structures by arguing for the inclusion of other languages can be seen as denying students full access to such power, particularly minoritised students who do manage to gain access to HE. These are the shifting sands that HE practitioners need to face when they engage in the process of developing academic literacies, and ways in which this particular problem may be solved will be discussed later.

From skills to critical positions: Possible frameworks for academic literacy courses

The degree to which language support courses or courses in (critical) academic literacy can 'suggest an opening' (Lave & Wenger, 1991: 35) in HEIs depends to a large extent on where and how language support or development is located. When Hyland and Hamp-Lyons (2002: 3) discuss the limitations of EAP, they also touch on the position of 'academic support practitioners' or 'language-in-education specialists' as 'support staff' that are seen as peripheral to the main business of academic faculty; 'it [English for Academic Purposes] has also inherited some of ESP's much discussed limitations, in particular: *a tendency to work for rather than with subject specialists*, a vulnerability to claims that it ignores students' cultures, and a reluctance to critically engage with the values of institutional goals and practices' (emphasis added).

Knapper (2000) maintains that academic 'development' remains a peripheral activity in HE, with Basturkmen (2012: 66) calling for the status of language practitioners to be raised from that of 'junior partner' to 'collaborator'. Jacobs (2005) attributes this phenomenon to perceptions of what can be regarded as 'core' activities in the academy, which is the inculcation of disciplinary knowledge and values; an essentially medieval orientation that depends on students from a homogeneous background with a stock of conventionalised knowledge that can be built upon by academics in HE. The fact that this orientation has survived for a few hundred years can at least partly be attributed to the lack of training of many HE lecturers in pedagogic practices and discourses. The widening of participation by 'non-traditional' and transnational students has not made any significant inroads into professionalising HE teaching with the result that discipline specialists can remain impervious to wider educational debates on situated learning, academic literacy and critical pedagogy.

Against this background, programmes that attempt to improve academic language proficiency or language(s) for academic purposes reflect elements of Street's autonomous or ideological approaches to literacy education to varying degrees; either mainly skills-based or moving in the direction of critical academic literacy. The orientation will depend on a variety of factors that may determine or interact with institutional ideology to determine the nature of academic language 'support' courses, for example:

- An academic development unit or language centre located outside the faculty may not have sufficient power or scope to develop collaborative partnerships with the faculty or academic department that requires such interventions.
- Whether language support is offered as a credit-bearing course may affect its scope and nature.
- The interest and commitment of academic staff 'in the disciplines' to academic literacy will determine the sustainability of academic literacy programmes.
- The timing of academic literacy support is crucial in its design and implementation. A first-year, first-semester course can easily fall into the trap of focusing on 'survival skills', whereas continued support can deepen understanding and develop a critical stance towards texts and meaning-making processes.

After my description of the various orientations between these two extremes, I attempt to show that a third space (in the sense of the concept developed by Bhabha (1994)) may be possible for HE practitioners who need to negotiate the tensions of student expectations, disciplinary requirements and their own convictions.

Scholarship as a kind of apprenticeship: The trainee applies skills practised under the auspices of experienced masters

The idea of the student as novice being led by the professor or somebody standing in for the professor may seem like Lave and Wenger's idea of peripheral participation (by putting the student on the periphery and the lecturer at the centre) but, as was indicated earlier, this is not what Lave and Wenger intended since such an idea of scholarship is essentially 'reproductive' (Canagarajah, 1999: 23, 24). Students copy the 'master' by acquiring a number of skills. Support by language practitioners may attempt to find out what academics require for particular assignments in terms of referencing style, register and format, trying to guide students towards fulfilling such requirements (Basturkmen, 2012).

When language practitioners are tasked to help with the development of language skills to satisfy disciplinary requirements, they essentially participate in a process that views 'language' as separate from 'content' and content.

Cases in point

(1) An example of how 'language' and 'content' are separated can be found in the introduction to a textbook *English for Law*, where the author (Riley, 1994: xxiii) provides guidelines for language teachers who will use the book by noting, 'No legal knowledge is required to teach the course'. The book is described as 'suitable as the course-book on an ESP course in English for law, or as a specialised supple-mentary text on a general English course' (Riley, 1994: xxiii).

(2) Jackson (2009) describes a process followed in a South African institution whereby a Department of English was tasked with the teaching of an academic writing course for Commerce students at the request of the School of Management Sciences. She notes of this initiative that 'it placed responsibility for the academic liter-acy development of Commerce students fully in the hands of SLC [School of Language and Culture] staff (with little expert knowl-edge of Commerce discourses), relieving Commerce staff of direct responsibility for explicitly inducting students into these discourses themselves' (Jackson, 2009: 65). As the pressure mounted on the SLC staff to focus on Humanities students (rather than the Com-merce students), the capacity for this course dwindled. Jackson concludes: 'Sustainable collaborative EAP course design and inter-vention between distinct academic units thus hinges on a very finely tuned balance between changes to, and maintenance of, the academic status quo; strong alignment between the goals of the venture and contributing disciplines' core orientations; sufficiency of institutional resources and incentives; and evenly distributed commitment to such curricular innovation' (Jackson, 2009: 74).

Finding 'a very finely tuned balance between changes to, and mainte-nance of, the academic status quo' (Jackson, 2009: 74) remains one of the biggest challenges for lecturers from outside the discipline, particularly when students are not convinced that language development is strictly rel-evant or that language practitioners have the necessary status as experts in disciplinary discourse. Even when students are motivated to develop their language proficiency for academic purposes (since success at academic level is crucial to enter the field), they face the next problem. They need to deal with the way in which disciplinary specialisms form their own communities of practice. The different units or departments in academic schools or faculties present the most obvious evidence of different communities of practice. Subject-specific glossaries attest to the differences at lexical level, but there can be a variety of practices that differ from one academic unit to the next and even within academic units. Such differences can be seen in styles of referencing, the imposition of a particular academic 'voice' (e.g. in the most basic sense, avoiding the use of personal pronouns in academic writing), the value attached to data collection and 'empirical verification' as opposed to writing that is conceptual, argumentative and 'philosophical'. For a student following a programme across academic units, a bewildering array of practices can lead to fragmentation of academic competencies. Students will find it hard to develop the ability to distinguish the particular (and sometimes peculiar) habits of one lecturer from more universally accepted practices, as argued in the section on critical academic literacy.

Scholarship as an orientation towards a community of practice: Becoming a professional

The idea of a community of practice in this case means focusing on professional discourses, that is, the world of work. In the case of ESP, there is a fundamental clash between what students *need* to do and know and value as junior members of the *academic* community and what they *want* to become: a member of the *professional* community: a successful teacher or lawyer or dental assistant. The language(s) used to qualify in a particular field may not be the language(s) required to practice in a particular field. In both cases, academic language acts as a powerful gate keeper, with increasing pressure

---

A case in point

A medical student in the Western Cape needs academic English to complete her or his study but has to be able to use Afrikaans and Xhosa to communicate academic concepts to patients. The problems of miscommunication and dependence on interpreters to convey critically important information accurately is described by Anthonissen (2010: 108):

> The communicative challenges in this context are quite daunting even when doctors and patients share the same first language; here they are compounded by the fact that often doctors and patients do not have a common first language, and they mostly do not have similar levels of proficiency in the *lingua franca*, which for most is English. In some cases Afrikaans functions as a *lingua franca*, as the preferred medium of communication, because patients appear to have better (though not necessarily advanced) proficiency in this relatively strong regional language.

on HE to produce graduates with job-related language proficiency. Although this approach may be reproductionist, the focus on job-related language proficiency ironically opens up the opportunity to raise the status of minoritised languages. As such, a specific purposes course would focus not only on the powerful language of learning and teaching (LoLT), but would take a critical stance towards its use in multilingual communities.

In circumstances like these, language development would need to focus on the interplay of various languages: less a language for specific purposescourse and more a multilingual professional communication course.

To repeat a point made in Chapter 1, the relation between language and power is complex, and resistance to the introduction of minoritised languages in HE (as preparation for the job market) may have less to do with opposition to the language per se and more with the (unspoken) conviction that speakers of a minoritised language should please just hurry up and learn the dominant language.

Scholarship to become a reflective practitioner: Radical and critical academic literacy

In the tradition of critical pedagogy, critical academic literacy requires that lecturers and students examine existing and conventional practices and reflect critically on the way in which they reproduce existing power relations. As indicated earlier, Street (2011: 61) criticises the view of literacy (academic literacy in this case) as a neutral technology that simply needs to be adopted and used. A more fundamental approach to academic literacy needs to be followed in this case, requiring that discipline specialists take co-responsibility for the development of academic language proficiency by reflecting on their own practice and deciding, for example:

- To what extent academic language practices differ fundamentally from one academic unit to another.
- To what extent they agree with colleagues on writing conventions and assess them similarly.
- Whether students have examples from which they can derive the required tone, register, lexical items and organisation. There would be little sense, for example, in teaching Economic and Management Sciences students how to write a report but they never get to see a good example of such a report, written by discipline specialists.

Authors who write in the same tradition as Street, such as Barton (2007), open up the possibility of seeing languages in HE not as an issue that can be dealt with by means of national policies or international imperatives, but one that needs to be managed institutionally or even at the level of academic units within the institution. Street (2011) aligns himself with Barton *et al.*'s (2000) recognition of the 'situatedness' of literacy and with Hornberger (2002) and her insistence on 'literacy as social practice'.

Clark (1992: 118) urges HE practitioners to 'critically explore with students the notion of academic discourse community and how it is that certain forms of knowledge and ways of telling that knowledge have evolved in the way they have'. Typical topics that have been discussed in this tradition are authorial presence and agency (Clark & Ivanič, 1997) as well as ideology, hegemony and identity (Fairclough, 1995). This approach requires that lecturers and students recognise, '[t]his tension between the need to acknowledge cultural difference and the need at the same time to give people access to the cultural, linguistic and discursive conventions that matter [which] is, of course, a classic tension in critical approaches to education' (Pennycook, 1997: 265).

Two practices militate against a radical academic literacy:

- The limits placed on and timing of academic literacy development: usually a first year or introductory course bearing minimum credits taught by English language practitioners from outside the disciplinary unit.
- The mental space that students inhabit, where they are anxious to succeed at their studies and at becoming specialists in their chosen field.

The success of an approach that requires critical and radical academic literacy is compromised if academic support (in the form of academic literacy) is limited to, for example, a semester module in the first year. The discoursal constraints on ways of writing, speaking, presenting and being in a particular discipline increase with cognitive demands as students move towards postgraduate studies. Wallace's (2001: 315) distinction of different types of critical literacy clearly demonstrates how the development of critical academic literacy is dependent on an ongoing engagement with texts, the concept of literacies itself and with 'wider social practices, arrangements, relations, allocations, procedures, and so on, which are mediated, made possible, and partially sustained through reading, writing, viewing, or transmitting texts'. A radical critical literacy would require sustained contact with students and their progress in their chosen field, supported by discipline specialists who integrate critical perspectives on disciplinary practices while raising awareness of the way in which they are realised in academic practices.

A case in point

Arguing for a 'transformative legal education' in South Africa, Quinot (2012) proposes self-awareness in lecturers as a starting point to question assumptions about learning and knowledge: 'This self-awareness can help us to unmask "characteristic rhetorical strategies" and "professional norms" in legal education that we may consider 'natural and fixed' but that are indeed socio-culturally contingent and that may stand in the way of true transformation'. On this basis, an integrated writing course has been developed in the Law Faculty at Stellenbosch University, whereby students are supported by peers and lecturers to develop writing proficiency in their subjects.

The idea of reflexive practice is central to professionalism in HE and such an approach will have to be managed in a way that acknowledges student identities as aspiring professionals, particularly in their early undergraduate studies. The extent to which language practitioners will be able to participate in such a process will depend on the orientation of discipline specialists to the development of academic literacy.

Scholarship as 'third space': A position where lecturers and students juggle academic requirements and an emerging, critical, own voice

As a pragmatic approach and one that attempts to manage the tension between academic demands and professional aspirations, a long-term approach to developing reflective practitioners requires that students and lecturers engage with dominant academic conventions and their position as novice professionals in a way that requires a critical as well as a developmental approach. Such a stance can be seen as a middle way, or a third space. As a possible framework for academic literacy development in multilingual HE, I find such an approach vital for academic as well as professional development. It is necessary to draw on the insights of subject specialists while maintaining a link with the professional (multilingual) world. This balance relativises the dominance of the LoLT and opens up spaces to acknowledge other languages as important for a multilingual workplace.

The concept of a 'third space' is described extensively by Bhabha (1994) in the context of powerless and/or minoritised groups' responses to majority or dominant culture. In view of the challenges described earlier, it seems necessary to find a position whereby students can satisfy their need to excel and succeed at their studies (by conventional and accepted practices), coupled with growing critical awareness. Gutiérrez (2008: 152), with reference to the development of academic literacy, describes the construction of a 'third space' as occurring at the point where 'teacher and student scripts – the formal and the informal, the official and the unofficial spaces of the learning environment intersect – creating the potential for authentic interaction and *a shift in the social organisation of learning and what counts as knowledge*' (emphasis added). Hybrid language practices can form an important part of this process. Canagarajah (2004) similarly finds hybrid and critically oriented practices in his analyses of multilingual writers in the academy as they try to find their voice. He concludes that

> critical modes of negotiating discourses don't have to be taught. Writers may develop these discourse strategies if they come to the communicative context with the frank and bold attitude of engaging with their conflicting discourse backgrounds to find a niche favourable to their purposes. (Canagarajah, 2004: 286)

Canagarajah may be over-optimistic about the fact that a critical orientation need not be taught. Airey (2009: 111), in his description of how Physics students become proficient in English as their second language of science, finds that, fluency in a given semiotic resource was a necessary (but not sufficient) condition for experiencing the facets of a disciplinary way of knowing that that resource allowed access to. When students were not fluent, it was found that they may *imitate* the disciplinary discourse. It was suggested that an element of discourse imitation may therefore be a natural stage on the way to students experiencing a disciplinary way of knowing.

However, the fact that multilingual students may already experience a degree of conflict in their academic practice may mean that their orientation is distanced from the self-evidence of these practices for mainstream and monolingual users of the dominant LoLT. The dissonance and hybridity that multilinguals experience in their academic and personal lives is a very obvious and convenient vantage point for a distanced stance to conventionalised (monolingual) academic practices. Airey's (2009) study shows how students adapt their study practices to compensate for teaching that takes place in English. A third space approach would have to guide students towards appropriating an academic voice in an almost ironical and distancing manner, as if becoming part of the discourse community means dismantling it from within, a form of what Canagarajah (2004: 282) calls *appropriation*: 'infusing the established conventions with one's own discourses in a direct act of resistance'.

A 'third space' offers the possibility of linking academic literacy development in the powerful LoLT with the use of 'non-standard', home or community languages. Students in multilingual education contexts can appropriate or be given the space to use interactional patterns that may not be accepted in very formal academic settings, like code switching and other forms of translanguaging. Compared with Bhabha's minority or colonised groups, HE students are not as powerless as school-going learners but they have much to lose by not conforming to academic conventions or to ways of making meaning in the academy. A third space approach is inherently subversive, just like using informal conversational norms (like code switching) in formal, classroom contexts. Resistance can take the form of using a home language that lecturers and students have in common rather than the dominant or expected LoLT, making it possible for the individual lecturer and student to engage with dominant practices by maintaining a critical distance in another language, as Söderlundh (2008) recounts. Another possibility is to avoid interaction in the LoLT. Yang (2010) describes a situation where Chinese students, '[t]o compensate for their limited sense of their English, made a thorough written analysis of the case, designed professional PPT slides, and left no more than five minutes for class discussion', which did not please their lecturer. Although the students did not use Chinese in their interaction with each other, Yang (2010: 157) speculates that 'that the competence or comfort of ESL students in group work may relate to their previous learning experiences in their home countries'.

A third-space perspective on critical academic literacy development will include multiple forms of literacy, and particularly the exploitation of previous academic literacies. Such an approach needs to be recognised even in HEIs where bi-/multilingualism is formally recognised but where languages are kept strictly separate.

A case in point

Moore (2010: 232), in a description of multilingual group work at the Autonomous University in Barcelona, observe that 'plurillingual classroom practices are not always contemplated at the level of course planning [...] courses were largely categorised as unilingual, in the sense that only one language was *explicitly* available for teaching and learning activities'.

In such cases, students show their willingness to use their available languages in formal classroom work and, although these practices did not occur in academic literacy classes, they show the possibilities for describing in very concrete terms what multiliterate academic practices could be.

In fact, the separation of languages and the insistence on using one language for academic work may support the misconception that bi-/multilinguals need to develop full control over a second or third language before they are regarded as bi-/multilingual. Although it is necessary for students to develop proficiency up to a certain point before a language is available for complex, academic work (Airey, 2009: 111), their use of such a language for academic purposes may not include using it for social purposes.

There are a number of ways in which multilingual students may choose to develop their languages for various purposes. It is entirely possible, for example, for a German-speaking student who follows a course in English at a Spanish university to develop basic interpersonal communication skills in Spanish for survival in service encounters while (further) developing cognitive academic language proficiency in English so as to cope with the course demands. Whether we call such a student bilingual or trilingual depends on whether we insist on multilinguals developing 'full' proficiency in all the languages to which they have access (in which case the student will probably not even be seen as bilingual, since her or his communication skills in English would probably not be developed fully) or whether we acknowledge the strategic deployment of language resources to deal with a demanding situation (in which case the student can be seen as trilingual). The ways in which we describe the various levels of language use by a trilingual need not exclude the label 'trilingual'.

In the case of students whose home or community language is a non-standard variety of the dominant LoLT, the development of academic language proficiency is essentially a case of consecutive bilingualism. It is a common misconception that, because we label a language 'Afrikaans' (for example), that all speakers of Afrikaans would thrive at Afrikaans schools. The standard form of the language, on which schooling depends, is a new language for speakers of (for example) Cape Flats Afrikaans. In Chapter 2, reference was made to Preece's (2009) observation of the devastating effects when home language speakers of varieties of English are deemed to require English language support at university level because academic literacy needs to develop in the school or HE language. As the next section will show, new academic literacy or literacies need to build on existing literacies, if not for ideological reasons, at least for reasons of effective learning and an efficient use of existing resources.

Applying the continua of biliteracy model to a 'third space' framework of academic literacies

Allowing for the use of more than one language in the classroom may be self-evident in one environment and totally taboo in another. Blackledge and Creese (2010: 206) point out, '[a]lthough we can acknowledge that across all linguistically diverse contexts moving between languages is natural, how to harness this pedagogically will depend on the socio-political and historical environment in which such practice is embedded and on the local ecologies of schools and classrooms'. The use of code switching, in particular, seems to be perceived negatively in most educational environments. Objections to the use of different languages in the classroom include the perception that code switching or even the use of bilingual (e.g. Afrikaans and English) PowerPoint presentations and OHP transparencies would inhibit academic language development in English (or any dominant, high-status LoLT). In cases where a dominant language is introduced, as is the case with English all over the world, the perception is that it would somehow threaten the minority or low-status language. The imagery of 'contamination' and 'impurity' is often invoked, for example, when people are exhorted to resist 'mixing' their languages. Derogatory or (depending on your point of view) humorous depictions of 'Franglais' or 'Spanglish' are typical of these perceptions.

However, in a third space approach to academic literacy in multilingual contexts, resistance to perceptions of languages 'contaminating' or 'restricting' one another should be addressed as part of raising awareness of the power of language. For HE practitioners, it is important to reflect and elaborate on the link between academic literacy and multilingualism by studying the way in which Hornberger's continua of biliteracy validate the use of more than one language across a variety of multilingual contexts. In this way, she enables context-sensitive discussions of language support or academic literacy development in bi-/multilingual education contexts, asking questions about the tensions created when traditionally less powerful aspects of classroom language use are in competition with traditionally more powerful aspects. To foreground these tensions, it is necessary to spend time on the different aspects that Hornberger (2002: 39) identifies as the opposing points on the various continua of biliteracy (Figure 3.1) by relating them to real-life contexts. As such, they may act as an organising tool whereby the macro and micro factors can be taken into account when developing academic literacies.

The *contexts of biliteracy* see micro, oral and bi-/multilingual contexts at the one end and macro, literate and monolingual contexts at the other. Along

Traditionally <u>less</u> powerful <----------> Traditionally <u>more</u> powerful

Contexts of biliteracy

Micro <-------------------------------------> Macro

Oral <-------------------------------------> Literate

Bi(multi)lingual <-------------------------------------> Monolingual

Development of biliteracy

Reception <-------------------------------------> Production

Oral <-------------------------------------> Written

L1 <-------------------------------------> L2

Content of biliteracy

Minority <-------------------------------------> Majority

Vernacular <-------------------------------------> Literary

Contextualized <----------------------------> Decontextualized

Media of biliteracy

Simultaneous exposure <---------------------> Successive exposure

Dissimilar structures <---------------------------> Similar structures

Divergent scripts <----------------------------> Convergent scripts

Figure 3.1 The elements of the various continua

this continuum, HE practitioners can take the macro context of the institution (e.g. nominally monolingual) as well as that of the world of work (multilingual) into account when planning for the level and types of language proficiencies that need to be developed. Although macro (e.g. policy) contexts need not be monolingual, just as bi-/multilingual contexts need not necessarily be oral, community convictions may militate against a multilingual education policy, just as community perceptions may prevent the use of textbooks and print materials in an indigenous language, as happens in South Africa. The context itself, as discussed in Chapter 2, will force a dichotomy for historical and political reasons and lead to ineffectual policies.

The *development of biliteracy* poses oral and receptive abilities in the home or community languages at the one end and the production of writing in a second language at the other. This is the scenario that García (2009: 342) describes as resulting in a convergent, monoliterate model of bilingual education or, as Banda (2009: 110) calls it, evidence of a monolingual bias whereby it is assumed that learners are monolingual when they start their schooling and move to become monoliterate in another language. According to this view, home and community languages are mere bridges to the dominant LoLT. Banda's view from Africa provides a more critical perspective on Hornberger's continua, arguing as he does that in 'multilingual contexts of Africa, people use linguistic repertoires rather than drawing on a singular monolingual system to communicate and perform different identity options, including hybrid ones'. The positioning of language practices at different ends of a continuum does, to an extent, inhibit the demonstration of hybridity or simultaneity.

In an attempt to help lecturers decide on the level and nature of language development, Airey (2009: 110) proposes a diagrammatic representation for natural science lecturers (see Figure 3.2). By deciding whether a specific language is necessary mainly for reading rather than for speaking, and another mainly for writing, lecturers can focus on areas that need urgent attention. The diagram will, however, have to be extended to include the world of work. Prior (2012), in her study to determine the workplace needs of students from the University of Bozen/Bolzano, found that emails constituted the most frequent kind of writing in English that students employed in industries in the region had to be able to do. Speaking English was required more rarely. If we think of the medical students at the University of Stellenbosch (mentioned in Anthonissen's study above), it is clear that they need to develop oral proficiency in Afrikaans, English and Xhosa to treat and counsel patients.

Minority, vernacular content, as used in contextualised settings (á la Bernstein), constitute the one end of the *content of biliteracy*, opposed by literary (and supposedly decontextualised, academic) texts in the majority language at the other end. *Content* is closely linked to the *development of biliteracy* dimension, building on the distinction between vernacular and oral communication, using content that is not necessarily intended for literary and decontextualised academic uses. The workplace examples provide ample evidence of such uses – emails, telephone calls, consultations, to

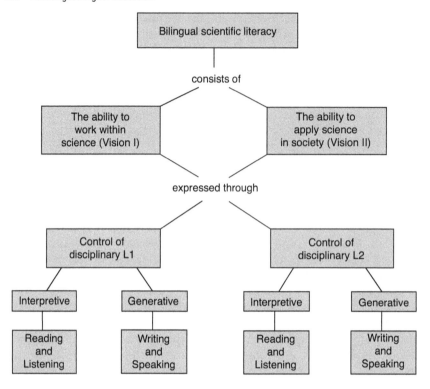

Figure 3.2 Making decisions about the development of academic competencies in two languages (Airey, 2009: 110)

name a few. However, a third-space perspective would also destabilise comfortable assumptions about the domains of use of certain languages: Xhosa for rural patients, English for an academic essay. Being able to explain academic concepts in Xhosa is one of the challenges for medical practitioners. Acknowledging the power of minoritised languages to be heard and seen in HE classrooms is a cornerstone of the continua of biliteracy.

The *media* of biliteracy is the innermost point along which a continuum of exposure to different languages is posited, either simultaneous or successively, taking into account the degree of dissimilarity in terms of structure and script. In terms of what happens in individual classrooms, the decisions taken along this particular continuum seem crucial and heavily dependent on research that investigates the successful acquisition of multiliteracies in languages and language varieties along these continua. The fact that many transnationally mobile students may already have developed advanced literacy in another language provides an obvious opportunity for the development of biliteracy (see Chapter 2). Research on Cummins's interdependence hypothesis (among many others Cummins, 2005), particularly recent findings such as those of Sparks *et al.* (2009) and particularly Melby-Lervåg and

Lervåg (2011), indicates the complexities inherent in assumptions that L1 proficiency predicts proficiency in other languages. This is the point at which resources and continuous professional development of lecturers and language practitioners become critical to manage fast-changing educational settings.

As pointed out earlier, Street (2011), in a tribute to Hornberger, relates the continua of biliteracy to New Literacy Studies because of their focus on literacy as social practice. This attempt is important for any endeavour to situate (critical) academic literacy in a multilingual education context because it provides a link between monolingual orientations to language teaching for specific purposes (ESP and EAP) on the one hand and an acknowledgement of the multilingual context of particular HEIs on the other. The continua of biliteracy model 'provides a heuristic for addressing the unequal balance of power across languages and literacies' (Hornberger, 2007: 182). Such a heuristic enables lecturers and teachers to determine the levels of language use in different languages and, subsequently, the extent to which such levels can be exploited to maximise learning, as can be seen in Figure 3.1.

Hornberger and Skilton-Sylvester (2000: 98) remind us that 'the more their learning contexts allow learners to draw on all points of the continua, the greater are the chances for their full biliterate development'. Although Hornberger and Skilton-Sylvester's point of reference is education at primary and secondary school levels, HEIs need to recognise the potential of existing academic literacies, particularly if they can support learning and improve throughput rates. By becoming more conscious of their students' linguistic resources and allowing for 'multiplicities of language practices' (García, 2009: 196), these linguistic resources can be tapped explicitly. In these contexts, a strict separation of languages makes little sense, since languages other than the LoLT that dominates at that stage are present: not always consciously but certainly as a potential resource. Arguing for the recognition of existing literacies in educational contexts where another language is the LoLT, Cummins (2005: 4) asks, '[i]f cross-lingual transfer is occurring anyway, and in fact is a necessary condition for successful bilingual development, surely we should attempt to encourage and facilitate this transfer rather than impede it?'

What would militate against the use of languages other than the LoLT in HE? The degree to which a language is available for learning in each individual student will depend primarily on two factors: the perceived suitability of a specific language for academic purposes and students' own beliefs about language learning and learning in a language other than an initial academic language. These perceptions make HE different from schooling, where teachers may have greater influence on perceptions of language domination.[3]

The perception that a language is not suitable for higher education

Many authors, but most significantly Bamgbose (2004), have written on the perception that African languages are not suitable for academic purposes, and these perceptions are shared by learners and students. Local varieties of English are similarly denigrated (Bobda, 2006).

A case in point

Bobda (2006: 58) describes notices that warn students about the 'dangers' of using Pidgin English at the University of Buea:

No Pidgin on campus, please.
Pidgin is taking a heavy toll on your English; shun it.
L'Anglais, un passport pour le monde; le pidgin, un ticket pour nulle part.
[English, a passport to the world; Pidgin, a pass for nowhere.]
The medium of studies at UB is English, not Pidgin. (UB=University of Buea)
If you speak Pidgin, you will write pidgin.
English is the password, not Pidgin.
No Pidgin on campus, please.
Speak less Pidgin and more English.
The better you speak Pidgin, the worse you will write English.
Speak a language well to write a language well.
Be my friend, speak English.
Succeed at UB by avoiding Pidgin on campus.
Commonwealth speaks English, not Pidgin.

Despite the fact that Pidgin English is the home language of a substantial number of students, its use is slated and not seen as worthy of use at HE levels. Popular perceptions of language variety as 'low class' or 'slang' would certainly exist among students too and would cause resistance (or just laughter) if a lecturer were to use such a stigmatised variety for 'serious' learning purposes. However, the use of a low-status variety can also decrease the distance between lecturer and students and in that way enhance the classroom climate for learning.

Multilingual HE students have also shared their belief that languages which they used at primary school level has not developed sufficiently to be of much use at HE level (Van der Walt, 2013). Even at school level, Setati *et al.* (2002) lend credence to this belief when they discuss the problem of learners not being able to develop from exploratory talk (in their home language) to discourse-specific (disciplinary) language use, particularly for purposes of writing in the LoLT: 'In summary, across English, mathematics and science classes the journey that needed to be navigated from learners' informal, exploratory talk in their main language [home or community language] to formal, discourse-specific talk and formal written work in English appeared to be incomplete' (Setati *et al.*, 2002: 139). The fact that teachers use academic terminology and discourse patterns in African languages (Wababa, 2009) means that these languages are available for such purposes. When students do not use their home language for these purposes, it has less to do with the language and more with their and the teacher's lack of attention to these forms in a language other than English. After all, some transference from academic forms in the home language(s) to English should be possible if teachers and learners are willing to build extensively on the resources of the home language(s).

The continua of biliteracy can address this issue by exploiting whatever students bring to class as a starting point for further literacy development and enhanced learning opportunities. By allowing the use of more than one language and explicitly teaching disciplinary discourse, it becomes feasible to move from exploratory talk in a home language to discourse-specific talk in the home language and, if necessary, in the LoLT. The purpose should always be to construct ways of using discourse-specific talk, note-making, summarising or presenting academic work in a home language as well as the LoLT.

The perception that languages should rather be kept separate

Separating languages is often the motivation for improved learning of another language, a conviction that is particularly strong in English language teaching, where 'reverting' to the home language is not tolerated and is sometimes even punished (Van der Walt, 2009). This belief, called the 'two solitudes assumption' by Cummins (2005: 4) is also at the root of the disapproval of code switching, partly because languages should be kept 'pure' and separate and partly because code switching is seen as social language use that has no place in formal education (Auerbach, 1993). This conviction is gradually changing, with Ferguson (2006: 193) arguing that at school level, '[t]here is a good case, then, for moderating official hostility to CS, for acknowledging its prevalence and, indeed, for incorporating awareness of CS as a resource into teacher education curricula'. Studies by Cook (2001), Üstunel and Seedhouse (2005) and myself (Van der Walt, 2009) attempt to show how teachers switch at school level to enable learning and to manage the classroom. Although the situation is qualitatively different at school level, there is evidence that it can support learning at HE level as well (Van der Walt, 2006), as will be discussed further in Chapter 4.

The necessity of active biliteracy

Resistance (for ideological reasons or because of individual convictions) to the use of a particular language in HE demonstrates that being multilingual does not automatically lead to the use of a language to make sense of texts in another language. The practice of activating another language for academic literacy purposes seems to depend on personal beliefs, habits and explicit encouragement from the multilingual context itself.

When students consciously use more than one language while they engage with text, they activate their languages and draw on the linguistic resources at their disposal. This visible and audible presence of other languages in the classroom is quite different from running a parallel programme in another language (as in officially bi-/multilingual HEIs) or merely acknowledging other speakers by providing additional support in the dominant LoLT (as in cases where English is used as the LoLT).

With reference particularly to educational institutions where there is a big difference in status between local languages and the powerful written and literary language, Hornberger (2007: 186) states that 'what is needed is attention to oral, multilingual interaction at the micro level of context and to learners' first language, oral, and receptive language skills development (that is, to the traditionally less powerful ends of the continua)'. The point that HE practitioners need to believe in is that two (or more) literacies are *not* in competition but that both have a role to play in promoting successful access to university study. They also need to acknowledge that having more than one language is an advantage when engaging critically and successfully (in academic terms) with complex academic material.

The active use of more than one language in the HE classroom implies a type of 'active biliteracy': a habitual activation of available languages by the student him/herself, sometimes supported or actively encouraged by the educational or community environment. Certain conditions seem to be required before students are willing to activate other languages in the classroom or when they study, of which the following have emerged from my own (Van der Walt, 2013) and Airey's (2009) work:

- They need to believe that the 'other' language is capable of supporting academic learning.
- They need to experience a variety of languages used regularly for teaching and learning purposes (in other words, translanguaging must be normal classroom and institutional practice).
- Bi-/multilingual material may be necessary, either in the form of support material or as examples of how one language can support learning in another, for example, in the form of glossaries or bi-/trilingual dictionaries.[4]

What would the chances of biliteracy development be in the official bilingual contexts discussed in Chapter 2? When we look at the European and Canadian contexts, we see bilingual institutions using high-status languages and receiving students from well-resourced schools. In this context, the introduction or increased use of English takes place against a solid schooling background. At the University of Fribourg (Switzerland), students can avail themselves of the opportunity to be awarded a qualification with a 'second language endorsement' (*Lizentiat/Diplom mit Zweisprachige-Zusatz*). In this way, students are encouraged to make use of a unique opportunity to develop bilingual academic proficiency, and they can, without a doubt, be said to be biliterate. Langner (2003: 60, 61) points out that it is compulsory for those students who do not have the proficiency to complete a degree in two languages to show a minimum of competence in the 'second' language. However, a language separation model seems to be in place at this and other bilingual HEIs, since programmes are offered in parallel, that is, in both languages.

In Africa, as in India, students come from a background that can vary from having few or no resources and limited academic literacy development in home/community languages or in a former colonial language to situations similar to European schools. In Africa, both English and French have co-existed with local languages for a long time. Former colonial languages occupy an ambiguous position as both coloniser and liberator (when one looks at struggle literature, for example) as well as languages of opportunity and access to HE. Currently, the colonial history of particularly English seems less important and the bright future it promises is the main motivation for using it in education. Literacy is seldom developed in a minority language beyond primary school level and where it is, the 'switch' to English is usually made as soon as possible. Hornberger (2002) refers specifically to a South African university context when she describes her observations of a multilingual class at (the former) Rand Afrikaans University. In looking at this university context, she applies her own model to a HE context, after having focused on the use of indigenous languages alongside a high-status language at school level. In her own words, 'the continua of biliteracy model, like the ecology of language metaphor, is premised on the view of multilingualism as a resource' (Hornberger, 2002: 32), but when pitted against parental and societal views of the value of English in HE, the use of a language other than English can be met with suspicion or even accusations of racism.

Chinese institutions depend on a strongly competitive system that allows only the very best and most dedicated students to proceed from one level of education to the next. The official language of instruction is still Putonghua, with some attempts to create a bilingual system (see Chapter 2). In Hong Kong, with its long history of association with Britain, informal switching between English and Cantonese is common and the use of both languages in HE has a longer and more sustained history than in mainland China (Swain et al., 2011). In these examples, there is little doubt that the contexts favour biliteracy development. But it is not clear whether teaching and learning practices work in that direction.

Conclusion

Being able to use languages well in an academic environment, that is, to view and read academic material and one's own writing critically, to respond in a variety of written and oral forms, to listen and engage in debate, are important ingredients for the successful completion of studies. Although Leibowitz (2004) argues that academic language proficiency is not the only condition for academic success, the ability to use language appropriately can be the deciding factor when lecturers consider borderline cases.

Serious criticism has been levelled at the EAP and the (bigger field of) academic literacies movement because of the impression that academic success can be guaranteed by introducing adjunct programmes that focus on improving 'academic skills' in the LoLT, which is, increasingly, English.

This chapter showed how such an approach not only stymies disciplinary socialisation but also fails to exploit the academic literacies already developed in other languages.

In contrast to the school environment, the continua of biliteracy concept (at HE level) is not limited to languages in which literacy still needs to be developed. If the HE LoLT is different from that developed at school level, HE practitioners can depend on academic literacy (in another language) on which they can build and depend for engagement with academic material. In other words, by using the continua of biliteracy as a heuristic tool to determine and manage the languages available for academic work, HE practitioners make the continuum from school or other HEIs explicit. Starting academic studies at another level and in another LoLT is therefore not seen as a break or negation of earlier competencies and abilities but an extension thereof.

The languages that students know need to be actively available for learning before they can be accessed successfully. The fact that students can use a language and may even have developed it to a high level does not mean that they may be able or willing to use it for academic purposes.

In response to Blackledge and Creese's (2010: 206) statement that it is difficult to 'harness' translanguaging practices pedagogically, the next chapter will suggest ways in which active biliteracy can be expanded and fostered in HE classrooms.

Notes

(1) 'Sie lernen nicht nur intensiv Deutsch, sondern auch Deutschland und seine Menschen im Alltag und in der Freizeit kennen' (Goethe Institute).

(2) In this book, 'task' is understood as language produced above sentence level for a specific communication purpose, the kind described by Ellis (2003: 319), in his conclusion to a book on task-based language teaching, as 'a tool for engaging learners in meaning making and thereby for creating the conditions for language acquisition'. Within communicative approaches to language teaching, a focus on communication is linked to task-based curricula, and Ellis (2003: 1) sees such tasks as representing 'real time communication' that is not overly concerned with accurate language use. Such a task-based approach eschews discrete-point, accuracy-focused language that is restricted to sentence-level transformations or insertions of lexical items. However, accuracy is not ignored. As Ellis (2003: 319) emphasises, a task-based approach does not sacrifice accuracy but constitutes the ideal tool 'to ensure that learners are motivated to attend to form – to notice new linguistic features in the input and to work with their interlocutors to construct new zones of proximal development'.

(3) However, in competition with parents, teachers may find that despite their influence on learners, parents will continue to demand education in English (Hornberger, 2002: 40).

(4) For example, the use of subject-specific trilingual glossaries or multilingual disciplinary dictionaries.

4 Multilingual Pedagogy in Higher Education Classrooms: Approaches and Techniques

Institutional Policies and Classroom Practices

Throughout this book the point is made that learning is situated and socially constructed: competency is developed (or not) towards the perceived goals of a particular course in a particular classroom setting, embedded in practices that develop there and often solidify over time. The demands of national governments and international agencies to widen access to HE institutions (HEIs) as well as global pressure to internationalise result in the student and staff profile diversifying, as shown in Chapters 1 and 2. Linguistic diversity emerges as one, crucial result of national and international pressures on HEIs and the one element that has a profound effect on learning and teaching interaction at HE level. Cots's (2008: 69) view of the international university as 'a complex multilingual and multicultural environment in which communicative and intercultural competences constitute a symbolic capital of the individuals' is equally true for HEIs that attempt to widen access for minoritised communities. Just like the so-called international universities, they have to manage 'the tensions between official policy, local policy and its [sic] (relatively) problematic enactment in routine assessments and teaching' (Roberts, 2008: 9).

In the previous chapter, the role of English and the development of a critical academic literacy were discussed against the background of various kinds of multilingual HEIs, as discussed in Chapter 2. The degree to which English is introduced to HEIs that are not English speaking can play out in different ways. The three descriptions below are not mutually exclusive, but each type will result in particular language use patterns.

- HEIs or particular faculties that decide to implement English as a language of learning and teaching (LoLT) for a more or less homogeneous group of students who share a home/community language, for example, the University of Maastricht, where decisions to internationalise the institution resulted in the introduction of English as a LoLT. In such contexts, many students and lecturers share a home language and the institution can depend on solid schooling and academic literacy development in one language, which will act as a base from which academic literacy in English can develop. Airey (2009: 89 and 110) finds that most of the Swedish students in his study managed to develop bilingual scientific literacy by the time they reached their second year of instruction in English.

- HEIs that attract substantial numbers of transnationally mobile students who will have developed academic literacy in another high-status language in their home countries. One example would be students in the ERASMUS programme who study for a semester abroad or who enrol for postgraduate studies at HEIs that are perceived as prestigious. This is the case in many European, US, UK, Australian and New Zealand HEIs. The use of English as a LoLT is generally seen as the answer to transnational student mobility, which means that students and lecturers seldom share a language other than English. However, unless particular initiatives are launched to foster interaction across different languages and cultures, students tend to socialise mainly with those who share their language and culture and, even then, cross-cultural communication and interaction may not occur (Leask, 2011: 15).

- HEIs that attempt to widen participation for local students from minoritised groups who may have been schooled in the same LoLT as that used in HE but who may struggle to manage studies at this level for a variety of reasons, of which academic language proficiency may only be one. An example would be post-colonial Africa, where English, French, Portuguese or Arabic is the high-status LoLT in HE but a home or community language is used outside educational institutions, that is, speakers exhibit a 'broad diglossia' (Kamwangamalu, 2010: 120). This situation would also obtain for first-generation immigrants who may still use the home language outside of formal educational contexts.

In all these cases, the linguistic diversity in the student population may vary from one year to the next, as the profile of the student population changes from one semester to the next. This means that the implementation of bi-/multilingual education practices, particularly in the case of a constantly changing, transnationally mobile student population, is dependent on a particular student population for a particular semester. It is this constant shifting of classroom populations that makes the development of an institutional language policy difficult and leads to institutions opting for a monolingual, usually English-only, policy.

If we accept, however, that multilingual teaching and learning strategies can be implemented and adapted at classroom level, irrespective of the changing language profile of the group, it becomes possible to look past the limits of a monolingual, institutional language policy. What this means is a contingency model of multilingual education that enables lecturers and students to *manage* teaching and learning based on the perceived needs and abilities of a particular group in a particular subject for a particular semester. To conceptualise this idea, we need to look at developments in language policy and planning literature.

Baldauf (2006) calls the management of language policy at classroom level 'micro-planning' and links up with Hornberger's *continua of biliteracy* to argue for ecological models of language policy and planning, that is, models according to which local practices form the starting point of policy and planning development, rather than the traditional view of language policy and policy as 'large-scale, usually national, planning, often undertaken by governments and meant to influence, if not change, ways of speaking or literacy practices within a society' (Baldauf, 2006: 148, 149). Following a trend of thought that also emerges in Pennycook's (2010) *Language as a Local Practice* and Canagarajah's (2005) *Reclaiming the Local in Language Policy and Practice*, this view of language policy and planning partly addresses Shohamy's (2006: 78) concern that teachers (lecturers in the case of HE) become 'soldiers' of the system who carry out orders by internalizing the policy ideology and its agendas as expressed in the curriculum, in textbooks and other materials and the very perceptions of language. As a result of the relative 'academic freedom' of HE practitioners and the relative unpredictability of student population profiles from one year to the next, language in education policy implementation is often contingent and ad hoc, relying on lecturers' experience and their perception of students' ability to make meaning of their course materials and academic activities. This is demonstrated in, for example, Moore's (2010) study of multilingual students at the Universitat Autonoma in Barcelona when she concludes that 'plurillingual classroom practices are not always contemplated at the level of course planning [...] courses were largely categorised as unilingual, in the sense that only one language was *explicitly* available for teaching and learning activities' (Moore, 2010: 232).

As pointed out in Chapter 2, teachers and lecturers may resist policies that they perceive as detrimental to the required academic standard or to the quality of learning of their students. For example, Martin (2005) shows teachers resisting Malaysia's 2003 language policy, which required that they had to teach Mathematics and Science in English. They did not use only English but code switched to ensure that their students understood them. As noted in Chapter 3, Yang and Lau (2003: 109) report that lecturers at a Hong Kong university use Cantonese instead of English (their language policy requires the use of English only). These examples reinforce García's (2009: 320) point that multilingual awareness 'must not only focus on how language works and how students use and learn languages, but also on the understanding of the social, political, and economic struggles surrounding the use of two languages'.

Baldauf's (2006: 154) point that micro-language planning inevitably raises issues about agency means that lecturers are not seen as unthinking bureaucrats (as Shohamy's term 'soldiers' implies), nor are HE students the hapless victims of a language policy. In our own investigations (Van der Walt & Dornbrack, 2011) Afrikaans- and English-speaking students use a number of strategies to manage the academic language demands of Afrikaans and English texts and lectures, including pairing up with proficient users of the language and using friends and family as 'funds of knowledge' (Moll, 2007: 274) on which they draw to write assignments and prepare for tests. Students report on having to translate 'everything' in their first year, but then become fluent users of English and Afrikaans. In Airey's (2009) study, mastering academic language is also shown to happen over time. Physics students struggle in their first year but then reach a 'threshold of competence' (Airey, 2009: 89, italics in the original):

> *above an initial threshold of competence in disciplinary English, students give descriptions with similar levels of disciplinarity in both English and Swedish, regardless of the language that has been used to teach them.*

This finding also seems to provide supporting evidence for Cummins's 'underlying cognitive/academic proficiency' (Cummins, 2005: 4).

From a socio-cultural perspective on learning, each classroom constitutes an intimate community of students and lecturers who, in a dialectical relationship, co-construct knowledge and academic practices over time. This classroom space is subject to tensions such as:

- the expectations of students, including their communities and families, and their performance;
- the lecturers' construction of what is required (e.g. the so-called standard that needs to be maintained) and student performance;
- classroom teaching practices and official university policies or regulations.

Within this space, attempts to support student learning and open up spaces for multilingual learning may not always succeed. Students (from minoritised communities) who gain access to HE as part of governmental drives to widen participation may have used the same LoLT in school as in HE, but may still be using a variety of the LoLT or an immigrant language at home. In such cases, they may not have developed literacy (academic or otherwise) in these varieties. However, they may still be able to use them for discussions about academic work. In this regard, two important considerations may act as conditions for the extent to which such languages are available for academic use.

First, the distinction made by Setati *et al.* (2002: 130) between *exploratory talk* (using mainly a home or community language) and *discourse-specific talk* (which, in their case, needs to be done mainly in English) must be kept in mind. Although exploratory talk may be useful to approach, contextualise and organise a particular academic task, students' lack of academic language proficiency in a minoritised language may hinder academic work in that language. The availability of academic texts and other types of input in that language will be crucial for its use in academic settings.

Second, students may feel that a particular language is not suitable for academic purposes, either because they feel that their language ability did not 'develop' enough for use at HE level (see Van der Walt, 2013) or they may feel that using a particular form of the LoLT may stigmatise them. This was the case in what Michael-Luna and Canagarajah (2007) call a 'failed experiment', where, despite encouraging students from minoritised groups to use vernacular discourses when discussing and debating academic topics online (seen as a 'safe' environment), students were not willing to use such discourses in class. Their awareness of societal perceptions and academic practices made students wary of flaunting them by using anything else than what they perceived as accepted academic conventions.

The intertwined nature of language, community and identity manifests itself in so many different ways that even the most general prescriptions in the form of guidelines or frameworks for multilingual pedagogy seem a futile exercise and I agree with Cuvelier (2010: xiii): 'it is quite clear that adaptation of language management (language policies) to real linguistic environments is very deficient'. The argument that policy is not particularly helpful in fluid educational settings and that micro-policy decisions need to be in the hands of HE lecturers may sound subversive, but it claims agency for HE lecturers who are often in the firing line (and the word is used advisedly) when throughput rates, internationalisation and widening access are at the top of administrators' agendas. In the following section, I will depend on existing frameworks of multilingual pedagogy in school contexts to discuss the way in which HE shows evidence of using similar approaches. The lecturer who faces incomprehension and disappointment when minoritised students struggle to manage their academic studies can draw on these insights to incorporate multilingual teaching and learning practice that can lead to academic biliteracy in HEIs, as described in the last section of this chapter. This argument does not absolve administrators from their responsibility to validate multilingual education practices in policy frameworks that are developed 'from below' (Cuvelier et al., 2010); the point is rather that individual lecturers' awareness and insight into multilingual education practices are far more valuable than a top-down policy.

In HE environments where multilingualism is evident, where users of many languages are visibly in positions of power and where individual students feel confident to 'activate' other languages (see the section on active biliteracy below and in the previous chapter), the development of academic biliteracy or, what Airey (2009) calls *bilingual scientific literacy* is possible and probable, even in the absence of bilingual policy frameworks. In her opening address to the conference on bi- and multilingual universities in 2007, Franceschini (2009: ix) notes that 'a multilingual university is an organisation where multilingualism is taken for granted' and although a multilingual language policy may show the commitment of HE managers to multilingual education, taking multilingualism for granted at least means acknowledging its existence – an acknowledgement that many HEIs are struggling to make and in some cases are actively suppressing.

Conceptualising Multilingual Pedagogy in Higher Education Classroom Settings

Baetens Beardsmore (2009: 157) discusses the many factors that lead to the development of bilingual education at school level and concludes:

> We know little about the purely linguistic elements of rate and route of learning two or more languages, depending on phasing and structuring of the curriculum, the effects of transfer, the role of translanguaging, the tolerance level of errors, the nature and quality of teacher-talk and pupil-talk in bilingual programs, to name but a few of the dark spots.

This is even more relevant to HE where, except for officially bi-/multilingual HEIs, multilingual students are seen mostly in deficit terms. Language proficiency entrance tests and/or compulsory academic literacy courses foster and support the perception that mastery of one language above all is required for academic success. Except for explicitly multilingual HEIs, where languages are often officially separated (see Chapter 2), using more than one language in spoken and particularly in written *academic* discourse remains one of the 'dark spots' in classroom research. It is worth repeating Blackledge and Creese's (2010: 206) point that harnessing multilinguals' ability to move among languages in educational settings 'will depend on the socio-political and historical environment in which such practice is embedded and on the local ecologies of schools and classrooms'.

An ecological approach has to deal with mainstream beliefs about language and language learning as well as with perceptions about the importance of high-status languages for social and professional advancement. As was pointed out in the introduction, beliefs about the necessity to separate languages or about the ability of the available languages to support academic discourse form part of the ecologies of classrooms and may stymie attempts by a lecturer or fellow students to 'activate' languages alongside the dominant LoLT. In short, the mere existence of another language does not guarantee that it will be used for academic purposes: an *active* biliteracy would imply students' willingness to actively incorporate other languages in learning practices. I referred to Bobda's (2006) descriptions of signs telling students how bad it is to use Pidgin English on the university campus (Chapter 3), a sentiment that is probably shared by many students. My own study with a small number of South African and international, multilingual students on their use of more than one language in academic settings has shown that students' beliefs about the usefulness of language or the importance to keep languages separate will result in them not using the language (Van der Walt, 2013).

In the next section, García's (2009: 312ff.) identification of the principles, objectives as well as bilingual practices that should drive a multilingual pedagogy will be discussed. However, the references to practice at HEIs will show that students' expectation of their training to result in well-paid job raises the language stakes and results in close scrutiny of the immediate relevance of pedagogical practices. Although García's focus is mainly on building and extending emerging *school* literacies, pointers can be deduced to manage the demands of critical academic literacy in HE contexts. Keeping the difference between HE and school-based bilingual education in mind, the next section will focus on multilingual practices and strategies for HE classrooms. Since published case studies on classroom practice in multilingual HE are on the increase, we need to keep García's (2009: 336) warning in mind for HE too:

> Oftentimes, schools pay a lot of attention to techniques and strategies while ignoring the social justice aspects of bilingual pedagogy ... Bilingual teachers thus need to be more than good technicians, effective bilingual educators must also be advocates for equity and justice ... bilingual teachers must develop practices that encompass both principles – that of social justice *and* that of social practice.

Language arrangements

In bi-/multilingual education, the concept *language arrangement* refers to allocations of languages in various ways, sometimes supported by official institutional, regional and national policies. As the previous discussion pointed out, we can only agree with Spolsky (2004: 8) when he says that, 'even where there is a formal, written language policy, its effect on language practices is neither guaranteed nor consistent'. This is evident particularly where a dominant LoLT is not spoken outside classrooms by students, lecturers and the community surrounding institutions. Language arrangements, as efforts to manage and enhance the use of languages, can be seen as attempts to empower minoritised languages, for example, when institutions require that examination papers be provided in languages other than the LoLT to improve comprehension. They can also be seen as sinister in the form of mechanisms of power and ideology, for example, when HE entrance tests are only available in one language, as described by Shohamy (2006: 55). Some of the arrangements described in the next sections have emerged from school contexts and their relevance for HE will be referred to throughout.

Strict separation of languages

Bilingual models of schooling offer glimpses into the possibilities of 'bilingual arrangements' (García, 2009: 291) in HE. These have all been developed in bilingual school contexts where learners have to develop initial literacy and academic literacy in two languages. A strict separation arrangement, as described by García (2009: 292), is based on the maintenance of both languages; that is, language acquisition follows an *additive* bilingual approach (one language is added to the learners' existing repertoire) rather than a *subtractive* approach whereby a home or community language is gradually phased out, to be replaced by dominant LoLTs. Since I have argued for the maintenance of existing literacies in HE, this point of departure in a language separation model may seem attractive, but separating languages in HE may not be feasible.

In bilingual school education, languages can be separated in different ways, according to

- time, for example, 'English' days and 'Spanish' days;
- subject, for example, teaching Mathematics and Science in English and the rest of the subjects in Bahasa Malay (Martin, 2005);
- the teacher's language use, so that each teacher uses only one language (which does not necessarily mean that they are monolingual);
- place, for example, classrooms or, in the case of HE campuses, are Dutch or French.

Officially bi- and trilingual universities (see Chapter 2) often follow a 'strict separation' arrangement, whereby modules and programmes are duplicated, for example, the Universities of Fribourg and Luxemburg. This is different from García's separation of languages on the basis of subjects, where learners are exposed to both languages but follow some subjects in one language and others in another. Such a bilingual school arrangement is not followed in exactly the same way at officially bi-/trilingual HEIs, where students can choose to follow a whole programme in only one language.

However, a separation based on subjects or programmes may intersect with a separation of languages based on lecturers' language proficiency, where their ability to use only one of the LoLTs may mean that students have to engage with another academic language. HEIs compete for experts in particular disciplines and fields and their ability to use local languages will not always be as important as their academic reputations. At the University of Fribourg (Switzerland), students' language proficiency in French and German is tested at the start of their academic studies and, although students are able to complete their course of study in only one language, the University does not guarantee provision of all modules in both languages, since lecturers may go on study leave or new lecturers may not be proficient in both LoLTs (which increasingly includes English – see Langner, 2003: 50). A similar arrangement obtained at the University of Ottawa, with university entrants being tested for proficiency in French and English. However, in an interview, a former rector of the university stated that they could not continue the practice because English-speaking students, who constitute approximately 60% of the student body, lack proficiency in French. As in the case of the University of Fribourg, students are not guaranteed that they will be able to follow their programme in English or French *only*, since lecturers who are able to use one of these languages effectively for instruction may not always be available. (See Brink & Van der Walt, 2005 for more detail in this regard.)

Another language arrangement based on programmes is followed at the University of Helsinki, where the Swedish minority provides funding for specific programmes to be offered in Swedish only. At the University of Luxemburg, lecturers who are proficient in only one of the LoLTs are given a period of two years to improve their proficiency in one of the other LoLTs. The role of English as *the* language of the academy means that English-plus multilingualism is the norm for lecturers at these officially bi-/multilingual institutions.

An example of bilingual arrangement according to place is evident in the case of the Catholic University of Leuven/Louvain, where the Flemish part of the University is situated at the centre of Leuven and the French-speaking one is located at Ottignies in the French-speaking part of the province Brabant. It is doubtful whether students and staff at these two campuses see themselves as belonging to one (bilingual) university. The HEI in Leuven started out as mainly French-speaking and, as a result of a series of protests by the Flemish-speaking population, gained 'autonomy' (Nys & Tollebeek, 2008: 50) as the Flemish-speaking Catholic University of Leuven (Katholieke Universiteit Leuven, or KUL). A new French-speaking university (Université Catholique de Louvain, or UCL) was built in Louvain-la-Neuve, Ottignies. Nys and Tollebeek (2008: 51) state that, despite the fact that the two institutions still existed as a legal entity KUL–UCL in the 1970s, very little cooperation occurred. In the early 1990s, this changed as the two universities 'formed a dynamic tandem in international organisations of catholic universities' (Nys & Tollebeek, 2008: 66[1]).

The North-West University in South Africa is in a similar situation after two HEIs were merged in the early 2000s by the then minister of education, Prof Kader Asmal, to form the new institution. The University of Bophuthatswana (which used English as a LoLT and was situated in Mahikeng, formerly known as Mafikeng, in the former homeland of Bophuthatswana) merged with the University of Potchefstroom, which used mainly Afrikaans as a LoLT on its Potchefstroom campus and Afrikaans and English on its Vaal Triangle Campus. As a result of the merger, there are three campuses: the Mahikeng Campus, which still uses only English as a LoLT; the Potchefstroom campus, which still uses mainly Afrikaans (except for scarce programmes for engineers and pharmacists); and the Vaal Triangle campus, where English and Afrikaans are used.[2] This is a very clear example of a merged institution where the separation of languages reflects the history and socio-political contexts of a nominally multilingual HEI.

An example of language separation in terms of time as well as place is a multilingual, International Business Management degree that is offered at three universities in Europe, as the Website of the University of Applied

Sciences and Arts Northwestern Switzerland explains (FHNW School of Business):

> International Business Management (IBM) is a unique trinational 3.5 year study programme which prepares students for an international career in a dynamic business environment ... The first and fourth semesters are mainly taught in French at the Université de Haute Alsace in Colmar, France, the second and fifth mainly in German at the Duale Hochschule Baden-Württemberg in Lörrach, Germany and the third and sixth mainly in English at the Basel campus of the School of Business, FHNW.

Entry requirements for the programme include language proficiency at level B2 of the Common European Framework (Council of Europe, 2001) in the three languages that are assessed in an interview with the candidates. Information about the programme states that 'students participate in classroom discussions, carry out group work, give presentations, and write papers and their examinations in all three languages'. Students' language proficiency is supported in language courses throughout their programme, with English and one other language (which should not be the home language) being compulsory in the first four semesters. In the final two semesters, only English is taught. Since students are probably mostly European and probably recruited from those regions of France and Germany where both national languages are used from an early age, the additional English language courses were probably identified as a particular need for these students (McMenamin, personal communication). It seems safe to say that students probably communicate in French and German with each other and their lecturers while using English for the semesters in Switzerland and to improve their internship and job opportunities.

It is clear that the multilingual contexts and their geographical location enable these arrangements and, although the languages are officially separated, students and lecturers probably use a variety of code switching and borrowing strategies in informal conversations or off-record communication.

Multilingual arrangements: Exploiting multilingualism for effective learning

In officially bi-/multilingual HE, where students' and lecturers' use of the institutional LoLTs is widespread, arguments for a strict separation of these languages may not appear useful or even possible. When students are able to actively use more than one language for learning, separating them may appear artificial or unnecessary. At HE level in particular, where the learning of a LoLT may not be uppermost in the minds of students, keeping languages separate may not seem functional either. García (2009: 295) makes a crucial distinction between two types of language arrangements where different LoLTs are used in the same classroom:

- A *flexible convergent* approach, where code switching is used randomly (mostly to translate or for affective reasons, for example, to emphasise efforts at disciplining a class or to engage emotionally with a learner) and/or where a low-status language is used to facilitate the development of literacy in a dominant LoLT, referred to as monoliterate bilingualism (García, 2009: 295). García places this within a theoretical framework that results in subtractive bilingualism and as such is evidence of a transitional bilingual model of schooling (2009: 310).
- A *flexible multiplicity* approach, where LoLTs are used in language practices that support meaning making in more than one language. These practices are evidence of a view of multilingualism as dynamic and recursive, resulting in the active use of LoLTs across the range of academic language practices.

In Chapter 2, an attempt was made to show how bi-/multilingual HEIs developed and flourished within their various historical, socio-cultural and psychological contexts. Their language arrangements reflect these contexts and their histories that testify to the dynamic nature of HE. The different types of multilingual institutions (in the introduction to this chapter) forecast at least two possible scenarios that different languages can play in their classrooms, in one case following a flexible convergent approach and in the other a flexible multiplicity approach.

However, the distinction between a flexible convergent and a flexible multiplicity approach blurs in the case of HEIs. At primary school level, learners will have minimal or no literacy in any language and are dependent on the language proficiency of their teachers. At higher levels of schooling, learners may have developed some literacy in a particular language, but, when they move to a different country or, as happens in many countries in Africa, when they switch to another LoLT, they are again dependent on their teachers to develop literacy in a different language.

In the case of HE, transnational students (and in some cases national students) will have developed academic language proficiency in another language and they are not as dependent on lecturers as are children who still need to develop literacies. Therefore, in the case of students who have developed literacy in a language other than the HE LoLT, a flexible convergent approach may not necessarily lead to monoliterate bilingualism. In fact, a flexible convergent approach, as described in Scenario A, can be one of the ways in which biliteracy is maintained irrespective of the lecturer's language ability, as will be shown below.

Flexible convergence in higher education

As was pointed out in Chapter 1, Hornberger's (2009: 198) continua of biliteracy framework shows that spaces can be opened up for minority and/or low-status languages along the contexts, content and media of biliteracy to enable the development of biliteracy (Hornberger, 2007: 184) or bilingual scientific literacy (Airey, 2009). In the case of HE, flexible convergence can be the first step in acknowledging the presence of other language groups at the institution.

In the introduction to this chapter, the point was made that student and lecturer attitudes must be taken into account if other languages are to be used successfully in the HE classroom. If lecturers and students regard the use of only English as a sign of their educational prowess, other languages will be avoided or will only be used in a flexible convergent approach. From the institution's point of view, the provision of academics who can manage a variety of languages for assessment and teaching purposes may seem daunting. Another perception may be that students have not developed enough academic literacy in home or community languages for HE study. In all these instances, the following scenario could support a multilingual approach to academic learning:

Scenario A: In cases where a particular LoLT is the only one that can be used for assignments and assessments (i.e. in the absence of an official multilingual policy) lecturers create space for informal and multilingual academic work in the form of, for example, classroom discussions, marginal notes and summaries in other languages as a preparatory stage for formal monolingual work (presentations, assignments, tests, exams) in the dominant LoLT. Monolingual academic work results from planning and drafting multilingually and the final product will be in English or another powerful LoLT:

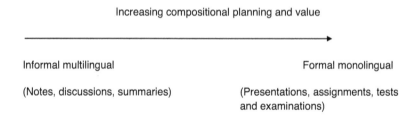

Increasing compositional planning and value

Informal multilingual   Formal monolingual

(Notes, discussions, summaries)   (Presentations, assignments, tests
                                         and examinations)

This scenario does not require that lecturers have proficiency in the languages used by their students, although multilingual proficiency is always advantageous. It does not even require more than one speaker of a particular language. It only requires that a multilingual space be opened in the form of the lecturer bringing multilingual learning strategies to the attention of students, for example, by providing multilingual glossaries or by guiding students to develop their own bilingual word lists, allowing discussions in other languages and providing examples of multilingual meaning-making activities. (See following text for more examples.)

This scenario may be the best that a lecturer can do in an environment that is restrictive in terms of institutional or student perceptions about the importance of the high-status LoLT. This is also the only multilingual space a lecturer can open up for students who have never written in a home or community language or may have stopped writing in it at primary school level. The danger of this first scenario is that, in a predominantly monolingual environment, the use of other languages would remain at the level of exploratory talk (as discussed by Setati *et al.*, 2002) and never progress to literacy practices in languages other than the LoLT. I maintain that informal chatting or code switching in a classroom does not constitute multilingual education (although such strategies may be important precursors): the use and active development of existing and emergent academic literacies (in whatever language) is the aim of multilingual HE and as such needs to be pursued consciously and responsibly.

Flexible convergence may appear to support multilingualism but it does not support the development of academic biliteracy and can even heighten the perception that other languages are not 'worthy' to be used for academic work. Preisler (2008: 246) predicts that even languages that have been in used in HE, in this case Danish, may come to be seen as 'less well suited as the language of higher education' as English is increasingly institutionalised.

A case in point

Michael-Luna and Canagarajah (2007) describe an attempt to create a multilingual space for students to discuss assignments in an academic writing course. They (Michael-Luna & Canagarajah, 2007: 70) call an approach where one language is considered useful for discussion or informal writing but not for formal academic writing that will be assessed, a 'monolingual ideology governing language use'. Although such an approach proved successful in getting students to use vernacular discourses in discussions of academic work online and in e-mail, students did not use them in class. They conclude (Michael-Luna & Canagarajah, 2007: 70):

> Vernacular discourses are often treated as unsophisticated by the social mainstream and the in-group norms of HE writing. The tension between safe house expression and formal HE writing in Canagarajah's (2004) study suggests that students are aware of these contextual norms and do not want to earn these associations by flaunting vernacular speech acts in the public sites of the classroom.

HEIs that attract a variety of transnational or national students who use languages other than the LoLT for daily communication may regard even flexible convergence as a bridge too far. However, both pragmatic and ideological forces argue for increased awareness of the power of a multilingual pedagogy. In pragmatic terms, increased pressure to improve throughput rates argues for far more than academic literacy support in the LoLT. In ideological terms, the acknowledgement and validation of diversity, including linguistic diversity, creates an empowering environment. As Michael-Luna and Canagarajah (2007: 72) conclude,

> HE teachers' increased awareness of the changing conventions of professional academic discourses may supply the strength to enact multilingual pedagogic strategies. A move toward valuing multivocal, multilingual rhetorical strategies and knowledge will serve to bring HE academic literacies into line with the linguistic pluralism of recent scholarly writing as well as of 'real world' communications.

Flexible multiplicity in higher education

In Chapters 1 and 3, Hornberger's continua of biliteracy was described and proposed as a framework for multilingual education in HEIs. The argument in favour of an approach that fosters and supports biliteracy, which includes what Airey (2009: 3) calls *bilingual scientific literacy*, is that linguistically diverse students may have participated in academic literacy practices in at least one other language or variety of a language, either at school or at undergraduate level. In contrast to the foundational levels of schooling, these students have concluded successful academic studies in other languages. In the case of transnationally mobile students, they will need to maintain their previously developed literacy competencies when they return to their communities and/or enter multilingual workplaces (see Chapter 3). In terms of Airey's (2009: 3) definition of scientific literacy as 'both the ability to work within science and the ability to apply science to the problems of society', the use of more than one code is inevitable. As job markets globally require *English-plus multilingualism*, an essential condition of internationalisation is that multilingualism is maintained in such a way that students' employment opportunities are enhanced. This inevitably means development of job-related academic competencies in more than one language.

A scenario that exploits and maintains existing academic literacy in a language other than the LoLT is foreseen in an approach that fosters flexible multiplicity:

Scenario B: This scenario would depend on the language abilities of lecturers and tutors or teaching assistants. Biliteracy would develop from informal and multilingual academic work to several points along the continuum, towards active biliteracy that is expressed in bi-/multilingual tutorial groups, allowing questions to the lecturer in other languages, responses by the lecturer to the class (or part of the class) in other languages, presentations by students and lecturers in more than one language, and submitting assignments (in tests, examinations) in more than one language:

Increased active use of two or more languages

Informal multilingual academic work ...   Active biliteracy
                                                            in tests and assignments

The maintenance and further development of two academic languages exploits and rewards students, academics and support staff who are able to use more than one language for academic purposes.

There are many arguments against academic biliteracy, mostly in terms of 'practicality' or 'logistics'.

- Who will ensure that the academic standard is maintained across languages in biliterate classrooms?
- How can we be sure that lecturers who teach, for example, Biochemistry or Ancient Cultures will know how to develop biliteracy?
- Where will we find the necessary experts who can teach and assess biliterally?

By substituting 'biliteracy' with 'English', these same questions can be asked of institutions that introduce English as a LoLT, or, as in post-colonial countries, of institutions that use mainly second language users of, for example, English or French for teaching. Despite a lack of training in HE teaching and learning, academics are generally expected to develop (critical) academic literacies and to socialise students into discipline-specific discourses. The majority (in the preceding contexts) are multilingual themselves and have no problem moving between languages in the course of their daily duties. Preisler (2008: 247) describes an HE situation in Denmark where English is increasingly used alongside Danish. A picture emerges of academics using English for publishing internationally and teaching transnational students and using Danish for local students and in academic meetings and committees. He argues that academics are duty-bound to consider local contexts when they publish:

> To a much greater extent than is the case today, scientific and scholarly research should be made accessible for different media aimed at a wide variety of local target groups. And not only should the flow of 'de-professionalized' information be stimulated in this way, for the benefit of non-specialist audiences. The interdisciplinary sharing of research results within the local research environments, too, constitutes a natural context for the use and further development of the national language.

Academic biliteracy is constructed as a problem by pretending that academics and students need to choose one language for academic work. This construction provides a lens that shows one LoLT as manageable and more than one as a headache, mainly because institutions may feel the need to formalise biliteracy practices as institution-wide policy. If institutions (in the form of their policies) acknowledge the potential and agency of lecturers to develop biliterate teaching and learning environments, the homogenising instinct may be mitigated by a focus on micro-language planning that aims at 'processes, relations and dynamic activities' rather than 'fixed objects or structures' (Baldauf, 2006: 153). What this would mean in practice is acknowledging the agency of lecturers and their students, as the following examples show.

Cases in point

(1)   In an environment where English is the LoLT for a majority of second language users of English, the University of Limpopo (South Africa) offers a bilingual degree programme in which students have to produce assignments and are assessed in English (for particular modules) and Sesotho sa Lebowa for others. Hornberger (2010: 549) notes how students code switch between English and Sesotho sa Lebowa, and Ramani et al. (2007) describe what is required of students in terms of reading and writing tests and assignments in two languages. This is the only programme of its kind in South Africa.

(2)   Although the University of Fribourg (Switzerland) keeps German and French course offerings separate, Langner (2003: 60, 61) points out that students who feel that they have high proficiency in these languages are able to qualify with a 'second language endorsement' (Lizentiat/Diplom mit Zweisprachige-Zusatz), which certifies that they completed a minimum of 40% of all their coursework (assignments, tests, reading materials, oral presentations and so on) in their second language (Langner, e-mail communication). According to the official university regulations of 8 June 2010 (Recueil systématique/Systematische Sammlung 7.1.3.1) faculties can develop their own guidelines in this regard. In this way, students are encouraged to make use of a unique opportunity to develop and showcase their biliteracy.

(3)   At the Universitat Autònoma in Barcelona, Moore and Dooly (2010) describe students using Catalan in group discussions and in marginal notes to problematise and clarify English concepts, drawing on this knowledge to build understanding of English texts and lectures.

In all three examples, academics and students are allowed to take the initiative to support and enhance academic biliteracy.

The two scenarios presented may not necessarily be different options; they can also be seen as phases towards official policy to manage multilingual learning and teaching. Their perspective is that of institutions creating the opportunity for multilingual learning, whereas my own research shows that multilingual students do not need interventions or sanction by the lecturer to use their linguistic resources when making meaning (Van der Walt & Dornbrack, 2011; Van der Walt, 2013).

The next section elaborates on this point and provides particular examples of multilingual teaching strategies.

Proposed Strategies and Practices in Multilingual Classrooms

The strategies that are discussed in this section are described by García (2009: 290–306) as they appear in primary and secondary school contexts. Their use in HE has not been researched to any significant extent, partly because interaction in HE classrooms, in contrast to HE students, are poorly researched. This may be because of the relatively exclusive nature of HE classrooms, the studies by Michael-Luna and Canagarajah (2007), Canagarajah (2011) and Airey (2009) being some of the notable exceptions. For these reasons I rely heavily on my own context for examples of code switching as well as co- and translanguaging practices in the hope that they may open up discussion and comparison with practices in other contexts.

In her discussion of bilingual education practices, García discusses five strategies:

- Responsible code switching both ways
- Translanguaging
- Co-languaging
- Preview–view–review
- Cross-linguistic work and awareness

In García's (2009: 303, emphasis added) discussion, she describes the strategy multilingual awareness and tolerance of other languages as resulting from cross-linguistic work and awareness, where

> a part of the curriculum is reserved for bringing the two or more languages together for contrastive analysis... there is an *instructional space* for bilingual children to do cross-linguistic work which allows them to translanguage ...

I would like to argue that awareness-raising needs to be separated from cross-linguistic work since I regard awareness-raising as a pre-condition (rather than a strategy) for HEIs that wish to widen access and acknowledge the linguistic diversity that result from internationalisation. Franceschini (2009: ix) regards awareness-raising among key role players in universities as one of the most important steps in the validation of multilingualism. An example of how this can be achieved at classroom level is provided by Airey (2009: 109) as one of his hints for lecturers, when he urges them at the start of a course to '[d]iscuss the fact that there are differences when lectures are in a second language'. Unless institutions and particularly lecturers and teaching assistants or tutors create space for multilingual practices, this resource will remain largely untapped. Although students, as adult learners, are able to use a wide range of sophisticated learning strategies, including using more than one language, they are not immune to institutional discourses that privilege monolingual learning and teaching, particularly when institutions see the introduction of English as an answer to the perceived problems posed by a multilingual student population. My discussion, therefore, elaborates on García's first four strategies to demonstrate how lecturers can create space for multilingual awareness in general and biliteracy in particular. I separate cross-linguistic work from awareness and subsume it under co-languaging practices.

Five strategies: code switching, co-languaging, translanguaging, preview–view–review strategy and interpretation strategies are discussed in the context of multilingual HE environments. The fact that multilingual HE students have developed (a degree of) academic literacy in other languages or at least have access to other languages means that they are not in the same vulnerable position as school-going learners. They have been successful students up to tertiary level, and this indicates potential to develop and use metacognitive and metalinguistic strategies to manage learning in more than one language. The challenge for multilingual HE environments, like school environments, is at institutional level; acknowledging the multilingual nature of a student population and raising awareness among staff and students of the ways in which other languages must be activated to support biliterate learning.

Instructional code switching

Studies on code switching in bilingual school settings seem to have moved from a very negative evaluation (Auerbach, 1993: 9) to some acceptance of it (Cook, 2001). Much of the research into instructional code switching has been done at primary and secondary school levels, and there is no reason to suppose that this would not be a phenomenon in multilingual HE contexts too. In contexts where secondary schools with bilingual language policies are feeder schools for such HE contexts, as is the case in the Western Cape, South Africa, the possibility that code switching will be used at HE level too is increased.

Code switching as a lecturing strategy is not officially endorsed at the bi-/trilingual HEIs in Europe. The practice of code switching seems to be limited to students, as shown, for example, in studies by Söderlundh (2008), Airey (2009) and Moore (2010). The problem with studying code switching, particularly by lecturers, is the fact that the 'conversation' in an HE classroom, particularly in the case of formal lectures and in big classes, will be quite one-sided. A description of code switching practices in such cases is difficult since explanatory frameworks of code switching are based on largely unplanned and spontaneous speech across a number of conversational turns. The examples provided by, for example, Myers-Scotton (2005), Swann (2000: 165–176), Finlayson and Slabbert (1997), and Gafaranga and Torras (2002) are all from spontaneous conversations, which form a small part of the interaction in formal lecture halls. Needless to say, instructional code switching in group work or in classrooms that are not lecturer-dominated will approximate spontaneous, conversational code switching as shown by Kamwangamalu (2010: 125). The focus in the discussion that follows is on lecturer code switching as a formal, lecturing practice in content subjects.

In a study of code switching practices at school level, it became clear to me that code switching for the purpose of enhancing learning and understanding cannot be done randomly by teachers (Van der Walt *et al.*, 2001). García (2009: 298) extends the concept of responsible code switching to include the idea that such switching should happen 'both ways' to build competence in both languages. This is a flexible multiplicity approach whereby proficiency is developed in both languages, rather than flexible convergence, where the dominant LoLT is developed to replace a home language, and code switching is merely an interim measure or bridge to the LoLT. The difference between random and responsible code switching can be found mainly in the degree of planning and explicit motivation for code switching. In the case of the former, switching is done almost intuitively as an aid to understanding. This is typical behaviour for bi-/multilinguals, which, according to García (2009: 296), 'is not always appropriate in educational settings where the development of academic language is necessary'. She links random code switching to transitional bilingual education where the child is expected to eventually become literate in one LoLT.

In HE, where students are expected to have developed academic literacy at least in the dominant LoLT, language development is not the first aim in content subjects. What responsible code switching in such contexts should look like must be determined by bi-/multilingual lecturers and students in HE because current explanatory frameworks of code switching are not intended to clarify the pedagogical impact of code switching in content subjects. Myers-Scotton (1993: 82), for example, distinguishes between 'unmarked' code switching – as 'neutral' in a particular context – and 'marked' code switching – the deliberate choice of a different code for a particular purpose. Kamwangamalu (2010: 124) points out that this distinction is too rigid to allow for the situation where a single utterance is both marked and unmarked. He describes an HE setting where a student switches from English to Swati when addressing his fellow students (for whom code switching is an unmarked choice) in the presence of the lecturer (who does not understand Swati and for whom this would be a marked choice and a distancing practice). See Extract 1 below for an example from the South African context.

Gafaranga and Torras (2002) argue for another and more productive way of looking at code switching, arguing that a monolingual view of code switching focuses simply on the use of various languages in one conversation. They refer to code switching, or language alternation (as they call it), itself as medium – in other words, language alternation as an unmarked choice. What this may mean is that language alternation as a mode of interaction may include switches from one language to another without signalling deviance. For example, one speaker starts in Language A and switches to Language B and back again to A in a manner that participants have agreed on tacitly. Deviance would be indicated by one speaker continuing in Language B against the conversational conventions of the group. The speaker indicates deviance by sticking to Language B, signalling 'interactional otherness' if avoidance of Language A is maintained.

However, in the course of a lecture where language alternation is the norm, switches can still signal 'interactional otherness', since teachers/ lecturers may use alternation for particular purposes that deviate from the 'medium' of code-switched academic discourse. The following example, from classes observed and recorded at Stellenbosch University by Visser, Anthonissen and Van der Walt,[3] shows a lecturer in full lecture mode, switching from English to Afrikaans when she or he observes a student (presumably Afrikaans-speaking) reading the local Afrikaans newspaper. This example illustrates the way in which educational code switching is similar to conversational code switching, where both the topic and function of communication requires a switch (as perceived by the lecturer), after which she or he continues in the teaching mode, *in English*, with a later switch to Afrikaans, still in teaching mode (numbering is only for ease of reference, with English in italics and the English translations in square brackets and in italics):

Example 1 (from a history lecture on Genghis Khan)

(a) *There is [sic] many ways of spelling Genghis. Chingis, the first one, that's the more traditionally correct one.*

(b) Kan jy vir ons vertel wat in Die Burger staan? Enigiets interessant? Okay, sit hom asseblief weg. En sien my na die tyd, asseblief. [*Can you tell me what* Die Burger *(name of newspaper) says? Anything interesting? Okay, put it away please. And come and see me afterwards, please.*]

(c) *Okay. Right. The great, the last great nomadic challenges, this is the last empire of nomads that developed into a civilisation or an empire.*

(d) *Genghis Khan, a lot of you are probably gonna do your assignments on Genghis, so you might as well get a bit of a head start.*

(e) Hy's gebore in 1162, rondom by, dis nie heeltemal seker van die presiese datum nie, en hy's oorlede in 1227. [*He was born in 1162, or around that time, the exact date is not a certainty, and he passed away in 1227.*]

From Gafaranga and Torras's perspective, code alternation is the medium in this HE context. In this extract, an example of deviance can be seen in the switch to Afrikaans at (b) and language alternation as the medium in the academic content of the lecture as it progresses from (a) to (c), (d) and (e). The lecturer switches to Afrikaans merely to order the student to put the newspaper away, he or she picks up the lecture again in the language that he or she was using before the interruption. The switch at (b) has nothing to do with the topic of the lecture and seems to constitute what Gafaranga and Torras would call deviance from the medium, which is repaired by switching back to English to return to what can be regarded as the 'academic medium' (which is code-switched Afrikaans and English). Language alternation as the medium is demonstrated in the switch to 'academic' Afrikaans, which only follows at (e), with more detail about the political context of Genghis Khan's birth.

In terms of code switching literature from school contexts, one could argue that the switch to Afrikaans was a disciplining device before moving back to English as the teaching language. It is clear that the lecturer has some kind of plan, explicit or intuitive, which organises the lecture into seemingly regular segments that are delivered in English, then Afrikaans, and back to English. Interruptions in the form of comments to particular students do not seem to interfere with that organisation (or 'medium') in the case of this lecturer.

Although Moore (2010) concludes that students (in her study) draw frequently on their knowledge of other languages 'as a locally deployable resource in the English medium classroom', much more research needs to be done on the contribution that the use of other languages may make to understanding. The lack of research on the effects of instructional code switching in HE is also evident in the lack of studies on what kind of code switching would be effective for learning. As can be seen in the following example from a class in Linguistics, intra-sentential code switching is also prevalent in formal lecture halls (English in italics, followed by a translation in English in square brackets):

Example 2 (from a lecture on Linguistics)

Hier is 'n paar, *there are a few interesting things you can discuss in the tutorials this week. And I think that many of the issues are of importance and some of them are important to us given the context in which we are.* Goed dames en here, komponente van taal, as jy enige taal, *if you take any language you can break it down into sounds, words, sentences and the ( ) context. This is where the language is spoken* nè, daar waar dit gebeur, waar die mense na jou luister of jy luister na hulle om sin te maak om te verstaan wat probeer die persoon sê ens.

[There are a few, *there are a few interesting things you can discuss in the tutorials this week. And I think that many of the issues are of importance and some of them are important to us given the context in which we are.* Okay ladies and gentlemen, components of a language. If you take any language, *if you take any language you can break it down into sounds, words, sentences and the ( ) context. This is where the language is spoken,* isn't it, that's where it happens, where people listen to you or you listen to them to make sense of and to understand what they say, etc.]

The length of language chunks that need to be maintained before a switch is made to the next language has not been researched at all. It could be that students will 'switch off' completely when lecturers present long stretches in the language with which they are not familiar or when they simply duplicate in Language B what they had just said in Language A (see Van der Walt, 2006). Such a strategy will not give students the opportunity to compare terminology, as the next lecturer does when he or she directly follows 'verskillende klanke' (underlined below) with a direct translation *'different sounds'*, just as she mentions and describes the concept of a 'mor-feem' *'morpheme'*:

Example 3 (from a lecture on Linguistics)

'n Woord is nou al bestaande uit verskillende klanke, *different sounds,* en ons noem dit 'n morfeem, die kleinste eenheid van betekenis. *So a morpheme is the unit of meaning such as root words, the core word, the suffixes and the prefixes.*

[A word has different sounds, *different sounds,* and we call that a morpheme, the smallest unit of meaning. *So a morpheme is the unit of meaning such as root words, the core word, the suffixes and the prefixes.*]

García (2009: 299) refers to unpublished research by O'Neill and Velasco, who suggest three points at which code switching would be useful in a lesson. It could support understanding of terminology (as the lecturer above does) or when providing a linguistic summary (a focus on language learning) or when providing a summary of the content to support meaning making. This view overlaps to some extent with Üstünel and Seedhouse's (2005) introduction of the term *pedagogical focus* to explain a language teacher's code switching behaviour. Both as an analytical tool and a justification for code switching, this term has the potential to help us decide when code switching would be most advantageous and productive. In terms of the organisation of a particular lecture, decisions can be made as to a focus on introducing key terms in different languages, using co-languaging practices to present the terms on a handout, or on a PowerPoint slide. The meaning and use of such terms can be reinforced by switching in the course of the lecture when they are used.

Much research has been undertaken on code switching by teachers and learners in schools (see Auerbach, 1993; Uys & Van Dulm, 2011) but the effect of code switching on learning or on affective states in learners and lecturers are in dire need of further research. Keeping in mind the negative attitudes to code switching in formal educational environments, we should not be surprised that data are not readily available. There is some evidence at HE level that code switching (by lecturers or by students) can have mixed results for learning. Banda (2007) describes the meaning-making practices of HE students who use Xhosa and English in study groups to discuss academic topics that have been introduced in English. He concludes that 'whatever advantage gained by the use of the L1 is lost if the study group is comprised of students not proficient in the language of academic writing, and worse still, unfamiliar with the subject matter at hand' (Banda, 2007: 17), thus confirming Setati *et al*.'s (2002) warning that exploratory talk in a language other than the LoLT will only be effective when students also move to disciplinary discourse in either of those languages.

There clearly is a need for investigations into what would constitute responsible code switching, where planned switches are made for learning purposes, either to explain concepts and content or to strengthen academic biliteracy by comparing terms and texts in different languages (Van der Walt *et al*., 2001; García, 2009: 299–301).

In a 2008 project on the influence of code switching on the development of listening comprehension in students' self-identified 'weaker' language, Visser, Anthonissen and Van der Walt investigated the language develop-ment of Stellenbosch University first-year students in bilingual classes. The initial results (reflecting so-called ethnic groups as required by current gov-ernment policy[4]) show that students who are proficient in Afrikaans and English predictably become used to this kind of teaching quickly. Equally predictably, students with no proficiency in one of the languages, in this case usually Afrikaans, do not feel that they make any comprehension gains when lecturers switch between these languages. Student responses to the statement 'I have become used to and comfortable with the bilingual lec-tures since the beginning of the year...' yielded the following responses in the categories (1) *Not at all;* (2) *To a small degree;* (3) *To a fair degree;* (4) *To a high degree;* (5) *To a considerably high degree:*

- Coloured[5] and White Afrikaans-speaking students chose option 3, with option 4 as a close second.
- Black English-speaking students overwhelmingly chose category 1.
- White English-speaking students mainly chose option 4, with 3 and 5 following closely.
- Coloured English-speaking students: the majority, by quite a margin, chose category 5.

The widespread perception among lecturers and students that a switch to English would accommodate students who do not know Afrikaans is obviously misplaced, although a portion of the class with presumably some receptive proficiency (English-speaking White and Coloured students) expe-rienced the switches more positively, as the statistics show.

Students have also expressed their frustration with this kind of teach-ing, as reported by Anthonissen (2006) and Van Heusden and Lambrechts (2008: 67), who note that students become bored or 'switch off'. In some cases the reaction is more extreme and Van der Walt's (2006: 366) survey among third-year students showed that as many as 35% of those polled felt that code switching was a waste of time. The following example shows how a particular lecturer used repetition while lecturing. In this case, no new information is presented after the switches, except for the underlined part (the first paragraph shows the switches to English in italics, followed by a translation in square brackets):

Example 4 (from a lecture on Geology)

Ons is klaar met plaattechtomie *we're finishing off with platetechtronics today and then we carry on to volcanoes and magmas which is part of the geological processes that start around page twenty three in your study guide.* So die eerste biologiese proses wat ons na gaan kyk is vulkane en magmas, vulkaniese uitbarstings <u>*and you'll see that it is chapter four*</u> <u>*and chapter five in the text book. So we are skipping chapter three for now*</u> <u>*and we'll come back to it,*</u> Ja? Tot hier. Woensdag se toets is tot op bladsy twee en twintig. *Wednesday's test up to page twenty two.*

[We have finished with platetechtronics today, *we're finishing off with platechtronics today and then we carry on to volcanoes and magmas which is part of the geological processes that start around page twenty three in your study guide.* So the first biological processes that we will look at are volcanoes and magmas, volcanic eruptions <u>*and you'll see that it is*</u> <u>*chapter four and chapter five in the text book.* So we are skipping chapter</u> *three for now and we'll come back to it.* Yes? Up to here. Wednesday's test is up to page twenty-two. <u>*Wednesday's test up to page twenty two.*</u>]

This particular lecture was presented to first-year students and one could argue that instructions about tests or about the topic of a lesson could bear repetition, even when it happens in the same language. However, it will probably become tedious in the course of 50 minutes.

Even in cases where students understand both languages, code switching as *accommodation* in the form of repetition is not necessarily seen as convergence with particular language groups, particularly when students judge the lecturer's language use as 'weak' or strongly accented. In Van der Walt and Steyn (2004b: 499), it was reported that *Afrikaans* students' 'request for English was linked to [the lecturer's] poor Afrikaans usage'. In such cases, code switching does not always achieve the goal of supporting students with limited proficiency either.

However, more qualitative data have been reported by Van Heusden and Lambrechts (2008: 49), who quote students in focus-group interviews commenting favourably on code switching practices by a particular lecturer:

'*I think I'd really like to salute him for doing the T-option* [using English and Afrikaans together] *and for like really taking into consideration the two languages, people with different languages in the class...*'

Code switching by the lecturer and by students is one strategy that can make a difference to multilingual orientations by enhancing learning when it is done responsibly and is supported by practices such as co- and trans-languaging, as discussed in the following section. It is important to note that although code switching by lecturers and students can enhance learning it will not necessarily develop biliteracy, unless it is supported by practices like co-languaging and by expectations that students present at least some of their written work in a language other than the dominant LoLT. The example set by the University of Fribourg is one that can be followed in this regard.

Co-languaging: Comparing and contrasting languages

Co-languaging is a strategy whereby languages are visually presented and compared to accommodate students from different language backgrounds by contrasting terms and phrases from these languages. The strategy can be used for various purposes at HE level, for example:

- In her book *English for law*, which is aimed at 'native speakers of other languages to understand and use the language of the law in English' (Riley, 1994: xix), the author compares the names of subjects in an English law course to the terms in French, German, Italian, Polish, Spanish and Swedish (see Example 5). This is an example of cross-linguistic work (García's fifth bilingual practice) because the author also compares cognate terms from these languages to English terms, distinguishing those that agree in meaning from 'false friends'. It is clear from the title that students are expected to gain proficiency in English and to read and write in English. This is an example of co-languaging but in a Flexible Convergent approach. Although the expectation seems to be that students will use English when reporting back from group work, individual 'oral practice' includes the instruction, 'If you want to practise speaking English, say your answers out loud or record them on tape, then listen to your recording' (Riley, 1994: 7). This looks like a Scenario A multilingual classroom.

Example 5

Table 1.1 Group I Subjects

Language	Paper 1	Paper 2	Paper 3	Paper 4
English	Roman *Law*	*Constitutional Law*	Criminal Law	Law of *Tort*
French	droit *romain*	droit *constitutionnel*	droit *criminel*	(*tort*)
German	*römisches* Recht	(*Konstitution*) Verfassungsrecht	(*Kriminal*) Strafrecht	–
Italian	diritto *romano*	diritto *costituzionale*	(*crimine, criminale*) diritto penale	(*torto*)
Polish	prawo *rzymskie*	prawo *konstytucyjne*	(*kryminalista, kryminalna*) prawo karne	–
Spanish	derecho *romano*	derecho *constitucional*	(*crimen, criminal*) derecho penale	(*tuerto*)
Swedish	*Romansk lag*	(*Konstitutionell*) Regeringsrätt	(*kriminal*) Straffrätt	–
Words you may know	Rome Roman	constitution	crime criminal	–

- When co-languaging is used to strengthen more than one language and when students are expected to read and write in more than one language, the strategy is used in a Flexible Multiplicity approach. This is the case in the bilingual degree at the University of Limpopo, where students need to show high levels of proficiency in English and SeSotho sa Leboa. In a discussion of the strategies used to develop terminology in SeSotho sa Leboa, Ramani *et al.* (2007: 213) show how lecturers on the programme contrast terms in the two languages (Example 6 below). This is clearly an example of a Flexible Multiplicity approach.

Example 6:

English   **Sesotho sa Leboa**

- Sample   Sampolo
- Variable   Bariepolo

The important point about this particular example is that lecturers and students on the programme were not deterred by the misconception that subject-specific terms cannot be expressed in African languages. Using the techniques of transference (borrowing a word as is), transliteration (adapting the features of a borrowed word to fit the phonology and morphology of SeSotho, as in Example 6) or omission (where a description was adequate to reflect the meaning of a term without a particular term being transliterated or transferred), Ramani *et al.* (2007: 216) conclude that 'teachers [i.e. lecturers] dig deep into their repertoire to find the terms in SsL [SeSotho sa Leboa] and in the absence of equivalents, the teachers employ the three strategies outlined above to cope with lack of terminology in their own language'. The article describes how lecturers and students analyse concepts in both languages to render a term suitably in SeSotho sa Leboa; an example of in-depth cross-linguistic work.

Co-languaging strategies can range from a simple bi- or trilingual poster (see e.g. Van der Walt & Ruiters, 2011) to a glossary that can be accessed by students on their mobile phones.[6] Although García (2009: 298) mentions co-languaging as a strategy that suits the Flexible Multiplicity approach, the fact that students have developed advanced literacy in other languages provides the opportunity for its use in a Scenario A (Flexible Convergent) context as well. Since literacy is well established in another language or languages, the possibility that a Flexible Convergent approach will lead to monoliterate bilingualism, as García (2009: 297) cautions, is considerably smaller at HE level. Furthermore, students can use co-languaging independently of their lecturers because of their competence in another language and in information-gathering skills. As my own studies with multilingual HE students have shown (Van der Walt & Dornbrack, 2011;

Van der Walt, 2013), bilingual students will make use of bilingual resources and strategies without the intervention of lecturers, although the success of this strategy will be enhanced when the lecturer creates awareness of and spaces for multilingual learning. The fact that students have developed advanced academic literacy in another language is the crucial difference between bilingual schooling and bi-/multilingual HE, and this fact increases the agency of both students and lecturers.

The examples of co-languaging mentioned so far may create the impression that this strategy is mainly used to contrast terminology from different languages. However, there are many examples of extended bi-/multilingual writing in daily life. Banda (2009: 102) notes that 'posters, notices and other official documents in the Western Cape Provincial Government are written in three languages'. In Venice, Italian–English notices warn tourists that certain stops of the water bus will not be available during flood times. At international airports, notices are in local language(s) and English. International train schedules may be printed in more than one language. These practices introduce another aspect of co-languaging and that is the formatting and placement of different languages in one space: be that on a road sign or a bilingual examination paper. In official signs and documents, this is usually done by providing a text in both languages, what Sebba (2012: 14) calls *parallelism*. The assumption is usually that readers can read the language they prefer or that they know. The arrangement of more than one language on the printed or projected page is crucial for ease of reading. Compare Example 7 (an extract from a train schedule) to Example 8 (an e-mail notification of a cancelled meeting) in terms of effectiveness:

Example 7:

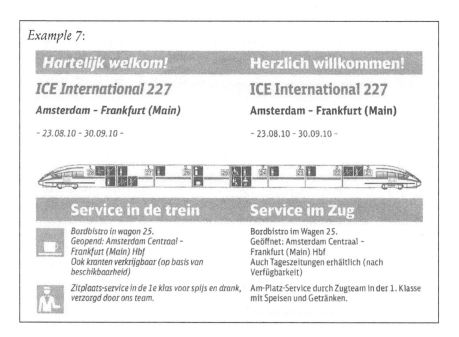

Hartelijk welkom!

ICE International 227

Amsterdam - Frankfurt (Main)

- 23.08.10 - 30.09.10 -

Herzlich willkommen!

ICE International 227

Amsterdam - Frankfurt (Main)

- 23.08.10 - 30.09.10 -

Service in de trein

Bordbistro in wagon 25.
Geopend: Amsterdam Centraal -
Frankfurt (Main) Hbf
Ook kranten verkrijgbaar (op basis van
beschikbaarheid)

Zitplaats-service in de 1e klas voor spijs en drank,
verzorgd door ons team.

Service im Zug

Bordbistro im Wagen 25.
Geöffnet: Amsterdam Centraal -
Frankfurt (Main) Hbf
Auch Tageszeitungen erhältlich (nach
Verfügbarkeit)

Am-Platz-Service durch Zugteam in der 1. Klasse
mit Speisen und Getränken.

A clear separation of languages facilitates scanning and skimming as well as comparison of the two languages, because of the thematic and iconic separation on the page.

In Example 8, the use of italics is meant to separate the two languages.

Example 8:
Goeiemore
Good morning
Neem asb kennis dat hierdie funksie gekanselleer
Please note that this function has been cancelled,
is, die Dekaan kan dit nie bywoon nie.
the Dean cannot attend.

The alternation of English and Afrikaans as one continuous paragraph, with italics being the only indication of a particular language being used, slows down reading. Effective and fast reading is crucial when assignments or examination papers are provided to students. Although bi-/multilingual students may compare the different language versions of test or examination questions (for clarification purposes, as described in Van der Walt, 2006 and Van der Walt & Dornbrack, 2011), they still need to be able to skim and scan fast and effectively. A layout that alternates one language after the other in continuous text seems counter-intuitive because it requires that the eye skips every second line to make meaning. My own attempts to create a bilingual text in this way took far longer than putting each language in a separate block, either side by side or directly below one another. This reinforces Sebba's (2012: 12) claim that 'many bilingual written texts cannot be satisfactorily analysed without paying attention to layout and typography'. For him, a conceptualisation of *text-as-image* (Sebba, 2012: 11) is required to analyse and describe multilingual texts, a conceptualisation that is immediately clear in Example 7.

Even less research has been done on how lecturers and teachers develop or reinforce ideas while writing on whiteboards, smartboards or any kind of media that allows 'live writing' (as opposed to prepared and planned writing). I have taken a look at the way in which lecturers organise their multilingual writing on white boards at my own institution. Lecturers' writing also shows how they separate languages by using forward slashes or arrows – again an illustration of *text-as-image* – as Example 9 shows. In this explanation of conjunctions in Xhosa, both Afrikaans and English translations are provided, separated by a forward slash or placed directly below one another.

This writing is, of course, accompanied by oral explanations, which will clarify the meaning and relationships of concepts. There may not be a separation or repetition of languages, a type of language arrangement that Sebba

Example 9:

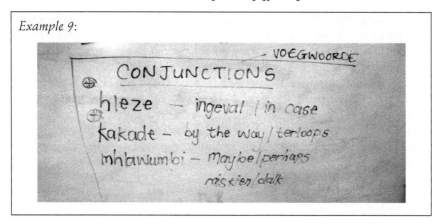

(2012: 15) calls *complementarity*, where the assumption may be that readers are multiliterate. In Example 10, Afrikaans and English appear randomly, probably as students brainstormed on the meaning and implications of a module in Environmental Studies for education students.

Example 10:

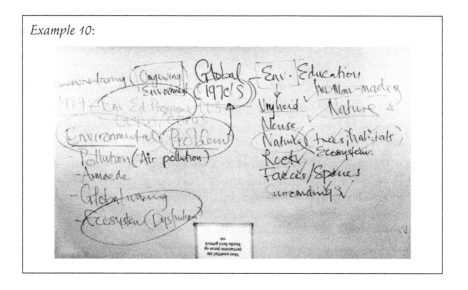

The title *Lewensoriëntering Omgewing* [Life Orientation Environment] at top left links the study of the environment to a current school subject called Life Orientation. The list of environmental problems under the heading Environmental Problems, shows how students came up with different problems in Afrikaans and English (*armoede* is Afrikaans for poverty). On the right-hand side, a list of issues again uses both Afrikaans and English words, *Vryheid* [Freedom], *Mense* [People] and what looks like the Afrikaans *Natuur*, but which could also be English 'nature'. The list shows how some words in the two languages are cognates, which can support learning, but the important point is that no attempt is made to provide parallel translations since the discussion that supports the text will presumably have clarified any comprehension problems.

For PowerPoint presentations, there is currently a bilingual template (Example 11) that lecturers can use to structure their presentations. Again, aspects such as font, colour and spacing structure and facilitate comprehension. The problem remains that word processing programmes are not particularly good at code switching and checking spelling can become time consuming.

Example 11:

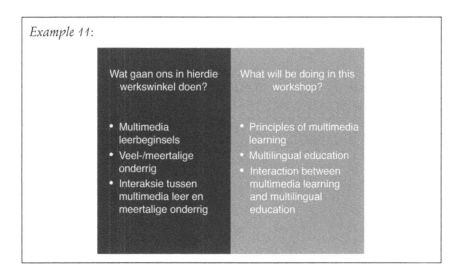

As is the case with instructional code switching, there is little research evidence of the effectiveness in terms of reading efficiency or successful learning of different types of layout. If co-languaging is used merely to clarify meaning (in a Flexible Convergent approach) it may not be all that important to use a layout that would make comparison and effective skimming and scanning possible. For Flexible Multiplicity, where students may need to go back to compare and reinforce their knowledge of terms and content in both languages (as in Example 11), an efficient layout will be more important.

Translanguaging: Ensuring the functional interrelationships of languages

Responsible code switching both ways, in the sense of deliberate switches to strengthen biliteracy, is closely linked to translanguaging practices that require a carefully structured approach to comprehension and production activities in both languages. This means that textbooks and academic articles are presented in two (or more) languages and written assignments are required in two (or more) languages. This is purposeful development of biliteracy that goes beyond code switching. Baker (2006) points out that such a language arrangement ensures that there is no functional separation of languages, for example in the sense that a minoritised language is only used for exploratory talk and the dominant LoLT for reading and writing purposes. Both languages need to be used in all domains and for all purposes. For HE students who need to develop additional academic literacy in English, while maintaining academic literacy in another language, bilingual arrangements that ensure the maintenance of both literacies enhance their chances of academic and professional success.

García (2009: 298, her emphasis) makes the point that

> ... it is not a flexible bilingual arrangement itself that leads to language shift or language maintenance or addition, but *the uses to which these practices are put.* Bilingual education programs which have monolingualism as a goal encourage language mixing in ways that lead to language shift. But bilingual education programs which develop bilingualism not as the full wheels of a bicycle but as an all-terrain vehicle adjusting to the ridges and craters of multilingual communication ... build on translanguaging practices that ensure the functional interrelationship of the languages used in school.

Translanguaging, therefore, encourages learning and meaning making in the way that Hornberger's *continua of biliteracy* require, which is that 'the more their learning contexts allow learners to draw on all points of the continua, the greater are the chances for their full biliterate development'. However, the difference between school-going learners and HE students is a crucial factor that complicates existing bi-/multilingual education frameworks and models.

In the case of HEIs that need to widen access to speakers of minoritised languages, reading material in the form of textbooks and academic articles may not be readily available in such languages. Even in the case of international programmes, academic material in high-status European languages is becoming increasingly scarce because publications in English are regarded as financially advantageous. Journal articles appear mainly in English, as shown in Chapter 4. This advantage results in the perception that writing in other languages is not necessary or useful. Theses and dissertations, where academic language is used and developed, are increasingly written in English with a view to international publication.

However, the picture is not all gloom and doom. Lillis and Curry (2010: 115ff.) discuss the decisions that multilingual academics make when they have to decide whether to publish in English or in a local language. One of the reasons why some academics may decide to publish in a local language is to provide reading material for their students. With reference to the academics whom they interviewed, they conclude that 'their [the academics'] goal is to take part in global disciplinary conversations, and for this to happen, such disciplinary conversations need to be maintained and developed at a local level, through local languages' (Lillis & Curry, 2010: 165).

In officially bi-/multilingual HEIs or in bi-/multilingual programmes, opportunities for translanguaging abound, because material is available in the languages mandated by the various language policies. However, not all institutions will necessarily support translanguaging.

In Africa, scholars often lament the fact that African languages do not have the requisite terminology or reading materials to allow for academic teaching in those languages. However, as Ramani *et al.* (2007: 213) show, this problem is easily overcome when lecturers and students are committed to a programme of study. They report,

> In the first year of teaching, i.e. 2003, there were very few scholarly texts in SsL [SeSotho sa Leboa], and the teacher had to rely on English originals. However, the domain of classroom interaction was entirely in SsL, and the assessment as well. Teacher-produced activity sheets and assessment instructions were always in SsL. So there was a minimal exposure to SsL materials in the form of these activity sheets. The MUST [Multilingual Studies] teachers estimate that from a 30% use of SsL materials (translated by the teachers themselves) in 2003, they have moved to a 70% use of SsL translations in 2006. In other words approximately only 30% of scholarly materials used in MUST are in English.

Paxton (2009: 351) describes how students, in an effort to improve understanding of concepts in an Economics module at the University of Cape Town, use both English and their home languages to discuss and write down their understanding in both languages. The lack of a specialist term in students' home languages is not seen as a disadvantage, as Paxton (2009: 352, 353) explains:

> It is important that translating into the home language 'is more difficult that it is in English' because this means that students are really grappling with conceptual meanings. If the translation 'gives you a whole paragraph in Xhosa when it is only one term in English' as the student explains, then it is more likely that students are providing a personal reconstruction of the concept and gaining a richer understanding of it.

Although students are eventually assessed in English (Scenario A), the oral and written use of African languages are important steps in strengthening academic performance by drawing on students' multilingual competence. The use of tools such as Google Translate even makes it possible for lecturers to check on assignments written in languages that they do not know.

When translanguaging practices include writing in more than one language, lecturers may have to face the possibility that students will 'code switch' when writing, using terms or phrases from various languages in an assignment or test. This may very well be a bridge too far, even for supporters of multilingual HE. However, if students are required to build and demonstrate academic biliteracy, it may be necessary to decide to what extent such a practice will be accommodated.

In their report on students' unwillingness to use local vernacular forms in academic writing, Michael-Luna and Canagarajah refer to the practice of 'code meshing', 'a communicative device used for specific rhetorical and ideological purposes in which a multilingual speaker intentionally integrates local and academic discourse as a form of resistance, reappropriation and/or transformation of the academic discourse'. The unmarked use of more than one language in an academic essay will certainly qualify as a form of resistance, reappropriation as well as transformation of 'accepted' academic writing conventions. However, how do we assess the student writing in Example 12?

This sample of student writing was created in 2009, when a module in Multilingual Education was introduced as part of a teacher certification programme. (See Van der Walt & Ruiters, 2011 for more detail.) Although the topic of the classroom discussion was the use of code switching, students were not asked to write in more than one language. Of the 22 students in the class, only two switched between English and Afrikaans in their essays and when they were asked why they did so, they could not really explain, except that 'it was faster' than sticking to one language.

Managing the assessment of code-meshed/code-switched academic essays remains a challenge. One requirement could be that students use well-formed, academic discourse, whatever the language may be.

Preview–view–review: A form of language separation?

As a form of language separation, the strategy to 'preview' in one language (introduce or contextualise a lesson), 'view' it in another (to explain and develop a particular concept or theme) and then 'review' (reinforcing the concept or theme in the same language as that used in the 'preview' phase) is used at bilingual secondary schools (García, 2009: 301). When a home language is used consistently for preview and review phases, the implication is that the language used for the most important and longest part of the lesson is the dominant LoLT, with other languages acting as bridges to the LoLT – an example of Flexible Convergence. When the choice of languages for the various phases varies, the implication is that biliteracy should develop in both languages, which makes this strategy an example of a Flexible Multiplicity approach. García (2009: 301) points out that for learners who are at the beginning stages of becoming biliterate, the

Example 12:

Na aanleiding van die artikel *Codeswitching in Multilingual Classrooms: a Teachers' debate* skaar ek myself by die gebruik **van** kodewisseling. My redes hiervoor sal vervolgens bespreek word.

Why is codeswitching important and necessary in the classroom?

As Faleni states in the above mentioned article, codeswitching is used for various purpose. This includes management and control of the classroom; where it is necessary for the teacher to instruct pupils in their mothertongue to insure that they understand the instructions they have to follow or to control any disruptive behavior in the language that is most effective, the language in which their parents discipline them as well. The second reason is to effectively increase the vocabulary of the pupils. Dit maak logies sin dat 'n leerder 'n nuwe konsep makliker sal kan verstaan indien hy of sy dit kan koppel aan sinoniem daarvoor in hul moedertaal. Dit is wel van uiterste belang dat die onderwyser slegs die konsep in die moedertaal deurgee as 'n beginpunt om die konsep onder die knie te kry. Die leerders moet dan verder onderrig word in die taal wat die vak aangebied word, sodat die res van die konnotasies in die addisionele taal aangeleer word. Laastens is dit belangrik dat die leerders kern konsepte verstaan. Dit koppel goed aan by die vorige punt bespreek, maar hier mag dit dalk nodig wees dat die onderwyser meer as net die sinoniem in die moedertaal moet gee. Futher explanation may be necessary and it can even be helpful to include idiomatic expressions in the mothertongue to bring the pupils to understand the key concept.

Wat is die faktore wat tot effektiewe kode wisseling sal lei?

Faleni noem die volgedende drie faktore. Conscious use (meaning that the teacher should continiously be aware of the use of codeswitching and know what impact it

advantage of starting off (previewing) in the second language would be to pre-teach subject-specific vocabulary. This strategy is recommended in CLIL contexts by Antonacci and O'Callaghan (2011).

The use of a home or community language to contextualise difficult concepts resonates with my own research in secondary school classrooms (Van der Walt *et al.*, 2001), but the languages were never as clearly separated as suggested by the preview–view–review approach. In the case of HE, where students have developed academic literacy in other languages, the preview phase could exploit literacy in another language by comparing and *contrasting* subject-specific vocabulary, rather than sticking to just one language. In cases where students use other languages outside the classroom without having developed academic literacy in them, explanations of terminology that use the home or community language will require code switching, which again provides the opportunity to compare and clarify concepts in different languages rather than separate them. In a flexible convergent approach, where assignments and examinations need to be delivered in English, the structure of a lecture would then probably be a code-switched preview phase, followed by the lecture phase in English, concluded by a code-switched review phase. In a flexible multiplicity approach, English (or any other dominant LoLT) would be alternated with another language.

Although this particular strategy is not, to my mind, entirely relevant to multilingual HE classrooms, it does present the opportunity for providing contextualising explanations in home or community languages. When the more familiar language also happens to be a low status language that is not used regularly for academic purposes, the challenge will be the same as when students use their home languages to discuss academic content: there must be a move from exploratory talk to discourse-specific academic language. As has been indicated in Example 6 above, the perception that academic terms do not exist in certain languages is only that: there is no reason why techniques such as transference, transliteration and even coining new words cannot be used in HE classrooms.

For lecturers who wish to use other languages but who may not feel that they are fluent enough in local languages or proficient enough for confident code switching, careful planning of lectures according to the preview–view–review strategy may be a way to start using such languages. Using a brief introduction and conclusion that can be read aloud (supported by notes or a PowerPoint presentation to compare terms explicitly) may show their willingness to use such languages and may decrease the distance between lecturer and students.

Interpretation strategies

Simultaneous translation as a teaching strategy is not widely known. However, it has been seen as a possible strategy to support students who are not fluent in the language of instruction, particularly in classes where formal lecturing is the mainstay of lecturer–student interaction.

This type of multilingual strategy is being tested mainly at the North-west University in South Africa and also at the University of Johannesburg, University of the Free State and Stellenbosch University, using various languages and assessing student comprehension and performance based on experimental and control groups. Van Rooyen (2005: 85) describes the system and procedure as follows:

With the Whispered Interpreting System, the interpreter sits among the audience, listening to the floor language like any other member of the audience, and does not require special equipment to hear the speaker(s). The interpreter then uses an ultra-sensitive radio-transmitter microphone to render the interpreted version of the message in a very low voice, which is received by listeners via the radio-receiver headphones.

I sat in on one of these classes myself and saw students entering the class and taking a set of headphones from the case in which the interpreter carries them. Although I could hear the interpreter behind me, I was not distracted by what essentially sounded like students whispering to each other. My impression has been supported by evidence reported by Verhoef (2006: 98) who also finds that students do not experience the interpreting service as disruptive. Van Rooyen (2005) reports on an experimental study with five groups of students:

- Mother-tongue speakers of an African language who received instruction in Afrikaans, making use of interpretation to English;
- Mother-tongue speakers of an African language who received instruction in English with no interpretation services;
- Afrikaans-speaking students who received instruction in English with no interpretation services;
- A control group of mother-tongue speakers of an African language who received instruction in Afrikaans with no interpretation services;
- A control group of Afrikaans-speaking students who received instruction in Afrikaans with no interpretation services.

Van Rooyen (2005: 86) finds in his study that 'African language speakers who received instruction in English improved 3.5% more than their counterparts, who attended Afrikaans classes with English interpretation, but this is not a statistically significant difference. Similarly, while there is a difference of 2.9% in favour of students listening to the interpretation into English (E1B) over those listening to the lecturer only in Afrikaans (C1B), this is not statistically significant'.

The use of simultaneous translation in this form also means that lecturers need to be aware of occasions where questions or comments from students may need to be repeated (by the lecturer), so that these can be interpreted too, thereby ensuring that students who use the service can also participate in the discussion (Verhoef, 2006: 92), which of course implies that the lecturer is bi-/multilingual.

Further empirical research is ongoing, as a 2008 volume edited by Verhoef and Du Plessis shows, since the impact of improved performance for government-subsidy purposes is not something that any South African university can ignore. However, Beukes and Pienaar (2006) conclude in their study on the use of whispering interpretation that '[t]he language attitudes and beliefs (ideologies) and the hegemony of English in the context of the linguistic diversity of the learner profile at a South African metropolitan university (in this case the University of Johannesburg) make such a service unlikely to benefit more than a very small percentage of learners'. The use of technology in delivering course content, particularly the ease and unobtrusiveness of the whispering interpretation, seems a very attractive option. Ultimately the hegemonic perception that proficiency in academic English is the mark of an educated person may be the one obstacle that such a solution cannot overcome.

Conclusion

Edstrom (2006: 337), in the context of language teaching at school level, appeals to teachers' moral obligation to identify the needs of their students and to make decisions as to what teaching and learning strategies may be most effective. Her appeal that teachers should develop awareness of real-life language use and not be bound by more traditional pedagogic practices links up with Baldauf's view of micro-language planning. Since institutional language policies cannot predict the language profile of each class, lecturers need to develop context-sensitive strategies to support learning in other languages. As Heller (1999: 274) says in the conclusion to her study,

> We can, in other words, put together what we see people doing with language with what we found out about the resources at their disposal and about their access to communicative situations where their participation, of whatever kind, might make a difference (in a variety of ways, both short term and long term) to themselves and to others.

As Chapter 1 indicated, the role of global market forces, national imperatives as well as students (as adults) and their parents mean that a view of multilingual education from the perspective of lecturers, programmes and institutions will have to be widened. Transnationally mobile students, as lucrative sources of income, may dilute the demands of national governments to provide epistemological access to minoritised groups of students. The argument in this chapter is that planning for multilingual practices needs to happen at classroom level by thinking beyond institutional language policies. It is certainly difficult for institutional managers to plan for a fluid and ever-changing context and the solution is often to formalise arrangements for two or three particular languages (that are kept separate) or to institutionalise monolingualism by pretending that one language, mostly English, will solve throughput problems.

In Europe, the entry requirements for university study include a specific level of performance in certain languages, as evidenced by the language portfolio and language passport (CiLT, 2006). Requirements for a specific level of performance in a local language as a prerequisite for university entrance in South Africa (and the rest of Africa) do not, to my knowledge, exist.

On the basis that home language proficiency may give an indication of a student's potential to transfer skills to a dominant language, it seems to be a relatively simple step for HEIs to develop tests of language proficiency for regional languages. The proposal is not that all home language speakers of these languages should take the test but that the performance of those students who studied the language up to school exit level may be indicative of their chances of success at developing academic biliteracy. As an exit requirement, particularly for students in education, health sciences and the law, knowledge of local languages for professional purposes will confirm the importance of such languages. The focus, in such cases, would not only be on proficiency in the powerful languages, notably English, but also on the degree to which all languages that the student has at her disposal can result in a productive engagement with academic content by using and developing biliterate academic language practices. Once more, the proposal is not that all students be forced to comply with a language requirement but to reward those who do by awarding a degree with a language endorsement.

As a result of the Stellenbosch University 'Code of conduct for language in the classroom' (2008), which enumerates the responsibilities and expectations of students and lecturers, classroom language use is negotiable particularly at the start of the course. This process foregrounds discussions about language use and perceptions about the kind of access that language affords. The fact that students and lecturers may sometimes continue negotiations throughout a course is an indication of their agency. That discussions like these may lead to subversion of official policy to improve learning, particularly through using more than one language or non-recognised varieties of language, is just one of the many ways in which multilingual practices flourish in HE classrooms.

Notes

(1) My translation. The original read: 'Overigens vormden de "twee Leuvens" een dynamische tandem in de internationale organisaties van katholieke universiteiten'.
(2) The history of merging HEIs in South Africa requires a separate book. There are many issues that still need to be resolved in the aftermath of these institutional changes.
(3) The data have not been reported on formally. First-year students were asked to comment on their ability to understand and develop academic vocabulary in code-switched lectures at the start of the semester and again six months later. The lectures themselves were recorded and transcribed.
(4) Current government policy still uses the divisive ethnic groupings legislated by the now defunct Population Registration Act in an effort to track the degree of transformation at South African universities. These universities have to report to the Ministry of Education regarding the demographic profile of staff and students.
(5) The term 'Coloured' is a controversial category for people who did not fit into the Apartheid government's race-based categories. All the so-called racial categories are still used today to determine whether people in these groups are better represented in the traditionally 'white' universities.
(6) This option has only recently become available (see Stockwell, 2007) and is being investigated at Stellenbosch University by Dr N. Klapwijk.

5 From *Mono* to *Multi*: New Thinking about Higher Education

Introduction: Higher Education, Prestige and Power

The prestige of higher education (HE) is evident, among others, in the lengths parents will go to to ensure that their children are able to attend HE institutions (HEIs): from the 'college fund' in the USA that is started as early as pre-school level to the tragic case of a parent queuing to register her child at a local university and getting trampled to death during the surge when the gates opened (see Chapter 2). Entrance requirements, pre-admission assessments, school-level preparation and high fees are just some of the organisational characteristics that signal exclusivity and stature. That such an enterprise should also be linked to high-status languages, and increasingly to English as *the* high-status language, is hardly surprising.

Multilingual HE, and English-plus HE in particular, requires a watering down of the power and prestige of one language while endowing lesser-used languages with the status of HE use. Multilingual HE privileges English-plus multilingualism and therefore challenges the perception that 'English is enough'. The status of English (and other powerful languages) has meant that its competent use up to now has acted as an automatic, international passport. In contrast, the perspective brought by English-plus multilingualism, as described in Chapter 4, implies more than just a passive and even patronising acknowledgement of multilingualism: it demands the active use of other languages and literacies. Despite the qualifier *English plus*, the emphasis is on the substantive *multilingualism*, which evokes the concept of multi-competence and the promise of 'various studies of the cognitive aspects of multilingualism in which bilinguals have turned out to be better language learners than monolinguals' (Jessner, 2008: 21). However, in this movement towards acknowledging the power of multilingualism in education, it is necessary to guard against oversimplifications of the role of language in learning and teaching.

From *Mono* to *Multi*: Arguments against False Dichotomies

The metaphor of ecology is often invoked in support of a multilingual perspective and the use of local languages in education, as Hornberger (2007) does, and which Street (2011) links to literacy as situated practice. I make the argument in Chapter 1 that HE is multilingual even when only one language is officially used for teaching and learning purposes. In subsequent chapters, I rely on Hornberger, Barton and Street's work to support my call for a multilingual HE, taking into account the specific role played by English. However, in this final chapter, it is also necessary to look critically at current arguments in support of the role of language and languages in education to avoid simplistic perspectives and solutions. In the sections that follow, two particular dichotomies will be discussed. First, the view of language as a tool as opposed to language as an identity marker will be discussed as a dichotomy that often emerges from the ecology metaphor. Second, the dichotomy of content and language and its embodiment as Content and Language Integrated Learning (CLIL) will be problematised as a form of literacy education that attempts to develop situated language proficiency.

Language as a tool and language as an identity marker

Although the central argument in this book is for the use of multilingual literacies in HE, the argument from the perspective of the situatedness of academic literacy practices is not primarily concerned with what has been called the 'sociodiversity argument' (Brink, 2006: 159) or, linking up with the ecology metaphor, an 'environmentalist position' (Coleman, 2006: 2). In other words, the primary task of HE is not to conserve minority languages, although an argument for multilingual HE would certainly support the continued existence of minoritised languages. The use of the ecology metaphor in multilingual HE needs to be framed by the view of learning as socially constructed, as has been argued throughout the book, and in a nuanced way, since nuance is what Edwards (2008: 19) calls for in the 'new' ecology of language discussions.

The *language as a tool for learning* perspective may sound diametrically opposed to the discourse of ecology. However, it is important from a view of learning and teaching as socially constituted and executed actions that *language as a tool*, and therefore *languages as tools for learning*, include *languages as identity markers* when the process of learning and eventual success or failure are related to the use of a particular language in a particular community.

From the *language as an identity marker* perspective, a unitary or an essentialist view of identity seems out of place in twenty-first century societies, where grandmothers learn to text and Skype, children of parents who live separately shuttle from one community to another in the space of a week and working parents rush from board meeting to kitchen. Although a different constellation of their identities may be required when changes occur in settings, participants and language, people will not necessarily experience their identities as fragmented. For many people, their multilingual ability is an aspect of their identity in the same way that a professional identity or a gendered identity would be. As Marx (2002: 277) notes, 'all people have multiple identities which change in interaction with other community members'.

Mills (2001: 8) describes the different ways in which bilinguals *synthesise* the worlds belonging to their different languages, either responding differently to each context in which a particular language is required (e.g. home and university) or not feeling the conscious need to change from one environment to the next. Language may be the defining factor in the various settings or it may be secondary to other identity markers like religion or class or ethnicity.

Conflating the linguistic expressions of these two mental representations in educational contexts may elicit the criticism that the easy 'middle ground' is sought or that the complexity of both positions is ignored. However, such conflation is necessary to avoid antagonistic and reductive perspectives on language so that the 'middle ground' can become a space in which the complexity of multilingual educational contexts is prioritised and acknowledged. In that uncomfortable position (on the fence as it were), we can see that in HE the distinction between language as an identity marker *or* as an instrument is not tenable. In the linear progression of a sentence, we can indicate this complex relationship by starting the sentence with *language as a tool* or with *language as an identity*, but we arrive at the same point, for example:

- Language is a *tool* that enables/prevents the development of an academic (even pre-professional[1]) *identity*, for example, when students are/are not proficient in the language of learning and teaching (LoLT).
- Language is an *identity* marker that enables/prevents the successful use of language as a *tool* to become a member of a particular academic community in the process of qualifying for a particular profession.

In both formulations, the unique and highly conventionalised nature of academic language is the centripetal element that transforms as it melds the instrumental and identity aspects. Like a whirlpool or a tornado, these aspects may still be perceived as separate along the edges but are increasingly integrated as they move towards the centre. The centre, perhaps the eye of the storm, would represent the point where multilingual students are successful users of more than one LoLT. This conceptualisation of identity, as it is linked to language in HE, is based on the view developed by Norton (2000), based on an idea mooted by West (1992): a view of identity as grounded in desire – 'the desire for recognition, the desire for affiliation and the desire for safety and security' (Norton, 2000: 8). For multilinguals and multi-dialectals, this perspective requires maintaining multiple identities that may be split according to such desires.

When we foreground and isolate (for argument's sake) the role of languages as tools to mark the identity of speakers, we can say that language functions as a tool at different levels of connectedness to identities or aspects of identity. This is a different view to that espoused by Kirkpatrick (2007: 12), who distinguishes between identity and communication and sees language users moving along an 'identity–communication continuum' – particularly in the sense of using 'broad' or 'basilectal' varieties of English in a personal (identity) setting and moving along to an 'educated' or 'acrolectal' variety for professional, communication purposes. The unfortunate and simplistic opposition of identity and communication as the two poles of a continuum suggests that varieties are somehow more indicative of identity than educated versions of such a variety and, conversely, that communication is more effective in an educated variety. O'Connor (2001: 159) laments the fact that the conceptualisation of identity in educational performance is so simplistic:

> [I]dentities are simultaneously structured and cultured and operate differentially across place and time. However, the traditions that generally characterize sociologists' efforts to make sense of group differences in achievement have differentially denied this more complex rendering of how people are positioned in the social world.

Although all attempts to make the link between language and identity visible in diagrammatic form are doomed to failure, I will attempt to illustrate the changeability referred to above as levels of connectedness or association (even affinity in the sense of similarity and empathy) by representing this phenomenon as unstable and overlapping circles that may wax and wane as the context of the speakers changes and their desire to be seen as a member of a particular community grows stronger or weaker (as the dashed lines indicate in some of the diagrams below). This is a social view of identity in an attempt to avoid the 'mistaken dichotomy', as Wenger (1998: 146) calls it, which is 'to wonder whether the unit of analysis of identity should be the community or the person'. I am in full agreement with Wenger that 'the focus must be on their mutual constitution' (1995: 146) and therefore refrain from using the term 'social identity' (as used by O'Connor, 2001; O'Connor et al., 2009). We can see this in the following examples of 'mutual constitution':

(1) For a bilingual person who grows up with Wolof and French in Dakar, Senegal, education and identity will coincide as products of language affiliation (a 'positive dual identity' according to Swigart (1994: 186)) and may remain stable as he or she completes schooling and HE by using French and obtains a job in the local community (e.g. a teacher) using Wolof for daily communication or for lower primary school teaching.

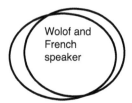

(2) For a bilingual child who grows up with Setswana and Tshivenda, or a monolingual child who has to learn a LoLT at school, the home and/or community language(s) may be the first circle(s) of identity

association, and the addition of English at school and HE level will add an additional layer of identity; both identities and associations may remain strong if he or she were to move to a city like Johannesburg and become a partner in an international law firm, with one or both of the other languages remaining as identity markers because of the geographical location and multilingual nature of Johannesburg.

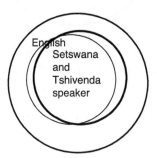

(3) For a monolingual German speaker who learns English at school and then completes an MBA at Harvard University in the USA, English will create a powerful identity pull, which may be particularly strong, and, then, depending on the job taken up at the end of the study period, may become even stronger or may weaken. (The challenge of integrating these two identities is obviously not as simple as the previous sentence may suggest – see Kramsch (2004) for a discussion of German and US English cross-cultural communication.) Should the speaker take up a job in an international firm in New York, the affinity with English may gradually overlap and in time may replace German as the first level of connectedness. Should the person return to a local firm in Germany, the identity affiliation with English may gradually wane.

(4) For a speaker of Turkish who emigrates to the USA and completes a professional qualification there, the initial identity affiliation with Turkish may be replaced by English, particularly when there is no further contact with a Turkish-speaking community. Should the person be involved in one of the so-called Saturday schools for Turkish-speaking children, the identity affiliation with Turkish can lead to a 'Turkish American identity' (Otcu, 2009: 32), which is part of the broader societal 'Americanness' without losing touch with the smaller community's 'Turkishness' (Otcu, 2009: 34).

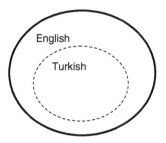

(5)   There are unwilling bi-/multilinguals who, despite having grown up bilingually, may feel no affiliation to a dominant language; for example, Irish speakers in the Republic of Ireland, who have a very strong identity of being Irish, without necessarily ever using Irish Gaelic. Similar examples are Flemish speakers who need to use French daily if they work in Brussels, but who would not claim a part of their identity as French in any way. In these cases only one language becomes essential for identity affiliation and such examples are often used as emblematic for a perceived direct relation between language and culture. These very personal and conflictual relations to language would be difficult to represent diagrammatically – perhaps something like the following:

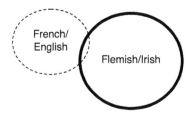

What these diagrams attempt to indicate is that identity is not stable or immutable and when seen from the perspective of language and education, will result in affiliations with language that change depending on the context and the use to which language can be put in that context. A dynamic model of bi-/multilingualism as proposed by García requires a 'flexible multiplicity' (2009: 297) as essential for flourishing in complex social arrangements. For students in HE who need to exhibit their membership of the academic community as they prepare for some kind of work-related professional community while they continue living in their own communities (at home, in a student residence, doing temporary jobs), 'identity is therefore not to be viewed as a fixed or stable characteristic of an individual, but rather as a process of continuous change and permutation which is comprised of cultural identity, social role, and discursive voice' (Marx, 2002: 266).

This statement by Marx can be applied to any HE student. However, the difference that multilingualism brings to this view of identity is that it complicates not only cultural identity but also social role and discursive voice. In the case of cultural identity, students may find that they move from mono- or multicultural school settings to a multicultural but homogenising HE setting where membership of an academic community may be a stronger facet of identity than a particular cultural membership. If I am the only person in my village attending HE, the academic aspect of my identity may feature much more strongly than my cultural or linguistic heritage. Such a part of my identity would create expectations for my social role as a possible leader in my community and that may, in turn, provide a motivational light for or cast a burdensome shadow over my attempts to succeed at my studies. My discursive voice will be a prism of various languages as a multilingual 'whose communicative practices include translanguaging' (García, 2009: 60 and 99): reading in one language, speaking in another, translating and switching. More importantly, cultural identity, social role and discursive voice can blend in acts of resistance to a monolingual HE culture, where students foreground their multilingual identities through 'transformational acts of resistance' whereby they attempt to 'pluralise the dominant academic discourse by bringing local, vernacular discourses into academic discourse' (Michael-Luna & Canagarajah, 2007: 57).

Language as a tool to develop a particular professional identity concentrates the attention and ambition of graduate and postgraduate students. Just like the German student (in (3) above) who hones her English to succeed at a prestigious American Ivy League university, the student doing a communication course in Tswana as part of his Business Management diploma at Boston College in Johannesburg would want to succeed at his business where he will employ mainly Tswana speakers. However, before these students reach their objectives, their respective ambitions for English and Tswana will take a backseat to their academic studies in German and English. The German speaker will have the advantage of having studied in German at school level. The South African may have had the advantage of schooling in English, but his home language could be any of the 11 official languages or one of the unofficial languages in the country. As described in Chapter 2, HE increasingly sees students coming from a particular language background, studying in another language and moving to a profession that will include and may demand the use of yet other languages. As Wenger (1998: 153, emphasis added) points out, 'membership in a community of practice translates into an identity *as a form of competence*'; therefore, if membership of the academic community and subsequently of a chosen profession is the desired identity marker, being competent in the requisite languages is probably the most important tool towards that goal.

However, what happens if, based on the superficial elements of identity (e.g. citizenship, gender, race or class), the competence in a particular language is assumed to be absent ab initio, or if assumed competence is gradually revealed as insufficient? The first instance, that is, the absence of competence, is often the case with minorities and transnational students who are assumed to lack the required level of linguistic knowledge and who are often expected to take language entrance tests. The second, and often more painful process, is when home language speakers of the LoLT do not master the academic discourse and fall behind. These two examples can and do, of course, coincide and their effect on identity 'as a form of competence' (in Wenger's words) is predictable. O'Connor (2001: 160) provides a useful terminology for the way in which identity is shaped, confirmed and re-confirmed by *reflection*, which 'registers how social identity is experienced as a consequence of how individuals interpret and subsequently perform their identities' and *refraction*, which 'registers how the same individuals experience social identity as a consequence of how others, given their own structured and cultured positionings, make sense of and, subsequently, respond to the individual'. The lack of response by the dominant culture to the individual is experienced by minority or international students all over the world and prevents the 'engagement of community members' by their 'acknowledgement of each other' (in Wenger's words). Norton (2000: 130) points out, 'Language is not just a neutral form of communication but a practice that is socially constructed in the hegemonic events, activities and processes that constitute daily life – the practices that are considered normal by the dominant society'.

A case in point

In her study of the experiences of international students at a German university, Schumann (2008: 38) reports the words of a Chinese student who had lived and studied in Germany 'for many years'. The lack of 'membership' of the community of practice is obvious (English in square brackets):

Ich finde es immer so schade. Ich habe so lange Jahre in Deutschland bleibe. Schon fast 5 Jahre. Meine Sprache is immer nicht so gut. Wenn ich mehr Kontakt mit Deutschen hätte veilleicht werde, könnte ich meine Sprache immer verbessern. Aber die Gelegenheit ist ein bisschen seltener. Ich habe nur Kontakt met Deutschen bei den Veranstaltungen. Aber die Veranstaltungen nur neunzig Minutes dauern. Nach der Veranstaltung alle weg. Fehlt mir einfach die Gelegenheit mit den Deutschen zu sprechen. [It's such a pity. I've been living for such a long time in Germany. Almost five years already. My German is still not good. If I had more contact with Germans, I could have improved. But there are so few opportunities. I only have contact with Germans at lectures which only last 90 minutes. After that everybody is gone and so is the opportunity to speak German.]

In the same study, a student from England, in a Department of English where language could not have been a stumbling block, notes that 'The fellow students in a course are often strangers, there is little feeling of belonging together' and another (or maybe the same) English student comments that 'a lot of foreign students seem to feel comfortable with the people of their country' (Schumann, 2008: 42).

When we look at the social circumstances of these students, it is not only the use of *a* language but also the language practices in social contexts that create the potential for success at HE level. Language practices can have an effect even before entrance to HE. In her studies of the narratives of students and lecturers at a South African university, Leibowitz (2009: 89) shows how early experiences with language – talking, arguing, listening to stories – can shape personalities that excel at HE, irrespective of the language in which this happens.

Reporting on British-born or UK-domiciled students who use a 'vernacular variety' of English, Preece (2009: 13) notes that these students are aware of the fact that they need to adapt to what they perceive as 'posh' or 'proper' English: 'adaptability appears to be one-sided in that they do not expect "posh" students to use "slang", the onus is on them to adapt'.

As this discussion shows, an argument for the use of more than one language is not simply an instrumentalist or an identity issue. Geeraerts (2003: 28) puts it succinctly when he says,

> [T]hose welcoming international English as an opportunity for all to participate equally in a global culture may easily be blind to the fact that access to English is not equal for all. And the champions of linguistic diversity may readily overlook the fact that the people they purport to defend often prefer the educational and professional opportunities provided by the non-native language (as appears to be the case, for instance, in most African countries that are ex-colonies of Britain).

For multilingual HE, the management of identities is crucial for successful learning. Charting a course between the demands of academic disciplines and the management of burgeoning social and professional identities in a diversifying world is the challenge for HE.

Language and content: Separating the inseparable

It seems facile to make the point that language and content have always been integrated, but it is important to remember that their perceived separation has resulted from efforts to support language development in non-credit bearing courses, that were seen as outside the core of a particular course of study. The call for language support often came from lecturers in these core or 'content' subjects because they felt they did not have the know-how to do the job. It seems as if we have come full circle, with language education specialists insisting that language development belongs in the teaching of 'content' subjects.

Orientations towards language teaching and learning, including the development of literacy (in general), have developed to the point where it is recognised that engagement in a community of practice requires effective communication, in the case of HE, communication with peers and teaching staff. Such communication would entail different levels of discipline-specific discourse competence, which may be as problematic for home-language speakers of the LoLT as for non-home language speakers.

One of the solutions offered to this problem is that of CLIL, which argues for a kind of 'just in time' or 'no more than is needed' learning (Graddol, 2006: 72). The argument for the integration of language teaching with the so-called content subjects is summarised succinctly by Knapp (2011: 52):

> [T]he integration of content and language learning is seen to have many advantages: the acquisition of subject specific terminology in English as well as the acquisition of subject or domain specific linguistic means of communicating about subject matter, including the realisation of typical academic language functions in English. In addition, practical and economic reasons play a role for integrating content and language learning in university studies. The mismatch between the increasing demands on students in terms of knowledge and competences to be acquired and – at the same time – a shorter time span for university studies contributes to the attractiveness of a 'getting two for the price of one' solution.

In Chapters 1, 2 and 3, I point to some of the limitations of CLIL, but my concern in this chapter is, first, with the either/or nature of a choice between what is perceived to be 'generic' language support and 'subject-specific' or 'specialised' language support and, second, with the transitional model of bi-/multilingual education that CLIL seems to imply.

Longitudinal studies on the success of CLIL at the primary and secondary school level are starting to emerge, as discussed in Chapter 3. Claims for its success at HE level, particularly in the long term, require more research, and even when such data appear, any conclusions will be dependent on the context of the particular study. At school level, a number of factors support the possibility of CLIL being successful, with teacher training being the most obvious one. As Knapp (2011: 52) points out, school populations are generally more homogeneous than is the case in HE, and CLIL is supplemented by additional English-language teaching. Even under these circumstances at school level, a longitudinal study at secondary school level by Whittaker, Llinares and McCabe (2011) shows that the results for a CLIL approach are mixed. Commenting on various school-level studies that have attempted to measure differences in English ability in CLIL courses, Airey (2009: 22) concludes that 'no measurable difference could be shown'.

Airey's (2009) study on the way in which HE Physics students learn English in the course of attending lectures describes essentially a CLIL approach (SPRINT in Swedish), and he finds that students who have never been taught in English struggle at first-year level, to the extent that they are not able to discuss disciplinary concepts in English. However, Airey (2009: 89, italics in the original) concludes that *'above an initial threshold of competence in disciplinary English, students give descriptions with similar levels of disciplinarity in both English and Swedish, regardless of the language that has been used to teach them'*. These are important findings for HE because, while acknowledging the ease with which students manage two languages, they point to the problems that students will experience if there is no support beyond the CLIL approach for language development.

CLIL is essentially an immersion approach, which can become submersion if students are simply expected to cope with instruction in English or another dominant language without additional support. Additional support should acknowledge the need for more general language support in English and in other languages, to allow the student to draw on all available resources. If CLIL is shorthand for a move towards English-only instruction, as the increasing availability of textbooks in English seems to signify, its relevance to HE must be questioned.

The effort of becoming a member of the dominant academic community, which involves a particular language community as well, may ultimately be too much for students, despite the fact that they cope with academic material. If their multilingual identity (as argued above) is not engaged in the process of making meaning when engaging with texts, their integration into the academic community may be compromised. As Wenger (1998: 160) notes,

> The work of reconciliation may be the most significant challenge faced by learners who move from one community of practice to another. For instance when a child moves from a family to a classroom, when an immigrant moves from one culture to another, or when an employee moves from the ranks to a management position, learning involves more than appropriating new pieces of information. Learners must often deal with conflicting forms of individuality and competence as defined in different communities.

That a feeling of 'strangeness' or alienation can result in academic failure is a foregone conclusion, which is why HEIs invest much strategic energy and finance in induction, introduction or integration programmes. Nikolarea (2004: 253) calls for an 'eclectic' approach to English-language teaching in 'non-English universities', which puts 'very good knowledge of English and the language of instruction (and the scientific discourse in *both languages*) in [*sic*] *equal footing*'; this is essentially the argument that I make in Chapter 4.

CLIL does not only make great demands on students; it also assumes that lecturers can automatically teach in English. The degree to which lecturers can manage this kind of teaching is described by (among others) Airey (2004), Hellekjaer and Wilkinson (2003) and Knapp (2011) – each mentions the fact that HE lecturers are not necessarily trained for this task.

The extent to which HEIs are able to develop the teaching abilities of their academic staff is a sensitive issue, particularly because of the status of English in academic contexts. Training initiatives for lecturers, particularly when they have been publishing in English journals, may be seen to imply that they are not educated or that they are not specialists in their fields. As Yusof *et al.* (2004: 531) indicate, lecturers' perceptions of their abilities to teach in English often differ substantially from their students' experiences, with the most important problem being 'clarity of lecture content'.

Furthermore, there is probably a limit to the time and energy that academics can spend on developing their teaching abilities *and* their language proficiency. When these two are combined with raising awareness of multilingual teaching practices, language development initiatives can be linked to institutions' internationalisation drives and/or attempts to widen access to speakers of minoritised languages. By combining awareness-raising seminars with a focus on the development of multilingual proficiencies, the focus of academic staff development can move from personal inadequacies to the changing and increasingly multilingual context of HE.

As with students, lecturers' multilingual abilities can be exploited and expanded, as shown in the following example.

A case in point

To a large extent, lecturers at HEIs outside English-speaking countries have the ability to use more than one language for instructional purposes. Knapp (2011: 65), in her study of the way in which English is used as a LoLT at a German university, shows how one lecturer (L) co-constructs meaning with students to make up for English language deficits. In the extract below, one of the students (S1) comes from the USA (as indicated by the abbreviation US) but has a good command of German.

L: ok (..) you take a bucket, collect a sample.

(More explanations follow.)

L: you take a shovel. (--) do you say shovel‽
S1 (US):   yes,
Ss: yes, yes, shovel.

(More explanations follow.)

L: we put a Schablone (..) what is Schablone auf Englisch‽
S1 (US):   I don't know
L: who knows Schablone in English‽
Ss: no (..) no don't know
S1 (US):   ah, an array

Later on:

L: ditches (-) do you say that‽ (-) oh my English is so bad (..)
            I don't know (-) Gräben (..)
            it has ups and downs, valleys, high points
S1 (US):   oh troughs‽

The fact that there is one student who is able to supply English equivalents is fortunate in this case. However, the teaching strategy that requires students to contrast the two languages is useful in this case because it builds their understanding as well as their language proficiency. This is an example of cross-linguistic work, as described in Chapter 4.

In this case, the co-construction of meaning is a strategy that engages students and helps the lecturer. The lecturer is clearly not shy to admit to his or her inability to come up with the right term in English. Discussing classroom observations of this nature, as well as lecturers sharing multilingual practices that work for them, may be more effective than outside interventions to 'improve English language proficiency'. It is interesting that some of the objections by students to lecturers' language ability, as described by Yusof *et al.* (2004), relate to lecturers code switching when they teach and to the fact that their lecturers do *not* use English outside the classroom. Clearly, students share societal evaluations of language practices, for example, that code switching is not appropriate for educational settings and that CLIL implies a monolingual campus, that is, the use of the LoLT outside the classroom. In multilingual settings, such perceptions need to be managed by lecturers at the start of their courses to create the necessary space for translanguaging practices.

Moving Forward: Future Directions for Research in Multilingual Higher Education

In previous chapters, there have been references to practices that are successful or prevalent in particular, multilingual HE settings. It is clear that these practices require research in terms of their effectiveness for learning. All the strategies discussed in Chapter 4 need to be investigated in a variety of contexts and with a variety of languages so as to refine our understanding of a multilingual pedagogy for HE. The particular items mentioned next seem to be the most important because their use is either widespread or calls for their implementation are increasing.

The effects of multilingual strategies on learning

In the example of the lecturer who asks a student what the English translation for a German term is (see previous 'Case in point'), one can assume that the terms in English and German will be foregrounded for this student. However, we do not know how well the rest of the class will have understood this exchange and to what extent they will remember the two terms. Even in cases where lecturers contrast terminology more explicitly and where students are asked to repeat or write down the terms, it is not clear how much they will remember and to what extent the use of both languages deepens their understanding of concepts. Language use, teaching style and personal orientations to code switching are intricately linked and it may be difficult to separate judgements about language proficiency from the ability to understand code-switched speech. Even lecturers' status and the importance of a particular course may influence students' willingness to accept code switching and to learn from it. As was shown in the study by Van der Walt and Steyn (2004b), students quickly lose patience with lecturers' language use when they find a subject difficult or when the lecturer has a particular accent. As we have argued (Van der Walt & Kidd, 2012), merely making multilingual materials and strategies available does not mean that they will be used effectively.

A more formidable barrier, however, is the way in which understanding is assessed. If we want to assess the depth of students' understanding of code-switched lectures, we will have to accept their code switching as well, in both speech and writing. Hellekjaer and Wilkinson (2003) are concerned about the fact that students may not be able to read as much and cover the same amount of work in English as is possible in their home languages. Students appear to share this fear, since they indicate in the study by Knapp (2011: 56) that the reasons why they would rather attend the German equivalent of an English course offering are because of 'less participation on the part of the students, lack of subject-specific vocabulary, higher demands, problems of motivation, less discussion, reduction of contents, and need for reviewing the contents' in the English course offering. We need to investigate the possibility of students using their strongest language when completing tests and assignments (when the LoLT is English) in order to build on students' receptive proficiency in English without the concomitant fear of not being able to write well in English. As Haberland and Risager (2008: 47) point out with regard to multilingual competence, '[i]f you can read an article in French, but not actually speak the language, then read the article!' The degree to which receptive bi-/multilingualism can support learning is just one of the many aspects of multilingual teaching strategies that require investigation.

The possibilities of bilingual assessment have not been researched to any significant extent, and my own attempts have led to mixed results, as shown in the following case.

A case in point

In an attempt to determine the effect of bilingual support in a reading comprehension text, we used a summary in Afrikaans to improve comprehension of an English text (Van der Walt & Kidd, 2012). Both English and Afrikaans students were given a summary of the text: an English summary for English-speaking students and an Afrikaans summary for Afrikaans-speaking students. We found that,

> Afrikaans students made some use of their home language knowledge to improve their understanding of the text. The fact that English students did not improve their scores means that the mere presence of a summary was not the factor that influenced performance: the presence of a home language summary aided performance on the test to some extent for Afrikaans-speaking students.

It was also clear that students needed support *before* the test on how to use summaries to improve their understanding.

The fact that not all students benefit from code switching in lectures or from the availability of multilingual materials underlines the importance of research in this area, just like research efforts need to be directed to determine the effectiveness of CLIL programmes.

Multilingual texts as images

As pointed out in Chapter 4, there is very little research on the most efficient ways of deploying different languages in instructional materials. When the purpose of multilingual texts is to develop biliteracy and an in-depth understanding of concepts (by building on advanced literacies in another language), it is important to contrast and compare scientific language in study materials and electronic presentations such as PowerPoint.

However, teaching techniques need to be supported by teaching and learning practices that make the differences and similarities between languages explicit. It is not enough to hope that students will automatically make such comparisons. In fact, in cases where languages share strong similarities, a lack of explicit instruction may cause confusion among users/ students and result in mistakes and/or misinterpretation. In the example below, a student teacher developed a bilingual (Afrikaans–English) explanation of biological processes. The similarities and differences between the two languages require extensive support and constant awareness-raising (see Van der Walt & Ruiters, 2011 for more information on this module).

The text-as-image (Sebba, 2012) necessitates decisions about font colour (for example green for English, blue for Afrikaans and other colours for the formulae), and the placement of text (justified left or centre). These need to be assessed as effective communication, not only in one presentation but as a language arrangement for all presentations in a particular course. This is particularly important for languages that are closely related so that the association of colour with language can support the distinction.

Outside of our classrooms we need to ask whether the linguistic landscape on our campuses validates multilingualism as an academic resource. If we look at the advertising campaigns for international student exchange, the focus may be either on the excitement of foreign travel or on the opportunity to improve English language proficiency. In a poster for student exchange to Spain (see p. 179), the clothing, surfboard and diving flippers may indicate some of the reasons for a high dropout rate of international students (Schumann, 2008: 47).

On my own campus, the signage reflects the recent history of the campus as mainly Afrikaans, with some signs in Afrikaans only, many in Afrikaans and English and, only recently, official signs at the entrances to buildings in Afrikaans, English and Xhosa (the third official language of the region). Since the university's contact with international students occurs mainly in a specific building, posters of other countries can be found there for groups of German and Dutch students, as well as for students from African countries such as Botswana, Namibia and Gabon. Posters of exotic

A case in point

A bilingual Afrikaans/English explanation of a biological process:

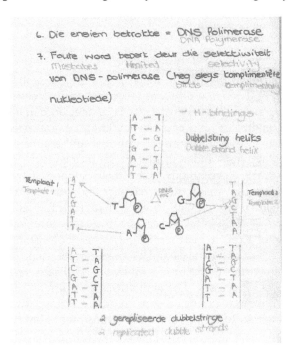

In terms like *polymerase*, *helix* and *template*, which are loanwords, only one letter differentiates the Afrikaans from the English term. In other cases, like *strand* (English) and *string* (Afrikaans), the fact that the Afrikaans word also appears in English, but with a slightly different meaning, requires explanation. It is also evident that Afrikaans spelling has had an influence on the student's English, in the *dubble* (Afrikaans spelling = dubbel) rather than *double* and the obvious self-correction of the 'c' in *complimentary* (Afrikaans spelling is '*komplimentêr*').

clothing, food and national characteristics do acknowledge the presence of such students, but do not necessarily give them the opportunity to use their languages for academic purposes.

Technology: Mobile learning and electronic learning support

There is probably no modern device more ubiquitous than the mobile phone. Investigations into the use of mobile phones in supporting learning are increasing daily. Smartphones, in particular, can provide access to subject content, podcasts, dictionaries and translation services. In addition,

Poster on a noticeboard at the Pompeu Fabra University in Barcelona. (Photo: Author)

their use for providing immediate feedback on questions in classroom con-texts (instead of the typical game show devices (the so-called clickers) that have already appeared in classrooms) means that no additional expense needs to be incurred for their use. In Africa, where mobile phone usage far outweighs computer access to the internet, the use of smartphones in particular seems an obvious choice as a learning resource.

For multilingual contexts, the use of mobile phones to check terminol-ogy in other languages or to download multilingual, subject-specific glossa-ries is a field that has not been researched in any depth. At well-resourced HEIs, the use of tablets offers similar opportunities to that of smartphones. Again, the use of mobile technology must be investigated, managed and integrated into daily teaching and learning in a meaningful way. In a current survey at Stellenbosch University of approximately 543 education students' preferences for the use of mobile phones on campus, the top six categories were as follows (Education Faculty Survey):

(1) View examination results: 83.74%
(2) View class or exam schedule: 80.98%
(3) View assignment information: 77.20%
(4) View calendar of important dates and deadlines: 75.17%
(5) Access educational content online: 70.06%

Students perceive their phones as a social tool first and only then as repositories of fairly static information rather than as an active tool for learning. Although they could benefit from getting assignment information in more than one language, the real value of multilingual resources is possible in category 5. For students to recognise the value of their phones as learning tools, multilingual teaching strategies will have to be designed to exploit the connectivity and accessibility of mobile devices in a meaningful way.

Conclusion

The possibilities for multilingual education are limited only by our own fixed ideas about language, language learning and the nature of education. As García (2007: xiii) asks in her foreword to Makoni and Pennycook's book *Disinventing and Reconstituting Languages*,

> What would language education look like if we no longer posited the existence of separate languages? How would we teach bilingually in ways that would reflect people's use of language and not simply people as language users?

If we argue from the perspective of students' use of language, we have to acknowledge that there are as many possibilities for engaging with academic material as there are students. With this realisation as the basis for education, we are essentially arguing from the perspective of constructivism, where instruction links up with the student's abilities, linguistic and otherwise, rather than expecting the student to meet a reified curriculum. We could, therefore, argue that multilingual education is what good education should be in any case.

However, such a statement masks a vast variety of convictions, such as that some languages are more suitable than others for HE, that multiple languages cannot be managed in class, that oral modes are less suitable than written ones, to name a few. Makoni and Pennycook (2007: 3) point to the need for 'rethinking language in the contemporary world, a need arising from an acute awareness that there is all too often a lack of fit between ostensible language problems and the language promoted as part of the solution'.

Ultimately, perhaps, those who doubt the value of multilingual HE should focus their discussions on these preconceived ideas about language and the problems they cause in HE. Until that happens, the multilingual world will continue to use the languages at their disposal to get the work done.

Notes

(1) The emphasis on professional qualifications pre-supposes a particular view of higher education, which may not sit comfortably with supporters of university education as a liberal and general programme. However, the argument for the acknowledgement of multilingualism in higher education requires that institutions remain aware of the world of work and the demands of globalisation, both of which result in students, lecturers, administrators and managers projecting a view of themselves and the institution as future role players in the world of work and the global stage.

References

Academic Cooperation Association (ACA) (2006) Official website accessed 8 February 2006. http://www.aca-secretariat.be/02projects/ELTDP.htm

Achieve. (2010) *Cambridge Assessment Newsletter*. Cambridge, MA: Cambridge University.

Achoka, J.S.K, Odebero, S.O., Maiyo, J.K. and Mualuko, N.J. (2007) Access to basic education in Kenya: Inherent concerns. *Educational Research and Review* 2 (10), 275–284. Online at http://www.academicjournals.org/ERR

Agasisti, T. (2008) Economic determinants of participation rates in university education. *Higher Education Quarterly* 63 (3), 287–307.

Airey, J. (2004) Can you teach it in English? Aspects of the language choice debate in Swedish higher education. In R. Wilkinson (ed.) *Integrating Content and Language: Meeting the Challenge of a Multilingual Higher Education* (pp. 97–108). Maastricht, MA: Universitaire Pers.

Airey, J. (2009) *Science, Language and Literacy: Case Studies of Learning in Swedish University Physics*. Uppsala: Uppsala University.

Alexander, N. (1995) Models of multilingual schooling for a democratic South Africa. In K. Heugh, A. Siegrühn and P. Plüddemann (eds) *Multilingual Education for South Africa*. Johannesburg: Heinemann.

Altbach, P.G. (2004) Globalization and the university: Myths and realities in an unequal world. In National Education Association (ed.) *The NEA 2005 Almanac of Higher Education* (63–74). Washington, DC: National Education Association.

Altbach, P.G. and Knight, J. (2006) The internationalization of higher education: Motivations and realities. *The NEA 2006 Almanac of Higher Education* 1–10.

Altman, P.G. and Knight, J. (2007) The Internationalization of Higher Education: Motivations and Realities. *Journal of Studies in International Education* 11 (3/4), 290–305.

Amaral, A. and Maassen, P. (2004) Preface. In P. Teixeira, D. Jongbloed, Dill and A. Amaral (eds) *Markets in Higher Education: Rhetoric or Reality?* (pp. xi–xiii). Dordrecht: Kluwer Academic.

Amritavalli, R. and Jayaseelan, K.A. (2007) India. In A. Simpson (ed.) *Language and National Identity in Asia* (pp. 55–83). Oxford, UK: Oxford University Press.

Anthonissen, C. (2006) Hoe gemaak in die meertalige konteks? [What should we do in a multilingual context?] Round table discussion on language in the classroom. Paper presented at the Second Annual Fall Academy, hosted by the Centre for Learning and Teaching. 30–31 May, Stellenbosch University, Stellenbosch.

Anthonissen, C. (2010) Linguistic diversity in a South African HIV/AIDS clinic. In B. Meyer and B. Apfelbaum (eds) *Multilingualism at Work: From Policies to Practices in Public, Medical and Business Settings* (pp. 107–140). Amsterdam: John Benjamins.

Antonacci, P.A. and O'Callaghan, C.M. (2011) *Developing Content Area Literacy*. Thousand Oaks, CA: Sage Publications.

Aponte-Hernández, E. (2008) Inequality, inclusion, and equity trends in higher education in Latin America and the Caribbean: Towards an alternative scenario for 2021. In A.L. Gazzola and A. Didriksson (eds) *Trends in Higher Education in Latin America and the Caribbean* (pp. 109–148). Caracas: IESALC-UNESCO.

Arar, K. and Haj-Yehia, K. (2010) Emigration for higher education: The case of Palestinians living in Israel studying in Jordan. *Higher Education Policy* 23, 358–380.

Aronin, L. and Singleton, D. (2008) Multilingualism as a new linguistic dispensation. *International Journal of Multilingualism* 5 (3), 1–16.

Astin, A. (1985) *Achieving Educational Excellence*. San Fransicso: Jossey Bass.

Auerbach, E.R. (1993) Reexamining English only in the ESL classroom. *TESOL Quarterly* 27 (1), 9–32.

Agence Universitaire de la Francophonie (AUF) (2012) Official website accessed 28 May 2012. http://www.auf.org/

Baetens Beardsmore, H. (2009) Bilingual education: Factors and variables. In O. García (ed.) *Bilingual Education in the 21st Century* (pp. 137–157). Oxford: Blackwell.

Bailey, S. (2011) *Academic Writing*. New York, NY: Routledge.

Bain, O. (2001) The cost of higher education to students and parents in Russia: Tuition policy issues. *Peabody Journal of Education* 76 (3/4), 57–80.

Baker, C. (1988) *Key Issues in Bilingualism and Bilingual Education*. Clevedon: Multilingual Matters.

Baker, C. (2006) *Foundations of Bilingual Education and Bilingualism* (4th edn). Clevedon: Multilingual Matters.

Baldauf, R.B. Jr. (2006) Rearticulating the case for micro language planning in a language ecology context. *Current Issues in Language Planning* 7 (2–3), 147–170.

Bamgbose, A. (2004) Sauce for the goose, sauce for the gander. In J.F. Pfaffe (ed.) *Making Multilingual Education a Reality for All: Operationalizing Good Intentions*. Proceedings of the joint Third International Conference of the Association for the Development of African Languages in Education, Science and Technology and the Fifth Malawian National Languages Symposium (pp. 18–36). Mangochi, Malawi, 30 August–3 September 2004. Zomba: University of Malawi.

Banda, F. (2000) The Dilemma of the mother tongue: Prospects for bilingual education in South Africa. *Language, Culture and Curriculum* 13 (1), 51–66.

Banda, F. (2009) Study groups and peer roles in mediated academic literacy events in multilingual educational contexts in South Africa. *Stellenbosch Papers in Linguistics* 37, 1–21.

Bartlett, L. and Holland, D. (2002) Theorising the space of literacy practices. *Ways of Knowing Journal,* Columbia Teachers College. Online at http://www.tc.columbia.edu/faculty/bartlett/publications/pdf/2_1WOK.pdf

Barton, D. (2007) *Literacy: An Introduction to the Ecology of Written Language*. Malden, MA: Blackwell Publishing.

Barton, D. and Hamilton, M. (2000) Literacy practices. In D. Barton, M. Hamilton and R. Ivanič (eds) *Situated Literacies* (pp. 7–15). London: Routledge.

Barton, D., Hamilton, M. and Ivanič, R. (2000) *Situated Literacies*. London: Routledge.

Bashir, S. (2007) Trends in international trade in higher education: Implications and options for developing countries. *Education Working Paper Series* no 6. Washington, DC: World Bank. Online at http://siteresources.worldbank.org/EDUCATION/Resources/278200-1099079877269/547664-1099079956815/WPS6_Intl_trade_higherEdu.pdf

Basturkmen, H. (2012) Languages for Specific Purposes: Curriculum Creation and Implementation in Australasia and Europe. *The Modern Language Journal* 96, 59–70.

Baumann, R. and Briggs, C.L. (2003) *Voices of Modernity: Language Ideologies and the Politics of Inequality.* Cambridge, MA: Cambridge University Press.

Beacco, J.-Cl. and Byram, M. (2003) *Guide for the Development of Language Education Policies in Europe: From Linguistic Diversity to Plurilingual Education*. Strasbourg: Council of Europe accessed 24 November 2005. http://www.coe.int

Beerkens, H.J.J.G. (2004) Global opportunities and institutional embeddedness: Higher education consortia in Europe and Southeast Asia. Phd thesis, University of Twente. Online at http://doc.utwente.nl/50803/1/thesis_Beerkens.pdf

Bekhradnia, B. (2004) Credit accumulation and transfer, and the Bologna process: An Overview. Report by the Higher Education Policy Institute. Online at http://www.bccat.ca/pubs/13CATFullReport.pdf

Benrabah, M. (2007) The language situation in Algeria. In R.B. Kaplan and R.B. Baldauf (eds) *Language Planning and Policy in Africa* (Vol. 2, pp. 25–148). Clevedon: Multilingual Matters.

Ben-Tsur, D. (2012) The impact of conflict on international student mobility: A case study of international students studying in Israel. *International Studies in Sociology of Education* 19 (2), 135–149.

Beukes, A. and Pienaar, M. (2006) Some factors influencing the use of simultaneous interpreting as an alternative to parallel-medium teaching in tertiary education. *Journal for Language Teaching* 40 (2), 127–138.

Bhabha, H. (1994) *The Location of Culture*. London: Routledge.

Black, S. (1999) Do better schools matter? Parental valuation of elementary education. *Quarterly Journal of Economics* 114, 578–599.

Blackledge, A. and Creese, A. (2010) *Multilingualism*. New York, NY: Continuum.

Blommaert, J. (1992) Codeswitching and the exclusivity of social identities: Some data from campus Kiswahili. *Journal of Multilingual and Multicultural Development* 13 (1 and 2), 57–70.

Blommaert, J. (2006) Ujamaa and the creation of the new Waswahili. In C. Van der Walt (ed.) *Living Through Languages: A Tribute to Rene Dirven* (pp. 5–22). Stellenbosch: SUN MeDIA.

Bobda, A.S. (2006) The emergence of "new mother tongues" in Africa and its implications: The example of Cameroon. In C. Van der Walt (ed.) *Living Through Languages: A Tribute to Rene Dirven* (pp. 55–70). Stellenbosch: SUN MeDIA.

Boughey, C. (2000) Multiple metaphors in an understanding of academic literacy. *Teachers and Teaching: Theory and Practice* 6 (3), 279–290.

Boughey, C. (2002) 'Naming' students' problems: An analysis of language-related discourses at a South African university. *Teaching in Higher Education* 7 (3), 295–307.

Bourdieu, P. (1986) The forms of capital. In J.G. Richardson (ed.) *Handbook for Theory and Research for the Sociology of Education* (pp. 241–258). New York, NY: Greenwood Press.

Bourdieu, P. (1991) *Language and Symbolic Power*. Cambridge, MA: Harvard University Press.

Bourn, D. (2010) Students as global citizens. In E. Jones (ed.) *Internationalisation and the Student Voice* (pp. 18–29). New York, NY: Routledge.

Boyer, E.L. and Levine, A. (1981) A quest for common learning. *Change* 13 (3), 28–35.

Brandenburg, U. and Zhou, J. (2007) *Higher Education in China in the Light of Massification and Demographic Change: Lessons to be Learned for Germany.* (Arbeitspapier 97). Gütersloh: Centrum für Hochschulentwicklung.

Bratt-Paulston, C. (1980) *Bilingual Education: Theories and Issues*. Cambridge, MA: Newbury House.

Brink, C. and Van der Walt, C. (2005) Multilingual universities: A national and international overview. *SA Journal for Higher Education* 19 (4), 822–852.

Brink, C. (2006) *No Lesser Place: The Taaldebat at Stellenbosch*. Stellenbosch: SUN ePress.

Brock-Utne, B. (2009) The adoption of a western paradigm in bilingual teaching: Why does it not fit the African situation? In K. Kwaa Prah and B. Brock-Utne (eds) *Multilingualism: An African Advantage* (pp. 18–52). Cape Town, South Africa: Centre for Advanced Studies of African Society.

Bunting, I., Sheppard, C., Cloete, N. and Belding, L. (2009) Performance indicators in South African higher education 2000–2008. CHET Summary Report. Online at http://books.google.co.za/books?hl=en&lr=&id=74LvNFHqyC8C&oi=fnd&pg=PA4&dq=higher+education+equity+Cloete&ots=wIaC7p5Nb6&sig=wkkZvpx5SRNKIXJ9ICv9NQ8lK8A#v=onepage&q&f=false

Canagarajah, A.S. (1999) *Resisting Linguistic Imperialism in English Teaching*. Oxford: Oxford University Press.

Canagarajah, A.S. (2004) Multilingual writers and the struggle for voice in academic discourse. In A. Pavlenko and A. Blackledge (eds) *Negotiation of Identities in Multilingual Contexts* (pp. 266–287). Clevedon: Multilingual Matters.

Canagarajah, A.S. (ed.) (2005) *Reclaiming the Local in Language Policy and Practice*. Mahwah, NJ: Lawrence Erlbaum.

Canagarajah, A.S. (2011) Codemeshing in academic writing: Identifying teachable strategies of translanguaging. *The Modern Language Journal* 95 (3), 401–417.

Candela, A. (1999) Students' power in classroom discourse. *Linguistics and Education* 10, 139–163.

Causa, O. and Chapuis, C. (2009) *Equity in Student Achievement Across OECD Countries: An Investigation of the Role of Policies*. Economics Department working papers no. 708. Official website accessed 5 April 2012. www.oecd.org/eco/working_papers

Cheng, K.K.Y. and Beigi, A.B. (2012) Education and religion in Iran: The inclusiveness of EFL (English as a Foreign Language) textbooks. *International Journal of Educational Development* 32 (2012), 310–315.

China Education and Research Network (CERN) (2010) Official website accessed on 19 October 2010. http://www.edu.cn/200109_1471/20060323/t20060323_16111.shtml

Chudgar, A. and Shafiq, M.J. (2010) Family, community, and educational outcomes in South Asia. *Prospects*. DOI 10.1007/s11125-010-9169-z. Online at http://www.springerlink.com.ez.sun.ac.za/content/d037004vq6778151/fulltext.pdf

Clark, R. (1992) Principles and practice of CLA in the classroom. In N. Fairclough (ed.) *Critical Language Awareness* (pp. 117–140). London: Longman.

Clark, R. and Ivanič, R. (1997) *The Politics of Writing*. London: Routledge.

Clay, M. (1991) *Becoming Literate: The Construction of Inner Control*. Auckland: Heinemann.

CiLT (2006) The National Centre for Languages. Online at http://www.cilt.org.uk/qualifications/elp/adultelp.htm

CLIL Compendium (2007) Website accessed 4 December 2007. http://www.clilcompendium.com/clilcompendium.htm

Cochran-Smith, M. (2001) Multicultural education: Solution or problem for American schools? *Journal of Teacher Education* 52, 91–93.

Coetzee-van Rooy, S. (2006) Integrativeness: Untenable for world Englishes learners? *World Englishes* 25 (3/4), 437–450.

Cole, M. (2006) Introduction. In M. Cole (ed.) *Education, Equality and Human Rights* (pp. 1–6). New York, NY: Routledge.

Coleman, J.A. (2006) English-medium teaching in European higher education. *Language Teaching* 39 (1), 1–14.

Conference Report. (2008) Developing links: EU–Africa cooperation in higher education through mobility. Online at http://ec.europa.eu/education/external-relation-programmes/doc/confafrica.pdf

Consortia in Europe and Southeast Asia, Center for Higher Education Policy Studies, University of Twente, accessed on 10 February 2006. http://www.utwente.nl/cheps/documenten/thesisbeerkens.pdf

Cook, V. (2001) Using the first language in the classroom. *The Canadian Modern Language Review/La Revue canadienne des langues vivantes* 57 (3), 402–423.

Cook, V. (2006) Linguistic contributions to bilingualism. In J. Altarriba and R.R. Heredia (eds) *An Introduction to Bilingualism: Principles and Processes* (pp. 245–264). New York, NY: Lawrence Erlbaum Associates.

Cooper, R.L. (1989) *Language Planning and Social Change*. Cambridge, MA: Cambridge University Press.

Cots, J.M. (2008) International universities in bilingual communities. In H. Haberland, J. Mortensen, A. Fabricius, B. Preisler, K. Risager and S. Kjaerbeck (eds) *Higher Education in the Global Village* (pp. 67–84). Roskilde: Roskilde University.

Council of Europe (2001) *Common European Framework of Reference for Languages: Learning, Teaching, Assessment*. Cambridge, MA: Cambridge University Press.

Craith, M.N. (2006) *Europe and the Politics of Language: Citizens, Migrants and Outsiders.* New York, NY: Palgrave Macmillan.

Crawford, J. (2007) Hard sell: Why is bilingual education so unpopular with the American public? In O. García and C. Baker (eds) *Bilingual Education: An Introductory Reader* (pp. 145–164). Clevedon: Multilingual Matters.

Crosier, D., Purser, L. and Smidt, H. (2007) *Trends V: Universities shaping the European higher education arena. An EUA Report.* Online at http://www.sowi-due.de/uploads/108.pdf

Cummins, J. (1979) Linguistic interdependence and the educational development of bilingual children. *Review of Educational Research* 49 (2), 222–251.

Cummins, J. (1981) *Bilingualism and Minority Language Children.* Ontario: Ontario Institute for Studies in Education Press.

Cummins, J. (1986) Empowering minority students: A framework for intervention. *Harvard Educational Review* 56 (1), 18–37.

Cummins, J. (1994) The socio-academic achievement model in the context of coercive and collaborative relations of power. In R.A. DeVillar, C.J. Faltis and J.P. Cummins (eds) *Cultural Diversity in Schools: From Rhetoric to Practice* (pp. 363–390). Albany: State University of New York Press.

Cummins, J. (2005) Teaching for cross-language transfer in dual language education: Possibilities and pitfalls. Paper read at the TESOL Symposium on Dual Language Education: Teaching and Learning Two Languages in the EFL Setting, Bogazici University, Istanbul, Turkey on September 23.

Cummins, J. and Hornberger, N.H. (eds) (2008) *Encyclopedia of Language and Education* (Vol. 5, 2nd edn, pp. xiii–xxiii). Dordrecht: Kluwer Academic.

Cuvelier, P. (2010) Foreword. In P. Cuvelier, T. du Plessis, M. Meeuwis, R. Vanderkerckhove and V. Webb (eds) *Multilingualism from Below* (pp. xxii–xvi). Pretoria: Van Schaik.

Cuvelier, P., Du Plessis, T., Meeuwis, M., Vanderkerckhove, R. and Webb, V. (eds) (2010) *Multilingualism from Below.* Pretoria: Van Schaik.

Dahl, K. and Freppon, P. (1998) A comparison of innercity children's interpretations of reading and writing instruction in the early grades in skills based and whole language classrooms. In C. Weaver (ed.) *Reconsidering a Balanced Approach to Reading* (pp. 271–320). Urbana, IL: National Council of Teachers.

Darn, S. (2006) *Content and Language Integrated Learning.* Izmir University of Economics, Turkey. Available online at: http://www.teachingenglish.org.uk/think/articles/content-language-integrated-learning

Davis, M. (2003) GDP by language. Unicode Technical Note #13, accessed on 29 May 2012. http://www.unicode.org/notes/tn13/

Dearing Report (1998) Higher education in the learning society. Official website accessed on 29 May 2012. http://www.leeds.ac.uk/educol/ncihe/

De Boer, H., Jongbloed, B., Enders, J. and File, J. (2008) *Progress in Higher Education Reform across Europe: Governance and Funding Reform.* (Volume 2: Methodology, performance data, literature survey, national system analyses and case studies.) European Community: Directorate General for Education and Culture of the European Commission.

De Mejia, A-M. (2002) *Power, Prestige, and Bilingualism: International Perspectives on Elite Bilingualism.* Clevedon: Multilingual Matters.

DeVillar, R.A. and Faltis, C.J. (1994) Introduction. In R.A. DeVillar, C.J. Faltis and J.P. Cummins (eds) *Cultural Diversity in Schools: From Rhetoric to Practice* (pp. 1–24). Albany: State University of New York Press.

Dewey, J. (1916) *Democracy and Education.* New York, NY: The Macmillan Company.

Didriksson, A. (2008) Global and regional contexts of higher education in Latin America and the Caribbean. In A.L. Gazzola and A. Didriksson (eds) *Trends in Higher Education in Latin America and the Caribbean* (pp. 19–50). Caracas: IESALC-UNESCO.

Dietsche, P. (2009) Small steps to a big idea: Personalising the post-secondary experience. In B. Leibowitz, S. van Schalkwyk and A. van der Merwe (eds) *Focus on First Year Success: Perspectives Emerging from South Africa and Beyond* (pp. 37–46). Stellenbosch: AFRICAN SUN MeDIASun.

Djité, P.G. (1992) The arabization of Algeria: Linguistic and sociopolitical motivations. *International Journal of the Sociology of Language* 98 (1), 15–28.

Doğançay-Aktuna, S. and Kiziltepe, Z. (2005) English in Turkey. *World Englishes* 24 (2), 253–265.

Dörnyei, Z. and Csizér, K. (2002) Some dynamics of language attitudes and motivation: Results of a longitudinal nationwide survey. *Applied Linguistics* 23 (4), 421–462.

Dustmann, C., Machin, S. and Schoenberg, U. (2008) Educational achievement and ethnicity in compulsory schooling. CReAM Discussion Paper No 12/08. Online at http://www.econ.ucl.ac.uk/cream/pages/CDP/CDP_12_08.pdf

Dzahene-Quarshie, J. (2010) English in contact with Swahili: Enrichment or threat? *Létünk* 4, 55–74.

Edelsky, C., Smith, K. and Wolfe, P. (2002) A discourse on academic discourse. *Linguistics and Education* 13, 1–38.

Edstrom, A. (2006) Oral narratives in the language classroom: A bridge between non-native, heritage, and native-speaking learners. *Hispania* 89 (2), 336–346.

Edwards, J. (2008) The ecology of language: Insight and illusion. In A. Creese, P. Martin and N.H. Hornberger (eds) *Encyclopedia of Language and Education* (2 edn, Vol. 9, pp. 15–26). Springer Science+Business Media LLC.

Egron-Polak, E. (2008) The Bologna Process – reflections from the international HEI perspective. Presentation to the International Association of Universities, Ghent, 19–20 May 2008. Online at http://www.ond.vlaanderen.be/hogeronderwijs/bologna/forum/Background_Paper_Policy_Forum-EEP-2008.pdf

Egron-Polak, E. (2009) Equitable Access and Success: Higher Education Institutions in Action. Paper read at the World Conference on Higher Education UNESCO, Paris, July 2009. Online at http://www.iau-aiu.net/association/pdf/EEP_WCHE.pdf

Ellis, R. (2003) *Task-Based Language Learning and Teaching.* Oxford: Oxford University Press.

Elyas, T. and Picard, M. (2010) Saudi Arabian educational history: Impacts on English language teaching. *Education, Business and Society: Contemporary Middle Eastern issues* 3 (2), 136–145.

Enyedi, A. and Medgyes, P. (1998) ELT in Central and Eastern Europe. *Language Teaching* 31, 1–2. Ethnologue.com. Online at http://www.ethnologue.com/web.asp

Fairclough, N. (1995) *Critical Discourse Analysis.* London: Longman.

Ferguson, C.A. (1977) Sociolinguistic settings of language planning. In J. Rubin, B. Jernudd, J. Das Gupta, J.A. Fishman and C.A. Ferguson (eds) *Language Planning Processes* (pp. 9–3). The Hague: Mouton.

Ferguson, G. (2006) *Language Planning and Education.* Edinburgh University Press, Edinburgh.

Field, R.F. (2008) Identity, community and power in bilingual education. In J. Cummins and N.H. Hornberger (eds) *Encyclopedia of Language and Education Volume 5: Bilingual Education* (pp. 77–89). New York, NY: Springer.

Findlow, S. (2006) Higher education and linguistic dualism in the Arab Gulf. *British Journal of Sociology of Education* 27 (2), 19–36.

Finlayson, R. and Slabbert, S. (2004) Is instruction in the mother tongue always the optimal choice? South African case studies with reference to the inclusion/exclusion debate, *Series A: General and Theoretical Papers* (602), Essen, LAUD.

Finlayson, R. and Slabbert, S. (1997) 'I'll meet you halfway with language': Code switching within a South African urban context. In M. Pütz (ed.) *Language Choices* (381–422). Amsterdam: John Benjamins.

Fischer, S.R. (2003) *A History of Reading.* London: Reaktion Books.

Fleisch, B. (2008) *Primary Education in a Crisis.* Cape Town: Juta.

Flowerdew, J., Li, D. and Miller, L. (1998) Attitudes towards English and Cantonese among Hong Kong Chinese university lecturers. *TESOL Quarterly* 32 (2), 201–231.

Français Interactif (2012) At the official website http://www.laits.utexas.edu/fi/fivideo/chapitre-06-la-ville-introduction.

Franceschini, R. (2009) Mehsprachige Universitäten sollten eine Selbstverständlichkeit werden. In D. Veronesi and C. Nickenig (eds) *Bi- and Multilingual Universities: European Perspectives and Beyond.* Conference Proceedings Bolzano-Bozen, 20–22 September 2007 (pp. vii–x). Bozen-Bolzano: Bozen/Bolzano University Press.

Frank, D.J. and Meyer, J.W. (2007) University expansion and the knowledge society. *Theory and Society* 36, 287–311.

Frank, R. and Pütz, M. (eds) *Cognitive Models in Language and Thought: Ideology, Metaphors and Meanings* (pp. 25–68). (Cognitive Linguistic Research 24). Berlin/New York: Mouton de Gruyter. Online at http://wwwling.arts.kuleuven.ac.be/qlvl/PDFPublications/03Culturalmodels.pdf

Friedenberg, J.E. (2002) The linguistic inaccessibility of U.S. higher education and the inherent inequity of U.S. IEPs: An argument for multilingual higher education. *Bilingual Research Journal* 26 (2), 213–230.

Gacel-Ávila, J. (2005) Internationalization of higher education in Mexico. In H. de Wit, I.C. Jaramillo, J. Gacel-Ávila and J. Knight (eds) *Higher Education in Latin America: The International Dimension* (pp. 239–280). Washington, DC: The World Bank.

Gacel-Ávila, J. (2007) The process of internationalization of Latin American higher education. *Journal of Studies in International Education* 11 (3/4), 400–409.

Gacel-Ávila, J., Jaramillo, I.C., Knight, J. and De Wit, H. (2005) The Latin American way: Trends, issues, and directions. In H. de Wit, I.C. Jaramillo, J. Gacel-Ávila and J. Knight (eds) *Higher Education in Latin America: The International Dimension* (pp. 341–368). Washington, DC: The World Bank.

Gadelii, K.E. (2004) Annotated statistics on linguistic policies and practices in Africa. Online at http://www.sprak.gu.se/digitalAssets/1310/1310354_annotated-statistics.pdf

Gafaranga, J. and Torras, M. (2002) Interactional otherness: Towards a redefinition of code switching. *International Journal of Bilingualism* 6 (1), 1–22.

Gajo, L. (2007) Enseignement d'une DNL en langue étrangère: de la clarification à la conceptualisation. *Tréma* [En ligne], 28. Online at http://trema.revues.org/448

Gallagher, K. (2011) Bilingual education in the UAE: Factors, variables and critical questions. *Education, Business and Society: Contemporary Middle Eastern Issues* 4 (1), 62–79.

García, O. and Baker, C. (eds) (2007) *Bilingual Education: An Introductory Reader.* Clevedon: Multilingual Matters.

García, O. (2007) Foreword. In S. Makoni and A. Pennycook (eds) *Disinventing and Reconstituting Languages* (pp. xi–xv). Clevedon: Multilingual Matters.

García, O. (2009) *Bilingual Education in the 21st Century: A Global Perspective.* Chichester: Wiley-Blackwell.

García, O. and Menken, K. (eds) (2010) *Negotiating Language Policies in Schools: Educators as Policy Makers.* New York, NY: Routledge.

Gaston, M.G. and Bruézière, M. (1974) *Le Français et la vie 3.* Paris: Hachette.

Gazzola, A.L. and Didriksson, A. (2008) Preface. In A.L. Gazzola and A Didriksson (eds) *Trends in Higher Education in Latin America and the Caribbean* (pp. 9–18). Caracas: IESALC-UNESCO.

Gee, J.P. (1996) *Social Linguistics and Literacies: Ideology in Discourses* (2nd edn). London: Taylor and Francis.

Gee, J.P. (2004) *Situated Language and Learning: A Critique of Traditional Schooling.* New York: Routledge.

Gee, J.P. (2008) *Social Linguistics and Literacies: Ideology in Discourses.* London: Routledge.

Geeraerts, D. (2003) Cultural models of linguistic standardization. In R. Dirven, R. Frank and M. Pütz (eds) *Cognitive Models in Language and Thought* (pp. 25–68). Berlin: Walter de Gruyter.

Ghaith, G and Diab, H. (2008) Determinants of EFL achievement among Arab college-bound learners. *Education, Business and Society: Contemporary Middle Eastern Issues* 1 (4), 278–286.

Gibbons, S. and Machin, S. (2003) Valuing English primary schools. *Journal of Urban Economics* 53, 197–219.

Gill, S.K. (2004) Language policy and planning in higher education in Malaysia: A nation in linguistic transition. In R. Wilkinson (ed.) *Integrating Content and Language: Meeting the Challenge of a Multilingual Higher Education* (pp. 109–125). Maastricht, MA: Universitaire Pers.

Goethe Institute. (2012) Official website at http://www.goethe.de/ins/de/spr/int/deindex.htm

Graddol, D. (1997) *The Future of English*. Plymouth: British Council.

Graddol, D. (2006) *English Next*. Plymouth: British Council.

Griesbach, H. and Schulz, D. (1976) *Deutsche Sprachlehre für Ausländer*. München: Max Hüber.

Groenewald, P. (1990) *Noord-Sotho vir eerstejaars*. Pretoria: Van Schaik.

Grosjean, F.n.d. The right of the deaf child to grow up bilingual, accessed 28 September 2010. http://deafstudies.gallaudet.edu/Documents/DSDJ_Grosjean_BSL.pdf

Grossman, G.M., Sands, M.K. and Brittingham, B. (2010) Teacher education accreditation in Turkey: The creation of a culture of quality. *International Journal of Educational Development* 30, 102–109.

Gurin, P., Dey, E.L., Hurtado, S. and Gurin, G. (2002) Diversity and higher education: theory and impact on educational outcomes. *Harvard Educational Review* 72 (3), 330–367.

Gutiérrez, K.D. (2008) Developing a sociocritical literacy in the third space. *Reading Research Quarterly* 43 (2), 148–164.

Haberland, H. and Risager, K. (2008) Two pilot studies of multilingual competence in international programmes at Roskilde University. In: H. Haberland, J. Mortensen, A. Fabricius, B. Preisler, K. Risager and S. Kjaerbeck (eds) *Higher Education in the Global Village* (pp. 41–66). Roskilde: Roskilde University.

Hamade, S.N. (2007) Acquiring information technology skills by freshmen students at Kuwait University: The language factor. Paper delivered at the International Conference on Information Technology (ITNG'07).

Hamdan, J.M. and Abu Hatab, W.A. (2009) English in the Jordanian context. *World Englishes* 28 (3), 394–405.

Hanks, W.F. (1991) Foreword. In J. Lave and E. Wenger (eds) *Situated Learning* (pp. 1–24). Cambridge, MA: Cambridge University Press.

Hamel, R.E. (2010) Engaging a plurilingual scientific community. *Anthropology News,* 17.

Hamers, J.F. and Blanc, M. (2000) *Bilinguality and Bilingualism*. Cambridge, CA: Cambridge University Press.

Hashim, A. (2009) Not plain sailing: Malaysia's language choice in policy and education. *AILA Review* (Multilingual, Globalizing Asia: Implications for policy and education.) 22, 36–51.

Hatcher, R. (2006) Social class and schooling: Differentiation or democracy? In M. Cole (ed.) *Education, Equality and Human Rights* (pp. 202–224). New York, NY: Routledge.

Heffernan, P.J. (2003) English-language hegemony in the language of publication and the referential discourse of Applied Linguists. In A. Coetzee (ed.) *Identity and Creativity in Language Education*. Proceedings of the World Congress of the World Federation of Modern Language Associations (pp. 339–350). 2–5 July 2003, RAU, Johannesburg, South Africa.

Held, D., McGrew, A., Goldblatt, D. and Perraton, J. (1999) *Global Transformations: Politics, Economics and Culture*. Stanford: Stanford University Press.

Heller, M. (1999) *Linguistic Minorities and Modernity*. London: Longman.

Heller, M. (2008) Bourdieu and "Literacy Education". In A. Luke and J. Albright (eds) *Bourdieu and Literacy Education* (pp. 50–67). Mahwah, NJ: Lawrence Erlbaum.

Hellekjaer, G.O. and Wilkinson, R. (2003) Trends in content learning through English at universities: A critical reflection. In C. van Leeuwen and R. Wilkinson (eds) *Multilingual Approaches in University Education* (pp. 81–102). Maastricht, MA: Valkhof Pers.

Herdina, P. and Jessner, U. (2002) *A Dynamic Model of Multilingualism: Perspectives of Change in Psycholinguistics*. Clevedon: Multilingual Matters.

Heugh, K.N.d. The case against bilingual and multilingual education in South Africa. *PRAESA Occasional Papers No. 6.* Accessed online at http://web.uct.ac.za/depts/praesa/OP.htm.

Hidalgo, M. (2008) Afterword: Indicators of bilingualism and identity: Samples from the Spanish-speaking world. In M. Niño-Murcia and J. Rothman (eds) *Bilingualism and Identity: Spanish at the Crossroads with other Languages* (pp. 333–358). Amsterdam: John Benjamins.

Higher Education Funding Frameworks in SADC. (2008) *Study Series* 2008. Accessed online at www.sarua.org.

Higher Education Monitor (2009) The state of higher education in South Africa. *Higher Education Monitor 8.* Pretoria: Council on Higher Education.

Hoffmann, C. (2000) The spread of English and the growth of multilingualism with English in Europe. In J. Cenoz and U. Jessner (eds) *English in Europe: The Acquisition of a Third Language* (pp. 1–21). Clevedon: Multilingual Matters.

Holm-Nielsen, L.B., Thorn, K., Brunner, J.J. and Balánet, J. (2005) Regional and international challenges to higher education in Latin America. In H. de Wit, I.C. Jaramillo, J. Gacel-Ávila and J. Knight (eds) *Higher Education in Latin America: The International Dimension* (pp. 39–17). Washington, DC: The World Bank.

Hornberger, N. (2002) Multilingual language policies and the continua of biliteracy: An ecological approach. *Language Policy* 1, 27–51.

Hornberger, N. (2007) Multilingual language policies and the continua of biliteracy: An ecological approach. In O. Garcia and C. Baker (eds) *Bilingual Education: An Introductory Reader* (pp. 177–194). Clevedon: Multilingual Matters.

Hornberger, N.H. (2009) Multilingual education policy and practice: Ten certainties (grounded in Indigenous experience). *Language Teaching* 42 (2), 197–211.

Hornberger, N.H. (2010) Language and education: A Limpopo lens. In N.H. Hornberger and S.L. McKay (eds) *Sociolinguistics and Language Education* (pp. 549–564). Bristol: Multilingual Matters.

Hornberger, N. and Skilton-Sylvester, E. (2000) Revisiting the continua of biliteracy: International and critical perspectives. *Language and Education* 14 (2), 96–122.

Hornberger, N.H. and Street, B. (2008) *Literacy.* New York, NY: Springer.

Howatt, A.P.R. (with H.G. Widdowson). (2004) *A History of English Language Teaching* (2nd edn). Oxford, UK: Oxford University Press.

Hrycak, A. (2006) Institutional legacies and language revival in Ukraine. In D. Arel and B.A. Ruble (eds) *Rebounding Identities: The Politics of Identity in Russia and Ukraine* (pp. 62–88). Baltimore, ML: Johns Hopkins University Press.

Hu, G. (2007) The juggernaut of English–Chinese bilingual education. In A. Feng (ed.) *Bilingual Education in China* (pp. 94–126). Clevedon: Multilingual Matters.

Hyland, K. (2006) *English for Academic Purposes: An Advanced Resource Book.* London: Routledge.

Hyland, K. and Hamp-Lyons, L. (2002) EAP: Issues and directions. *Journal of English for Academic Purposes* 1, 1–12.

Ichilov, O. (2009) *The Retreat from Public Education: Global and Israeli Perspectives.* New York, NY: Springer.

Jackson, F. (2009) EAP course design within a context of institutional change and cross-disciplinary collaboration: Factors shaping the creating of 'writing for commerce'. *Per Linguam* 25 (2), 61–81.

Jacobs, C. (2005) On being an insider on the outside: New spaces for integrating academic literacies. *Teaching in Higher Education* 10 (4), 475–487.

Jacobs, C. (2007) Mainstreaming academic literacy teaching: Implications for how academic development understands its work in higher education. *South African Journal for Higher Education* 21 (7), 870–881.

Jacobs, G.M. and Farrell, T.S.C. (2003) Understanding and implementing the CLT (communicative Language Teaching) paradigm. *RELC Journal* 34 (5), 5–30.

James, R. (2000) *Socioeconomic Background and Higher Education Participation: An Analysis of School Students' Aspirations and Expectations.* Melbourne: Commonwealth of Australia.

Jaramillo, I.C. (2005) Internationalization of higher education in Colombia. In H. de Wit, I.C. Jaramillo, J. Gacel-Ávila and J. Knight (eds) *Higher Education in Latin America: The International Dimension* (pp. 175–210). Washington, DC: The World Bank.

Jenkins, J. (2003) *World Englishes.* London: Routledge.

Jessner, U. (2008) Teaching third languages: Findings, trends and challenges *Language Teaching* 41 (1), 15–56.

Jiazhen, P. (2007) Facts and considerations about bilingual education in Chinese universities. In A. Feng (ed.) *Bilingual Education in China* (pp. 200–218). Clevedon: Multilingual Matters.

Jones, E. (ed.) (2010) *Internationalisation and the Student Voice.* New York, NY: Routledge.

Jones, E. and Caruana, E. (2010) Preface. In E. Jones (ed.) *Internationalisation and the Student Voice* (pp. xv–xxiii). New York, NY: Routledge.

Kamberelis, G. (2001) Producing of heteroglossic classroom (micro)cultures through hybrid discourse practice. *Linguistics and Education* 12, 85–125.

Kamwangamalu, N. (2010) Multilingualism and code switching in education. In N.H. Hornberger and S.L. McKay (eds) *Sociolinguistics and Language Education* (pp. 116–142). Bristol: Multilingual Matters.

Kaplan, R.B. and Baldauf, R.B. (1997) *Language Planning from Practice to Theory.* Clevedon: Multilingual Matters.

Kimizi, M. (2009) From a Eurocentric to an Afrocentric perspective on language of instruction in the African context – a view from within. In K. Kwaa Prah and B. Brock-Utne (eds) *Multilingualism: An African Advantage* (pp. 195–218). Cape Town, South Africa: Centre for Advanced Studies of African Society.

Kirkpatrick, A. (2007) *World Englishes: Implications for International Communication and English Language Teaching.* Cambridge, MA: Cambridge University Press.

Kirkpatrick, J. (2008) *Montessori, Dewey, and Capitalism: Educational Theory for a Free Market in Education.* Claremont, CA: TLJ Books.

Knapp, A. (2011) When comprehension is crucial: English as a medium of instruction at a German university. In A. De Houwer and A. Wilton (eds) *English in Europe Today* (pp. 51–70). Amsterdam/Philadelphia: John Benjamins.

Knapper, C. (2000) Editorial: The politics of academic development. *International Journal for Academic Development* 5 (1), 1–5.

Knight, J. (2005) An internationalization model: Responding to new realities and challenges. In H. de Wit, I.C. Jaramillo, J. Gacel-Ávila and J. Knight (eds) *Higher Education in Latin America: The International Dimension* (pp. 1–38). Washington, DC: The World Bank.

Kolesnikov, A. (2012) Berufsorientierende Komponente als Bestandteil der linguistischen mehrsprachlichen Ausbildung. Paper presented at an international conference on Multilingualism in Society, the World of Work, and Politics: New Challenges for Teaching at Institutes of Higher Education/ Universities, hosted by the Sprachlehr Institut, Freiburg University, Freiburg i. Br., Germany, from 18–20 April 2012.

Kramsch, C. (2004) The language teacher as go between. *Utbildning & Demokrati* 13 (3), 37–60.

Kumaravadivelu, B. (2006) Dangerous liaison: Globalization, empire and TESOL. In J. Edge (ed.) *(Re) Locating TESOL in an Age of Empire* (pp. 1–32). London: Palgrave/ Macmillan.

Landinelli, J. (2008) Scenarios of diversification, differentiation, and segmentation of higher education in Latin America and the Caribbean. In A.L. Gazzola and A. Didriksson (eds) *Trends in Higher Education in Latin America and the Caribbean* (pp. 149–172). Caracas: IESALC-UNESCO.

Langner, M. (2003) Fachsprachen als Fremdsprachen [Subject languages as foreign languages]. In C. van Leeuwen and R. Wilkinson (eds) *Multilingual Approaches in University Education* (pp. 47–64). Maastricht, MA: Valkhof Pers.

Language Policy for Higher Education (2002) Pretoria: Ministry of Education. Accessed online at http://www.wsu.ac.za/campuslife/indaba/documents/Language%20Policy%20for%20Higher%20Education.pdf

Larsen-Freeman, D. (2006) The emergence of complexity, fluency, and accuracy in the oral and written: Production of five Chinese learners of English. *Applied Linguistics* 27 (4), 590–619.

Lauridsen, K.M. (2012) Summation of session papers, presented at an international conference on Multilingualism in Society, the World of Work, and Politics: New Challenges for Teaching at Institutes of Higher Education/Universities, hosted by the Sprachlehr Institut, Freiburg University, Freiburg i. Br., Germany, from 18–20 April 2012.

Lave, J. and Wenger, E. (1991) *Situated Learning: Legitimate Peripheral Participation*. Cambridge, MA: Cambridge University Press.

Law, W.W. (2007) Legislation and educational change: The struggle for social justice and quality in China's compulsory schooling. *Education and the Law* 19 (3–4), 177–199.

Leask, B. (2010) 'Beside me is an empty chair'. The student experience of internationalisation. In E. Jones (ed.) *Internationalisation and the Student Voice* (pp. 3–17). New York, NY: Routledge.

Legère, K. (2006) Formal and informal development of the Swahili language: Focus on Tanzania. In O.F. Arasanyin and M.A. Pemberton (eds) *Selected Proceedings of the 36th Annual Conference on African Linguistics* (pp. 176–184). Somerville, MA: Cascadilla Proceedings Project. Accessed online at http://www.lingref.com/cpp/acal/36/paper1422.pdf

Lehikoinen, A. (2004) Foreign-language-medium education as national strategy. In R. Wilkinson (ed.) *Integrating Content and Language: Meeting the Challenge of a Multilingual Higher Education* (pp. 41–48). Maastricht, MA: Universitaire Pers.

Leibowitz, B. (2004) Becoming academically literate in South Africa: lessons from student accounts for policymakers and educators. *Language and Education* 18 (1), 35–52.

Leibowitz, B. (2009) Towards a pedagogy of possibility. In E. Bitzer (ed.) *Higher Education in South Africa: A Scholarly Look behind the Scenes* (pp. 85–102). Stellenbosch: African Sun Media.

Lemann, N. (1999) *The Big Test: The Secret History of the American Meritocracy*. New York, NY: Farrar, Strauss and Giroux.

Lewis, M.P. (ed.) (2009) *Ethnologue: Languages of the World* (16th edn). Dallas, TX: SIL International. Accessed online at http://www.ethnologue.com/

Li, Y. and Wang, L. (2010) A survey on bilingual teaching in higher education institute in the northeast of China. *Journal of Language Teaching and Research* 1 (4), 353–357.

Lillis, T. and Curry, M.J. (2010) *Academic Writing in a Global Context*. London: Routledge.

Liu, S. (2009) Globalization, higher education, and the nation state. In Proceedings of the China Postgraduate Network Conference 23–24 April 2009, Luther King House, Manchester (pp. 91–100). Accessed online at http://www.bacsuk.org.uk/cpn/wp-content/uploads/2012/01/Proceedings20091.pdf#page=91

Lohfink, M.M. and Paulsen, M.B. (2005) Comparing the determinants of persistence for first-generation and continuing-generation students. *Journal of College Student Development* 46 (4), 409–428.

López, D.A., López, D.C., Andrade, L.I. and López, B.A. (2011) Functional patterns in international organizations for university cooperation in Latin America and the Caribbean. *Journal of Studies in International Education* 15 (2), 203–215.

Maerhoff, G.I. (1982) Ties that do not bind. *Change* 14 (1), 12–17.

Maiworm, F. and Wächter, B. (2002) *English-Language-Taught Degree Programmes in European Higher Education*. Bonn: Lemmens.

Makoni, S. and Pennycook, A. (2007) Disinventing and reconstituting languages. In S. Makoni and A. Pennycook (eds) *Disinventing and Reconstituting Languages* (pp. 1–41). Clevedon: Multilingual Matters.

Marginson, S. and Rhoades, G. (2002) Beyond national states, markets, and systems of higher education: A glonacal agency heuristic. *Higher Education* 43, 281–309.

Marginson, S. and Van der Wende, M. (2007) Globalisation and higher education. (Education Working Paper No. 8). Paris: OECD Education Working Papers Series. Accessed online at http://doc.utwente.nl/60264/1/Marginson07globalisation.pdf

Marsh, D. and Laitinen, J. (2005) *Medium of Instruction in European Higher Education: Summary of Research Outcomes of European Network for Language Learning Amongst Undergraduates (ENLLU) Task Group 4.* Jyväskylä: UniCOM, University of Jyväskylä.

Martin, P.W. (2005) 'Safe' language practices in two rural schools in Malaysia: Tensions between policy and practice. In A.M.Y. Lin and P.W. Martin (eds) *Decolonisation, Globalisation and Language-in-Education Policy and Practice* (pp. 74–97). Clevedon: Multilingual Matters.

Marx, N. (2002) Never Quite a 'Native Speaker': Accent and Identity in the L2 and the L1. *The Canadian Modem Language Review/La Revue canadienne des langues vivantes,* 59 (2), 264–281.

Maseko, P. and Kaschula, R. (2009) Vocational language learning and teaching at a South African university: Preparing professionals for multilingual contexts. *Stellenbosch Papers in Linguistics PLUS* 38, 130–142.

Mazrui, A.A. and Mazrui, A.A. (1998) *The Power of Babel.* Oxford: James Currey.

McGhie, V.M. (2012) *Factors Impacting on First-Year Students' Academic Progress at a South African University.* PhDthesis, Stellenbosch: Stellenbosch University. Accessed online at http://hdl.handle.net/10019.1/20090.

McKay, S.L. (2002) *Teaching English as an International Language.* Oxford: OUP.

McSwan, J. and Rollstadt, K. (2005) Linguistic diversity, schooling and social class: Rethinking our conception of language proficiency in language minority education. In J. Cohen, K.T. McAlister, K. Rolstad and J. MacSwan (eds) *ISB4: Proceedings of the 4th International Symposium on Bilingualism* (pp. 329–341). Somerville, MA: Cascadilla Press.

Melby-Lervåg, M. and Lervåg, A. (2011) Cross-linguistic transfer of oral language, decoding, phonological awareness and reading comprehension: A meta-analysis of the correlational evidence. *Journal of Research in Reading* 34 (1), 114–135.

Michael-Luna, S. and Canagarajah, A.S. (2007) Multilingual academic literacies: Pedagogical foundations for code meshing in primary and higher education. *Journal of Applied Linguistics* 4, 55–77.

Mills, J. (2001) Being bilingual: Perspectives of third generation Asian children on language, culture and identity. *International Journal of Bilingual Education and Bilingualism* 4 (6), 383–402.

Ministry of Basic Education (2011) *Curriculum News: Improving the Quality of Learning and Teaching, Strengthening Curriculum Implementation from 2010 and Beyond.* May 2011.

Miranda, X.Z. (2008) Regional integration and internationalization of higher education in Latin America and the Caribbean. In A.L. Gazzola and A. Didriksson (eds) *Trends in Higher Education in Latin America and the Caribbean* (pp. 173–232). Caracas: IESALC-UNESCO.

Mohanty, A. (2012) MLE and the double divide in multilingual societies: Comparing policy and practice in India and Ethiopia. In T. Skutnabb-Kangas and K. Heugh (eds) *Multilingual Education and Sustainable Diversity Work* (pp. 138–150). New York, NY: Routledge.

Moate, J. (2011) Reconceptualising the role of talk in CLIL. *Apples – Journal of Applied Language Studies* 5 (2), 17–35.

Moll, L.C. (2007) Bilingual classroom studies and community analysis: Some recent trends. In O. García and C. Baker (eds) *Bilingual Education: An Introductory Reader* (pp. 272–280). Clevedon: Multilingual Matters.

Momanyi, C. (2009) The effects of 'sheng' in the teaching of Kiswahili in Kenyan schools. *The Journal of Pan African Studies* 2 (8), 127–138.

Montgomery, S. (2004) Of towers, walls, and fields: Perspectives on language in science. *Science*, 1333–1335, doi: 10.1126/science.303.5662.

Moore, E. (2010) Exploring plurilingualism as a teaching/learning resource in English medium higher education. In O. Guasch and M. Milian (eds) *L'educación lingüística i literària en entorns multilingües* (pp. 221–236). Barcelona: Unìversidad Autònoma Barcelona.

Moore, E. and Dooly, M. (2010) How do the apples reproduce (Themselves)? How teacher trainees negotiate language, content, and membership in a CLIL science education classroom at a Multilingual University. *Journal of Language, Identity, and Education* 9, 58–79.

Morrow, W. (1993) Epistemological access in the university. *Academic Development Issues* 1 (1), 3–4.

Mouton, J. and Hunter, M. (2002) 'n Ondersoek na die inskakeling van bruin studente aan die Universiteit van Stellenbosch: 'n geval van twee kulture. [An investigation into the incorporation of brown students at the University of Stellenbosch: a case of two cultures.], A Stellenbosch University unpublished report.

Mufwene, S. (2002) Colonisation, globalisation, and the future of languages in the twenty-first century. *International Journal on Multicultural Societies* 4 (2). Protecting Endangered Minority Languages: Sociolinguistic Perspectives. Ed. by Matthias Koenig. UNESCO.

Muskens, G. (2009) *Inclusion and Education in European Countries*. INTMEAS Final report: 2. Comparative conclusions. Accessed online at: http://www.docabureaus.nl/INTMEAS.html

Muthwii, M.J. and Kioko, N.D. (2004) Editorial: A fresh question for new language bearings in Africa. In M.J. Muthwii and N.D. Kioko (eds) *New Language Bearings in Africa*. Clevedon: Multilingual Matters.

Myers-Scotton, C. (1990) Elite closure as boundary maintenance: The case of Africa. In B. Weinstein (ed.) *Language Policy and Political Development* (pp. 25–42). Norwood, NJ: Ablex.

Myers-Scotton, C. (1993) *Social Motivations for Code Switching: Evidence from Africa*. Oxford, UK: Oxford University Press.

Myers-Scotton, C. (2005) *Multiple Voices: Introduction to Bilingualism*. Malden, MA: Blackwell Publishers.

Nastansky, H.-L. (2004) National strategy in the internationalisation of higher education: The German perspective. In R. Wilkinson (ed.) *Integrating Content and Language: Meeting the Challenge of a Multilingual Higher Education* (pp. 49–54). Maastricht, MA: Universitaire Pers.

Nelde, H.P. (1991) Language conflicts in multilingual Europe: Prospects for 1993. In F. Coulmas (ed.) *A Language Policy for the European Community: Prospects and Quandaries* (pp. 59–74). Berlin: Mouton de Gruyter.

Nikolarea, E. (2004) ELT for social sciences students at non-English Universities. In R. Wilkinson (ed.) *Integrating Content and Language: Meeting the Challenge of a Multilingual Higher Education* (pp. 251–263). Maastricht, MA: Universitaire Pers.

Northedge, A. (2002) Organizing excursions into specialist discourse communities: A sociocultural account of university teaching. In G. Wells and G. Claxton (eds) *Learning for Life in the 21st Century. Sociocultural Perspectives on the Future of Education* (pp. 252–264). Oxford, UK: Blackwell Publishers.

Norton, B. (2000) *Identity and Language Learning. Gender, Ethnicity and Educational Change*. Essex, UK: Pearson Education.

NSFAS Annual Report (2009) NSFAS. Accessed online at https://www.nsfas.org.za/resources/226/ANNUALReport2009.pdf

Nys, L. and Tollebeek, J. (2008) *De stad op de berg. Een geschiedenis van de Leuvense universiteit sinds 1968*. [The city on the hill. A history of the University of Leuven since 1968.], Universiteit Leuven: Leuven.

Nzimande, B. (2012) Message from Minister of Higher Education and Training, Dr Blade Nzimande. Accessed online at http://www.jet.org.za/events/fet-college-round-table-and-summit/message-from-minister-of-higher-education-and-training-dr-blade-nzimande.

Oberhuemer, P. (2005) International perspectives on early childhood curricula. *International Journal of Early Childhood* 37 (1), 27–37.

O'Connor, C. (2001) Making sense of the complexity of social identity in relation to achievement: A sociological challenge in the new millennium. *Sociology of Education*, 74, (Extra issue: *Currents of Thought: Sociology of Education at the Dawn of the 21st Century*), 159–168.

O'Connor, C., Hill, L.D. and Robinson, S.R. (2009) Who's at risk in school and what's race got to do with it? *Review of Research In Education* 33 (1), 1–34.

OECD (2006) *Education at a Glance 2005*, OECD, Paris, France.

OECD (2008) *Reviews of National Policies for Education – SA*. Accessed online at http://www.oecd.org

Omar, A.H. (2007) Malaysia and Brunei. In A. Simpson (ed.) *Language and National Identity in Asia* (pp. 337–359). Oxford, UK: Oxford University Press.

Oreopoulos, P. (2007) Would more compulsory schooling help disadvantaged youth? Evidence from recent changes to school-leaving laws. Accessed online at http://www.chass.utoronto.ca/~oreo/research/school%20leaving%20age%20to%2018/should%20we%20raise%20dropout%20age%20to%2018%202007%20july.pdf

Ortega, L. (2010) *The Bilingual Turn in SLA*. Plenary delivered at the Annual Conference of the American Association for Applied Linguistics. Atlanta, GA, March 6–9. At http://www2.hawaii.edu/~lortega/ on 12 March 2010

Osborne, M. (2003) Increasing or widening participation in higher education? — A European overview. *European Journal of Education* 38 (1), 5–24.

Osmond, J. and Roed, J. (2010) Sometimes it means more work In E. Jones (ed.) *Internationalisation and the Student Voice* (pp. 113–124). New York, NY: Routledge.

Otcu, G.B. (2009) Language maintenance and Cultural Identity Construction in a Turkish Saturday school in New York city. Doctoral dissertation, Teachers College Columbia University, New York.

Ouane, A. (2009) My journey to and through a multilingual landscape. In K. Kwaa Prah and B. Brock-Utne (eds) *Multilingualism: An African Advantage* (pp. 53–61). Cape Town, South Africa: Centre for Advanced Studies of African Society.

Parry, G. (2008) Patterns of participation in higher education in England: A statistical summary and commentary. *Higher Education Quarterly* 51 (1), 6–28.

Pattanayak, D.P. (2003) Multilingual contexts and their ethos. In A. Ouane (ed.) *Towards a Multilingual Culture of Education* (pp. 29–33). Hamburg: UNESCO Institute for Education.

Paxton, M.I.J. (2009) 'It's easy to learn when you using your home language but with English you need to start learning language before you get to the concept': Bilingual concept development in an English medium university in South Africa. *Journal of Multilingual and Multicultural Development* 30, 345–359.

Pennycook, A. (1997) Vulgar pragmatism, critical pragmatism, and EAP. *English for Specific Purposes* 16 (4), 253–269.

Pennycook, A. (1998) *English and the Discourses of Colonialism*. London: Routledge.

Pennycook, A. (2001) *Critical Applied Linguistics: A Critical Introduction*. Mahwah, NJ: Lawrence Erlbaum.

Pennycook, A. (2010) *Language as a Local Practice*. London: Routledge.

Pfaffe, J.F. (ed.) *Making Multilingual Education a Reality for All: Operationalizing good intentions*. Proceedings of the joint Third International Conference of the Association for the Development of African Languages in Education, Science and Technology and the Fifth Malawian National Languages Symposium (pp. 18–36). Mangochi, Malawi, 30 August–3 September 2004. Zomba, University of Malawi.

Peters, M. and Lankshear, C. (1996) Critical literacy and digital text. *Educational Theory* 46 (1), 51–70.

Pillay, P. (2008) Higher education funding frameworks in SADC. Study Series 2008. Accessed online at http://www.sarua.org/files/publications/TACF/Chapter3_full.pdf

Preece, S. (2004) Language and identity issues with home students on EAP writing programmes. In L. Sheldon (ed.) *Directions for the Future: Issues in English for Academic Purposes* (pp. 169–173). Oxford: Peter Lang.

Preece, S. (2009) Multilingual identities in higher education: Negotiating the 'mother tongue', 'posh' and 'slang'. *Language and Education* 24 (1), 21–39.

Preisler, B. (2008) Deconstructing 'the domain of science' as a sociolinguistic entity in EFL societies: The relationship between English and Danish in higher education and research. In B. Preisler, A. Fabricius, H. Haberland, S. Kjaerbeck and K. Risager (eds) *The Consequences of Mobility* (pp. 238–248). Roskilde: Department of Culture and Identity, Roskilde University.

Pressley, M. (1998) *Reading Instruction that Works: The Case for Balanced Teaching.* New York: The Guilford Press.

Prior, G. (2012) 'All you need is....': investigating the university-workplace interface. Paper presented at an international conference on Multilingualism in Society, the World of Work, and Politics: New Challenges for Teaching at Institutes of Higher Education/Universities, hosted by the Sprachlehr Institut, Freiburg University, Freiburg i. Br., Germany, from 18–20 April 2012.

Progress in Higher Education Reform across Europe (2008) Directorate General for Education and Culture of the European Commission, Vol. 2.

Purser, L. (2000) The bilingual university – General reflections on its origins, mission, and functioning. *Higher Education in Europe* 25 (4), 451–459.

Qorro, M.A.S. (2009) English only versus bilingual education in Africa: With a focus on Tanzania. In K. Kwaa Prah and B. Brock-Utne (eds) *Multilingualism: An African Advantage* (pp. 219–236). Cape Town, South Africa: Centre for Advanced Studies of African Society.

Quinot, G. (2012) Transformative Legal Education. *South African Law Journal* 129, 411–433.

Ramani, E., Kekana, T., Modiba, M. and Joseph, M. (2007) Terminology development versus concept development through discourse: Insights from a dual-medium BA degree. *Southern African Linguistics and Applied Language Studies* 25 (2), 207–223.

Ramsden, P. (1997) The context of learning in academic departments. In F. Marton, D. Hounsell and N.J. Entwistle (eds) *The Experience of Learning* (pp. 198–216). Edinburgh: Scottish Academic Press.

Resnik, M. (1993) ESL and language planning in Puerto Rico. *TESOL Quarterly* 27, 259–273.

Riley, A. (1994) *English for Law.* Ismaning: Max Hueber.

Ritzen, J. (2004) Across the bridge: Towards an international university. In R. Wilkinson (ed.) *Integrating Content and Language: Meeting the Challenge of a Multilingual Higher Education* (pp. 28–40). Maastricht, MA: Universitaire Pers.

Roberts, C. (2008) Introduction. In H. Haberland, J. Mortensen, A. Fabricius, B. Preisler, K. Risager and S. Kjaerbeck (eds) *Higher Education in the Global Village* (pp. 7–16). Roskilde: Roskilde University.

Romaine, S. (2008) Multilingualism. In M. Aronoff and J. Rees-Miller (eds) *The Handbook of Linguistics* (pp. 512–532). Oxford, UK: Blackwell.

Ruiz, R. (1984) Orientations in language planning. *NABE Journal* 8 (2), 15–34.

Ruiz, R. (1994) Language policy and planning in the United States. *Annual Review of Applied Linguistics* 14, 111–125.

Sanchez, C.R. (2005) Internationalization of higher education in Chile. In H. de Wit, I.C. Jaramillo, J. Gacel-Ávila and J. Knight (eds) *Higher Education in Latin America: The International Dimension* (pp. 149–174). Washington, DC: The World Bank.

Schofer, E. and Meyer, J.W. (2004) The world-wide expansion of higher education in the twentieth century. CDDRL Working Papers Number 32. Accessed online at http://iis-db.stanford.edu/pubs/20801/Schofer-Meyer_No32.pdf

Schumann, A. (2008) Interkulturelle Fremdheitserfahrungen ausländischer Studierender an einer deutschen Universität. [Intercultural experiences of being foreign students at a German university.] In A. Schumann and A. Knapp (eds) *Mehrsprachigkeit und Multikulturalität im Studium [Multilingualism and Multiculturality in Academic Studies.]* (pp. 30–45). Frankfurt: Peter Lang.

Scott, P. (1998) Massification, internationalization and globalization. In P. Scott (ed.) *The Globalization of Higher Education* (pp. 108–129). Buckingham: The Society for Research into Higher Education/Open University Press.

Scott, P. (2000) Globalisation and higher education: Challenges for the 21st century. *Journal of Studies in International Education* 4 (3), 3–10.

Scott, I. (2009) First year experience as terrain of failure or platform for development? In B. Leibowitz, A. van der Merwe and S. van Schalkwyk (eds) *Focus on First-Year Success: Perspectives from South Africa and Beyond* (pp. 17–36). Stellenbosch: Sun MeDIA.

Scholes, R. (1998) *The Rise and Fall of English: Reconstructing English as a Discipline.* New Haven: Yale University.

Sebba, M. (2012) Researching and theorising multilingual texts. In M. Sebba, S. Mahootian and C. Jonsson (eds) *Language Mixing and Code-Switching in Writing* (pp. 1–26). New York, NY: Routledge.

Seelen, L. (2002) Is performance in English as a second language a relevant criterion for admission to an English medium university? *Higher Education* 44, 213–232.

Seidlhofer, B. (2003) "English for Europe, or European English?" In A. Rüdiger (ed.) *Europäische Sprachenpolitik. [European Language Policy]* (pp. 123–138). Winter: Heidelberg.

Seidlhofer, B. (2004) Research perspectives on teaching English as a lingua franca. *Annual Review of Applied Linguistics* 24, 209–239.

Setati, M., Adler, J., Reed, I. and Bapoo, A. (2002) Incomplete journeys: Code-switching and other language practices in Mathematics, Science and English language classrooms in South Africa. *Language and Education* 16 (2), 128–149.

Shavit, Y., Arum, R. and Gamoran, A. (2007) More inclusion than diversion: Expansion, differentiation and market structure in higher education. In Y. Shavit, R. Arum and A. Gamoran (eds) *Stratification in Higher Education* (pp. 1–38). Stanford: Stanford University Press.

Sheorey, R. (2006) *Learning and Teaching English in India. Volume 7 of Research in Applied Linguistics.* New Delhi: Sage Publications.

Shohamy, E. (2006) *Language Policy: Hidden Agendas and New Approaches.* London: Routledge.

Simpson, A. (2007) Language and national identity in Asia: A thematic introduction. In A. Simpson (ed.) *Language and national identity in Asia* (pp. 1–30). Oxford: Oxford University Press.

Skutnabb-Kangas, T. and Cummins, J. (1988) *Minority Education: From Shame to Struggle.* Clevedon: Multilingual Matters.

Skutnabb-Kangas, T. Phillipson, R., Mohanty, A.K. and Panda, M. (eds) (2009) *Social Justice through Multilingual Education.* Bristol: Multilingual Matters.

Smit, T.C. (2009) *The Role of African Literature in Enhancing Critical Literacy in First-Generation Entrants at the University of Namibia.* PhD thesis, available at http://scholar.sun.ac.za/handle/10019.1/741/search

Smith, M.K. (2003) *Communities of Practice: The Encyclopedia of Informal Education,* www.infed.org/biblio/communities_of_practice.htm

Söderlundh, H. (2008) Language practices in Swedish higher education: Results from a pilot study. In H. Haberland, J. Mortensen, A. Fabricius, B. Preisler, K. Risager and S. Kjaerbeck (eds) *Higher Education in the Global Village* (pp. 97–102). Roskilde: Roskilde University.

Sparks, R., Patton, J., Ganschow, L. and Humbach, N. (2009) Long-term crosslinguistic transfer of skills from L1 to L2. *Language Learning* 59 (1), 203–243.

Spaull, N. (2011) *Primary School Performance in Botswana, Mozambique, Namibia and South Africa.* Paris: Southern and Eastern African Consortium for Monitoring Educational Quality (SACMEQ) Working Paper no. 8.

Spolsky, B. and Cooper, R.L. (1978) *Case Studies in Bilingual Education.* Rowley, MA: Newbury House Publishers.

Spolsky, B. (2004) Language policy failures – why won't they listen?, Series A: General and Theoretical Papers (584), Essen, LAUD.

Spolsky, B. (2005) Language policy. In J. Cohen, K.T. McAlister, K. Rolstad and J. MacSwan (eds) *ISB4: Proceedings of the 4th International Symposium on Bilingualism* (pp. 2152–2164). Somerville, MA: Cascadilla Press.

Stellenbosch University 'Code of conduct for language in the classroom' (2008) Online at http://www.sun.ac.za/university/taal/dokumente/gedragskodeklaskamer_eng.doc

Stern, D. and Briggs, D. (2001) Changing admissions policies: Mounting pressures, new developments, key questions. *Change* 33 (1), 34–41.

Stevenson, J. and Willott, J. (2010) Refugees: Home students with international needs. In E. Jones (ed.) *Internationalisation and the Student Voice* (pp. 193–202). New York: Routledge.

Stockwell, G. (2007) Vocabulary on the move: Investigating an intelligent mobile phone-based vocabulary tutor. *Computer Assisted Language Learning* 20 (4), 365–383.

Street, B.V. (1984) The autonomous model. In B.V. Street, P. Burke and R. Finnegan (eds) *Literacy in Theory and Practice* (pp. 1–11). Cambridge, MA: Cambridge University Press.

Street, B.V. (2011) New literacy studies and the continua of biliteracy. In F.M. Hult and K.A. King (eds) *Educational Linguistics in Practice: Applying the Local Globally and the Global Locally* (pp. 59–67). Bristol: Multilingual Matters.

Summary Report. (1997) *Higher Education in the Learning Society.* The National Committee of Enquiry into Higher Education. Accessed online at http://www.leeds.ac.uk/educol/ncihe/.

Swann, J. (2000) Language choice and code switching. In R. Mesthrie, J. Swann, A. Deumerts and W.L. Leap (eds) *Introducing Sociolinguistics* (pp. 148–183). Edinburgh: Edinburgh University press.

Swain, M., Kirkpatrick, A. and Cummins, J. (2011) *How to Have a Guilt-Free Life Using Cantonese in the English Class: A Handbook for the English Language Teacher in Hong Kong.* Hong Kong: Research Centre into Language Acquisition and Education in Multilingual Societies, Hong Kong Institute of Education. Accessed online at http://www.ied.edu.hk/rcleams/view.php?secid=1399

Swigart, L. (1994) Cultural creolisation and language use in post-colonial Africa: The case of Senegal. *Africa: Journal of the International African Institute* 64 (2), 175–189.

Talbot, M., Atkinson, K. and Atkinson, D. (2003) *Language and Power in the Modern World.* Tuscaloosa: The University of Alabama Press.

'The three commitments of ICU' (2012) Online at http://www.icu.ac.jp/english/info/history/commitment.html

Torres-Guzmán, M.E. (2007) Dual language programmes: Key features and results. In O. García and C. Baker (eds) *Bilingual Education: An Introductory Reader* (pp. 50–62). Clevedon: Multilingual Matters.

Tucker, G.R. (1998) A global perspective on multilingualism and multilingual education. In J. Cenoz and F. Genessee (eds) *Beyond Bilingualism: Multilingualism and Multilingual Education* (pp. 3–15). Clevedon: Multilingual Matters.

UKCISA. (2010a) *Higher education statistics.* Accessed online at http://www.ukcisa.org.uk/about/statistics_he.php#table3

UKCISA. (2010b) *International students in the UK: Facts, figures – and fiction.* Accessed online at http://www.ukcisa.org.uk/files/pdf/about/international_education_facts_figures.pdf

UKCOSA: The Council for International Education. (2007) *Benchmarking the provision of services for international students in higher education institutions.* Accessed online at http://www.ukcisa.org.uk/files/pdf/pmi/benchmarking_report.pdf

UKZN academics lead the way in language policy. (2012) Accessed online at http://www.ukzn.ac.za/news.aspx?type=ukr&id=18

Ulrich's Periodicals Directory. (2001) Bowker's Ulrichsweb.com—the global source for periodicals. R.R. Bowker. Available at http://ulrichsweb.serialssolutions.com/login

UNESCO Institute for Statistics (2007) Education counts: Benchmarking progress in 19 WEi countries. Montreal. Accessed online at http://www.uis.unesco.org/Pages/default.aspx

UN Universal Declaration of Human Rights (Article 26:1 and 2) Accesssed online at http://www.un.org/en/documents/udhr/index.shtml#a26

UNESCO's study abroad guide (98) Accesssed online at (http://portal.unesco.org/education/en/ev.php-URL_ID=21997&URL_DO=DO_TOPIC&URL_SECTION=201.html

Usher, A. and Cervenan, A. (2005) *Global Higher Education Rankings 2005.* Toronto, ON: Educational Policy Institute.

Üstunel, E. and Seedhouse, P. (2005) Why that, in that language, right now? Code-switching and pedagogical focus. *International Journal of Applied Linguistics* 15 (3), 302–325.

Uys, D. and van Dulm, O. (2011) The functions of classroom code switching in the Siyanda District of the Northern Cape Province. *Southern African Linguistics and Applied Language Studies* 29 (1), 67–76.

Van der Walt, C. (2004a) The challenge of multilingualism: In response to the language policy for higher education. *South African Journal of Higher Education* 18 (1), 140–152.

Van der Walt, C. (2006) University students' attitudes towards and experiences of bilingual classrooms. *Current Issues in Language Planning* 7 (2–3), 359–376.

Van der Walt, C. (2009) The functions of code switching in English language learning classes. *Per Linguam* 25 (1), 30–43.

Van der Walt, C. and Dornbrack, J. (2011) Academic biliteracy in South African higher education: Strategies and practices of successful students. *Language, Culture and Curriculum* 24 (1), 89–104.

Van der Walt, C. and Ruiters, J. (2011) Every teacher a language teacher? Developing awareness of multilingualism in teacher education. *Journal for Language Teaching* 45 (2), 84–99.

Van der Walt, C. and Kidd, M. (2012) Acknowledging academic biliteracy in higher education assessment strategies: A tale of two trials. In A. Doiz, D. Lasagabaster and J.M. Sierra (eds) *English-Medium Instruction at Universities: Global Challenges* (pp. 27–43). Bristol: Multilingual Matters.

Van der Walt, C. (2013) Active biliteracy? Students taking decisions about using languages for academic purposes. In H. Haberland, D. Lønsmann and B. Preisler (eds) *Language Alternation, Language Choice and Language Encounter in International Education.* Heidelberg: Springer.

Van Heusden, M. and Lamprecht, H. (2007) Doeltreffende onderrig in die tweetalige klaskamer met die fokus op taalgebruik [Effective teaching in the bilingual classroom with a focus on language use], draft report to the Centre for Learning and Teaching, to be published on the University website at http://sun025.sun.ac.za/portal/page/portal/Administrative_Divisions/SOL/CTL%20Home%20page, Stellenbosch University, South Africa.

Van der Walt, C., Mabule, R. and De Beer, J.J. (2001) Letting the L1 in by the back door: Code-switching and translation in Science, Mathematics and Biology classes. *SA Language Teaching Journal* 35 (2–3), 123–134.

Van der Walt, C. and Steyn, M. de V. (2004b) Student perceptions and frustrations with bilingual education at Stellenbosch University, South Africa. In R. Wilkinson (ed.)

Integrating Content and Language: Meeting the Challenge of Multilingual Higher Education (pp. 493–507). Maastricht, MA: Universitaire Pers Maastricht.

Van Leeuwen, C. (2004) Multilingual universities in Europe: Models and realities. In R. Wilkinson (ed.) *Integrating Content and Language* (pp. 576–584). Maastricht, MA: Universitaire Pers.

Van Leeuwen, C. (2007) Feasibility of policy in university language teaching today. Netherlands, Maastricht University. Available online at: http://www.unimaas.nl/default.asp?template=werkveld.htm&id=I33135POUMB13HE0M0R0&taal=nl

Van Rooyen, B. (2005) The feasibility of simultaneous interpreting in university classrooms. *Southern African Linguistics and Applied Language Studies* 23 (1), 81–90.

Van Schalkwyk, S.C. (2008) Acquiring academic literacy: A case of first-year extended degree programme students at Stellenbosch University. PhD thesis, available at http://scholar.sun.ac.za/handle/10019.1/741/search

Van Schalkwyk, S., Bitzer, E. and Van der Walt, C. (2009) Acquiring academic literacy: A case of first-year extended degree programme students. *Southern African Linguistics and Applied Language Studies* 27 (2), 189–201.

Varghese, N.V. (2008) *Globalisation of Higher Education and Cross-Border Student Mobility*. Paris: International Institute for Educational Planning.

Verhoef, M. (2006) Tolking as afleweringsmodus in universiteitsklasse. 'n Bespreking en analise van die Dagbreektrusttolkprojek aan die Potchefstroomkampus van die Noordwes-Universiteit. [Interpreting as delivery mode in university classes: A discussion and analysis of the Dagbreek Trust interpretation project at the Potchefstroom campus of North-west University.] *Tydskrif vir Geesteswetenskappe: Moedertaalonderrig: Supplement* 46 (2), 89–99.

Verhoef, M. and Du Plessis, T. (eds) (2008) *Multilingualism and Educational Interpreting*. Pretoria: Van Schaik.

Wababa, Z. (2009) *How Scientific Terms are Taught and Learnt in the Intermediate Phase*. M Ed dissertation. Accessed online at http://hdl.handle.net/10019.1/2189

Wallace, C. (2001) Critical literacy in the second language classroom: Power and control. In B. Comber and A. Simpson (eds) *Negotiating Critical Literacies in Classrooms* (pp. 209–228). Mahwah, NJ: Lawrence Erlbaum.

Walters, P.B. (2001) Educational access and the state: Historical continuities and discontinuities in racial inequality in American education. *Sociology of Education* (Extra Issue), 35–49.

Wang, T. and Li, L.Y. (2011) 'Tell me what to do' vs. 'guide me through it': Feedback experiences of international doctoral students. *Active Learning in Higher Education* 12 (2), 101–112.

Watson, D., Amoah, M. and Blackstone, T. (2007) *The Dearing Report: Ten Years on*. Sterling: Stylus Publishing.

Wenger, E. (1998) *Communities of Practice: Learning, Meaning, and Identity*. Cambridge, MA: Cambridge University Press.

West, C. (1992) A matter of life and death. *October* 61, 20–23.

Whittaker, R., Llinares, A. and McCabe, A. (2011) Written discourse development in CLIL at secondary school. *Language Teaching Research* 15 (3), 343–362.

Wilkinson, R., Zegers, V. and Van Leeuwen, C. (eds) (2006) Bridging the assessment gap in English- medium higher education, Bochum, AKS-Verlag [Series: Fremdsprachen in Lehre und Forschung (FLF); Band 40], 211–34.

Woods, P. (2006) 'The hedgehog and the fox': Two approaches to English for the military. In J. Edge (ed.) *(Re)locating TESOL in an Age of Empire* (pp. 208–226). New York: Palgrave Macmillian.

World Higher Education Database (2010) International Association of Universities: MacMillan Web Services.

Yang, R. (2001) An obstacle or a useful tool? The role of the English language in internationalizing Chinese universities. *Journal of Studies in International Education* 5 (4), 341–358.

Yang, L. (2010) Doing a group presentation: Negotiations and challenges experienced by five Chinese ESL students of commerce at a Canadian university. *Language Teaching Research* 14 (2), 141–160.

Yang, A. and Lau, L. (2003) Student attitudes to the learning of English at secondary and tertiary levels. *System* 31, 107–123.

Yusof, R.N., Tayib, M. and Mansor, M. (2004) English medium instruction in non-English higher learning institutions: Accounting lecturers' experience versus students' perception. In R. Wilkinson (ed.) *Integrating Content and Language: Meeting the Challenge of a Multilingual Higher Education* (pp. 523–535). Maastricht, MA: Universitaire Pers.

Zajda, J. (ed.) (2006) *Decentralisation and Privatisation in Education: The Role of the State.* Springer: Dordrecht.

Subject Index

Country Index

Lightning Source UK Ltd.
Milton Keynes UK
UKHW021402270922
409525UK00017B/294